the best of
Mauritian cuisine

dedicated to the fans of Madeleine worldwide

by Madeleine Philippe

with

Clancy Philippe

Madeleine Philippe with Lindsay Noë

Maddy's Cookbook – Foreword by Lindsay Noë

"Maddy and I would love you to write a preface for the Cookery Book we are producing". Clancy's email did not really surprise me as I am used to him speaking of his dearest wife, Madeleine, in the present tense. Although physically departed from this world, Maddy's spirit will live on forever for those who loved her...and still do.

"All, ...everything that I understand...I understand because I love you". These words from none other than Victor Hugo - whose mother, by the way, was born in Mauritius – must have been written for Maddy and Clancy whose love affair has survived the ravages and worldly pressures of time and even the harsh reality of death.

Clancy keeps her alive, and cheerful, in all his actions and writings and one cannot but feel the communion - that united them all these past years - continue to flow into his daily life.

So what better way to honour her memory than to publish a book on her inimitable cuisine? The cuisine of her homeland, Mauritius, one of the rare places in this world where different ethnic groups live in near-perfect harmony. Sharing their cultures and religions whilst maintaining a very strong sense of belonging to a little island-dot lost in the middle of the Indian Ocean. A very special island, steeped in history, which appears on the first world map ever published – Alberto Cantino's planisphere (1502). No Australia yet and only pieces of America...!

These diverse elements from Asia, Africa, India and Europe (France in particular) find their way in the cuisine of Mauritius in a happy, spicy and often intriguing blend... always succulent.

Maddy had mastered the subtleties of this cuisine and in this book, she reveals through her soul mate Clancy, the secrets of its intricacies leading to the final taste explosion.

Those who were not fortunate enough to have crossed her path will have the lucky opportunity, here, to discover the jovial and fiery character mingled with her incredible warmth and generosity that pervade these recipes. She would desperately want you to enjoy them, as sharing was an innate part of her persona.

This is not just any Cookery Book....this one was written in Heaven !

Marcel Lindsay Noë

Editor's Note:
Lindsay is a promoter of all things Mauritian and long term friend of Madeleine and Clancy.

Madeleine Philippe

Introduction by Liz Coates

The fact you are reading this introduction tells you that the book's author, Clancy Philippe, has realised a dream - to share with the world his immense passion and love for Mauritius and its Cuisine.

It goes even deeper than that - this was a dream he shared with his late wife Madeleine and it is thanks to her love and presence since her passing in 2011 that Clancy has been able to bring it to fruition.

Madeleine and Clancy Philippe

You may already have enjoyed visiting the "Mauritius Australia Connection" and "Recipes from Mauritius" web sites set up in 1994 by Madeleine and Clancy Philippe when they saw the potential to use internet to promote both Mauritius and Mauritian Cuisine.

The Mauritian Cuisine element came to the fore after numerous requests from Mauritians scattered worldwide looking for recipes to cook to remind themselves of their homeland.

Born and bred in Mauritius, Clancy travelled to UK to attend University where he graduated as a Civil Engineer. It was during this period, he realised how much he missed the tastes and smells of home. Understanding this from personal experience has made him more determined than ever to ensure that no matter where in the world people may be, being able to taste home can and will lift spirits and stimulate memories of family times and loved ones.

Returning to Mauritius, he met the love of his life Madeleine and was immediately bowled over by her immense personality and electrifying smile. Even better, she was the most fantastic cook.

"She would create dishes that had her special signature and left invitees to her table yearning for more".

At that time Clancy could not even boil an egg and even Madeleine joked "So you married me for my cooking!"

In 1987, when Madeleine and Clancy settled in Australia, they found that not very much was known about Mauritius and its cuisine. Many misconceptions existed, including the impression that Mauritian Cuisine involved a hotchpotch of strange foods that included an assortment of greens, some of which were considered weeds and could kill you if eaten! Around the same time, Australians began to start appreciating ethnic foods from the different migrant communities that had settled in Australia. This inspired Clancy to look back in time to try to identify exactly where, why and how other cultures have influenced the Mauritian cuisine and added to its style and taste of cooking. With the result this book includes not only the recipes people savour today but the results of his fact finding mission as to where it all began.

This is no ordinary recipe book! Following on from his first book, a very moving, tear jerking autobiography: "Madeleine - Losing A Soul Mate to Cancer", Clancy has brought together an exceptional collection of recipes, presented in an easy to follow format, for the whole world to try

Throughout the entire book one ingredient predominates and is clearly the mainstay of not only the recipes but is the essence of life itself. In an interview not long before her passing, Madeleine was asked: "What is the most essential ingredient for the preparation of good food?" Her emphatic answer: "Love!"

Whilst the Mauritius Australia Connection web site is now a Mauritian Community Portal web site for the Mauritian Community in Australia, Clancy and Madeleine always want to make available the very best of Mauritian Cuisine in print.

Mauritian cuisine will titillate your taste buds like no other cuisine. This unique cuisine is a combination of French, African, Malagasy, English, Indian, Tamil, Telegu, Muslim and Chinese gastronomic delights that will bring to your table a whole new spectrum of tastes and flavours. Evolving from this, the Mauritian Creole cuisine is also unique in that it evokes a subtle and flavoursome blend of its constituent cultural mix, supercharged with a rich culinary heritage.

It has been a long held dream of Madeleine and Clancy to share their passion for Mauritian Cuisine worldwide. This book does just that and will also share with you the rich culinary history of Mauritian Cuisine, honouring the people who left their own motherlands to call Mauritius home.

Note from Clancy Philippe:
Special thank you to Liz and Norman Coates for their invaluable assistance in the production of this book.

Fried bread in batter with tomato chutney (page 35)

Contents

Foreword by Lindsay Noë	iii
Introduction by Liz Coates	v
History of Mauritian Cuisine	3-24
Snacks and Gajacks	25-62
Soups and Bouillons	63-84
Condiments, Sauces, Chutneys and Pickles	85-112
Main Courses	113-176
Vegetables and Pulses	177-222
Seafoods	223-254
Sweets and cakes	255-278
Acknowledgements	279
Index	280

Poisson salé (saltfish with onions and green chillies-page 241)

History of Mauritian Cuisine

honouring the people who left (sometimes unwillingly) their own motherlands to call Mauritius home

"Tell me what you eat, and I will tell you who you are."
~Anthelme Brillat-Savarin

Origins of Mauritian Cuisine

Mauritian cuisine is loved by everyone and has been recognised as being within the top three dietary patterns based on more healthful foods / nutrients consumed in 187 countries. This finding is correlated with common observations that Mauritians, women in particular, maintain their youthfulness until very late in their lives. This high rating is driven by the high consumption of ten healthy food selections consumed within traditional Mauritian cooking. Those ten healthy food selections include the consumption of fruits, vegetables, beans and legumes, nuts and seeds, whole grains, milk, total polyunsaturated fatty acids, fish, plant omega-3's and dietary fibre. This is very evident within the wide spectrum of Mauritian everyday foods that include French, African, Malagasy, English, Indian, Tamil, Telegu, Muslim and Chinese influences.

Malagasy and African cuisines' contributions to Mauritian cuisine have stayed undocumented as the Malagasy and African slaves who were forcibly taken to the island had no say in the foods available to them. The history of Malagasy and African cuisines is not well documented either. The Malagasy and African slaves had to make do with what was available to them. They prepared foods in accordance with the preference of their masters. A good description of the foods consumed by the slave workforce and others under British occupation is contained in an official report written by Charles Telfair, dated Jan 15, 1830 (Some Account of the State of Slavery at Mauritius since the British Occupation in 1810):

> *"Manioc and other root crops and grains which possess farinaceous qualities, such as potatoes, yams, cambars and sweet potatoes were generally given to the well behaved slaves. Breakfast would consist of a full meal chosen from boiled rice, Indian corn, wheaten bread (called makacthia), manioc cakes, roasted yams, sweet potatoes, cambar of Java or potatoes. Lunch and dinner would be boiled haricots, lentils, pois du cap, beetroot, parsnips, eggplant or dhal, with either manioc, potatoes, yams, cambars or sweet potatoes, accompanied with a soup. A glass of rum would also be allowed with dinner. On Sundays, dinner would include as treats some of the following: dried or salt beef, dried fish, fresh beef, salt pork, fresh pork, dried dates, raw, baked or boiled fruits, molasses, soup made from some of the following ingredients: brédes martin, turnips, cabbage, carrots, lettuces, eggplant, chilli, tomatoes, leeks, garlic, chives, spinach, parsley, hog's lard or ghee. Salads would also be served to the well behaved slaves consisting of some of the following ingredients: radishes, onions, leeks, lettuces, cucumbers, celery, watercresses, sorrel or endives, prepared with vinegar and sugar".*

You can relate the aforementioned ingredients with the traditional day to day foods consumed by Mauritians today. The culinary landscape for Mauritian Cuisine originated from way back in the 1830's. Other dishes like Italian pasta were introduced by passing sailors and travellers on ships, and other immigrants who stopped and settled in Mauritius. The well known Mauritian Cimiotti family has Italian heritage. After the Second World War, many expatriates from Europe were sent to Mauritius and they also introduced their cuisines to others. Expatriate soldiers from the colonising countries, who never returned home, adopted Mauritius as their home. Similarly, English expatriate soldiers, civil servants and traders in India also resettled to Mauritius when changes in the administration of East India Company took place and it was no longer safe for them to stay there. One of my ancestors Joseph Nunn was born to an English trader who moved from the Bengal region in India to Mauritius. They also made their contribution to Mauritian cuisine.

An English lady visiting Mauritius in 1830 wrote the following:
> "The Port Louis bazaar, or market, is a very good one, abundantly supplied with everything; the meat I think quite equal to that in England; European and tropical vegetables and fruits abound there ; peaches and pine-apples, in particular, are very plentiful and very cheap, although certainly inferior in excellence to those raised in this country. The finest fruit in the Island, in my estimation, is the litchi; its external aspect is not at all inviting, as it is covered with a rough, coarse, dusky red skin, but, on that being pulled off, discovers within a snow white pulpy substance, containing a most delicious juice; the fruit has then much the appearance of a hard boiled egg, and is nearly of that size and shape; its flavour is exquisite, and quite unlike that of any other fruit I ever tasted."

The successive settlement in Mauritius by the Dutch, French and British, brought into the island people and products from very many diverse places, including South America, France, England, Africa, India, China and to a lesser extent other countries such as Italy, Germany and Portugal. These people carried with them their dietary habits and introduced foods from their motherlands and other places. The current Mauritian cuisine has evolved from such settlement that reconciled cultural habits with the availability of products. In particular, inhabitants from very different culinary backgrounds learned from each other how to use available products to feed themselves, when supplies were low and they had to survive droughts, cyclones and crop failures. That was the first blueprint for the original Mauritian cuisine that was to evolve through the colonial settlement periods and after.

The true roots of Mauritian Creole cooking come from traditional French foods influenced by Malagasy and African cuisines, very similar to New Orleans' Creole cuisine. This description of New Orleans' cuisine by Elizabeth M. Williams in 'New Orleans A Food Biography 2013', could well be applicable to Mauritian cuisine:
> "All of the peoples who lived or settled in New Orleans, whether free or enslaved, brought with them their sense of identity as defined by food. Clinging to old foodways is a common experience of immigrants everywhere. And all of the peoples contributed to what has become the cuisine of the city. The city was the crucible filled with all those component cuisines and with raw ingredients. The mixture was transformed into a unique cuisine, connected to its component parts, but distinctly different from them."

The makeup of traditional Mauritian cuisine comprises fresh vegetables purchased on a weekly trip to the market, pork or beef, chicken in various cuts, pulses such as red or black lentils, beans, fish and other seafoods such as green prawns and delicacies such as salted fish, dried octopus, black pudding, deli quality sausages. Sometimes, pasta dishes, French dishes such as gratins, Chinese fried rice or noodles would be prepared as special treats. Curries can be prepared with almost every ingredient available, seasoned with various blends of spices and herbs. Some curries are made solely with spices and herbs, others include crushed tomatoes to provide thicker curry sauces. The Mauritian rougaille whose main ingredients include crushed tomatoes, onions, garlic and ginger with herbs, is similar to the curries, in that it can be made with a wide range of ingredients. The Mauritian bouillon brèdes, made with greens, is a most popular and cheap fallback dish that can be prepared quickly and eaten with a rougaille or pickle on rice.

Of special significance to Mauritians are pre-dinner or "with drinks" snacks, referred to as gajacks. This habit has been picked up by many Australians who enjoy Mauritian foods. The true story is told of an Aussie who has a Mauritian partner. At his next Aussie family get-together, drinks were being served with no gajacks. He queried his mother suggesting that it would be appropriate for gajacks to be served, as he was feeling peckish. His mother responded and said: "What are you talking about! - Never heard the word before." He had to explain that Mauritian customs demanded that snacks referred to as gajacks be served before dinner.

The origin of the name gajack (gajak in India) is probably Indian, adopted by Mauritians to refer to snacky foods. Gajak is a dry sweet dessert found in northern India, where it is most commonly consumed in the winter months. It is made from sesame and sugar. Gajak is also the name given to a Punjab sweet, prepared with different dry fruits, it is rich in almonds, peanuts, walnuts and cashew nuts. These foods can also be used as snacks between meals. In Mauritius, the name gajack is used for snacks prepared from all the different cuisines. In French, gajacks are also called "amuse gueles" or in Creole to something that "arrange la bouche". The Chinese equivalent would be "dim sums".

Other important components in Mauritian cuisine are the numerous snack foods and cakes that are served from street vendors and stalls. These snacks and cakes originate from across the whole spectrum of Mauritian cuisine. The most popular being the famous dhal puri (delicate pancakes) with ground dhal inside with various sauces and pickles. Many restaurants sell simple dishes like plain noodles (referred as mines touni) with some seasoning and very few ingredients that constitute a cheap and quick lunch.

Madeleine Philippe dressed for a Bollywood party

Garlic, ginger and onions are used in the preparation of almost every Mauritian dish and are consumed on a daily basis by most Mauritians. The health benefits in their consumption are widely known and it is no wonder that Mauritians benefit from their consumption.

In summary, Mauritian cuisine cuts across French, African, Malagasy, English, Indian, Tamil, Telegu, Muslim and Chinese cuisines, picking up a very diverse combination of fresh ingredients with an array of fresh herbs and spices. The use of these quality products contributes considerably to the healthiness of Mauritian Cuisine.

However, the introduction of fast foods, processed and manufactured foods in Mauritius during the last decade has seen the quality of foods eaten by the younger Mauritians deteriorate. In Australia, the same observation is made with the exception that Mauritians who have been brought up on Mauritian cuisine crave for Mauritian foods. They all love their Mauritian fried noodles, curries, bouillon brèdes and rougailles. My own granddaughter Annabelle claims that her best dish is still a rougaille poisson salé. The continuing popularity of our web site "Recipes from Mauritius" www.cjp.net is testimony that Mauritian cuisine is still very popular among Mauritians and non-Mauritians worldwide.

Mauritius Australia Connection www.cjp.net

Mauritian cuisine will awaken your taste buds with new flavours and sensations. The sense of taste can be categorized into sweetness, sourness, saltiness, bitterness, and umami. There are between 2000 and 5000 taste buds that are located on the back and front of the tongue. Others are located on the roof, sides and back of the mouth, and in the throat. Mauritian cuisine has a very wide taste spectrum that reflects the constituent ingredients used in its preparation. It is particularly rich in the umami taste created by natural glutamates in seafoods, meats and vegetables.

Umami has only been brought into modern culinary circles recently. Mauritian cuisine, incorporates this umami taste mainly through its inclusion of foods from many cultures. Naturally occurring glutamate can also be found in meats and vegetables. In 1985, the term umami was officially recognized as the scientific term to describe the taste of glutamates. It can best be described as a pleasant brothy or meaty taste, with a long lasting, mouth watering and coating sensation over the tongue. Glutamate has a long history in cooking. Fermented fish sauces (garum), which are rich in glutamate, were used widely in ancient Rome, fermented barley (murri) rich in glutamate were used in medieval Byzantine and Arab cuisines, and fermented fish sauces and soy sauces have histories going back to the 3rd century in China.

In the late 1980's, French chef Auguste Escoffier created meals that combined umami with sweet, sour, salty and bitter tastes. He did not know the chemical source of this unique umami quality. This umami taste was first scientifically identified in 1908 by Kikunae Ikeda, a professor of the Tokyo Imperial University. The synthetic equivalent of umami is monosodium glutamate, commercially known as MSG. This artificial product is not recommended for consumption. Good Mauritian cuisine contains good natural umami compounds, that explain the flavoursome character of Mauritian foods.

Cauliflower pickle, with choko fricassée and chatini pomme d'amour on rice

A dish of cauliflower pickle, choko beef fricassée and chatini pomme d'amour served on rice colourfully illustrates the concept of multiple flavours on a plate, made up of a combination of umami with sweet, sour, salty and bitter tastes.

Madeleine Philippe at an interview with the Melbourne Mauritian Community radio station 3ZZZ, was asked: "In all your cooking, what would you consider to be the most important ingredient?" She answered without hesitation:
> *"The love that you put in your cooking. If you cook with love, your dishes will undoubtedly be nice because of the care and attention to detail that you would put in your food preparation."*

Love in your cooking will generate its own umami. The next most important aspect is the freshness of the products and ingredients. Avoid at all costs packaged and manufactured foods that contain loads of filler materials, additives and chemical preservatives.

The integration of the various cultures calling Mauritius home is summed up in a travel review article by Michael Gray published in The Sunday Times (UK) circa 1996.
> *"The feeling is of space and sociability, among a people greatly variegated. Has anywhere else on earth such racial harmony: where people celebrate and respect each other's religious festivals, eat each other's foods ....? It gives the visitor a charge of optimism about what's humanly possible."*

Sir Aneerood Jugnauth, Prime Minister of Mauritius also said:
> *"Mauritius has indeed won recognition as a land of peace and stability where traditions and cultures drawing their origins from various sources have been developing in harmony and mutual enrichment, thus providing to the world a living example of 'Unity in Diversity."*

This Unity in Diversity is strongly reflected in Mauritian Cuisine.

Portuguese Settlement Influence on Mauritian Cuisine

Ile de France (Mauritius under French Rule) and Mauritius was also a strategic stopover where ships stopped and trade was conducted in the pre-Suez Canal days. Mauritius was an official settlement of the Dutch East India Company between 1638 and 1710, and used as a refreshing station for passing ships. It was already frequented by Dutch ships from 1598 onwards, but only settled in 1638, to prevent the French and the British from settling on the island. They found sea turtles, wood pigeons, parrots and the famous dodo bird. On one occasion, they found twenty five of these birds with very small wings under a tree.

Dodo bird

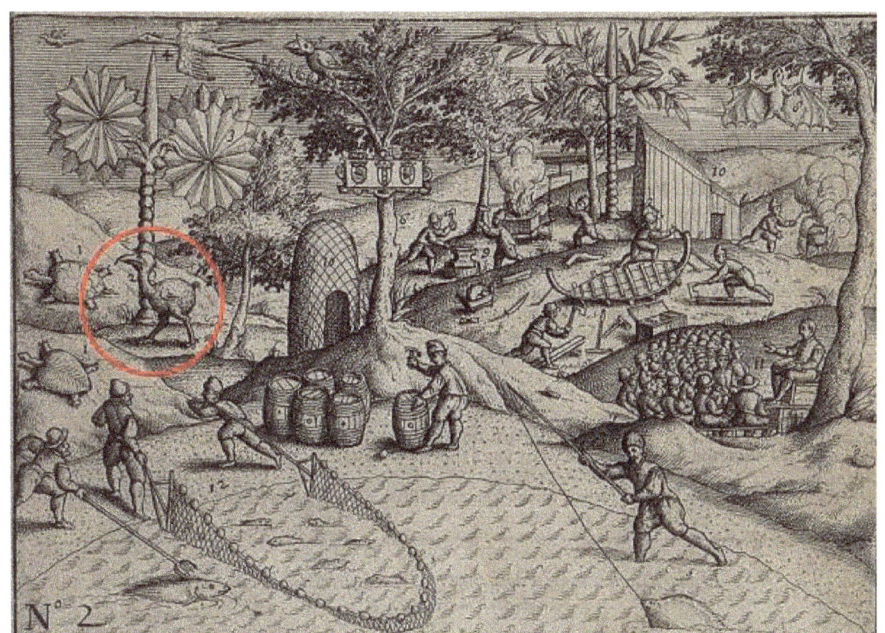
Drawing of a Dutch expedition which landed in Mauritius in 1601 showing the Dodo

They named the island Mauritius. Sydney Selvon in his book *"A comprehensive History of Mauritius, 2001"* explains:

> *"During their colonisation of Mauritius, the Dutch introduced the plantation of sugarcane using sugarcane from Java (Indonesia). Rice, tobacco, orange and mango trees were also cultivated. Deer brought from Java (Indonesia) was also released in the forests of Mauritius and rabbits, sheep, goats, chicken and ducks were reared. They also introduced the wild boar (cochons marrons) and monkeys now found in the forests of Mauritius. Slaves from Madagascar were also brought in to toil the fields. They also attempted to grow cereals like wheat, barley and oats. On 17 February 1710, the last Dutch colonists found life too harsh and left the island, with only runaway slaves left behind."*

French Settlement Influence on Mauritian Cuisine

On 27 August 1715, Captain Guillaume Dufresne d'Arsel officially took possession of Mauritius in the name of Louis XIV and renamed the island Isle de France. On 5 April 1722, The French Compagnie des Indes installed Denis de Nyon as governor of the island; with a group of sixteen settlers from the neighbour island Bourbon (now Reunion Island). They brought in people from Africa, Madagascar and India as artisans, slaves or sailors. These people, along with runaway slaves from the Dutch settlement formed the original core population of Mauritius. You can already picture the Mauritian dietary pattern evolve with French, African, Malagasy and Indian cuisine to make the best use of available and imported products. However, they faced the same challenges as the Dutch. Namely, they had to face severe climatic conditions, pests destroying crops and runaway slaves. In 1726, the Compagnie des Indes encouraged families and artisans to migrate from France to Isle de France. French peasant girls were also brought in to marry the bachelors of Isle de France. Land concessions were made to the new settlers for the establishment of farms to grow crops and rear livestock, both for local consumption and to supply passing ships. One of my ancestors Pierre Alifond (Aliphon) aged 24, stonemason was one of those settlers from Mirabel aux Baronnies in South East France who settled in Isle de France in 1740. His engagement contract read as follows:

"Service Historique de la Marine a Lorient (56) - Serie 1P76-F 22. Contrat d'engagement pour l'Ile de France. 'Je sousigne Pierre ALIFOND fils de Joseph et Margueritte LIDIERRE, natif de St Julien, eveche de Vezon, age de 24 ans, taille 5 pieds. Macon et tailleur de pierres de mon metier, reconnois m'etre engage a raison de 450 (livres sterlings) par an". A Paris, le 02.12.1740." He owned land concessions in the Flacq district and used same for livestock and crops.

The Compagnie des Indes also brought in products such as rice from their settlements in India and other islands, to supplement local products and feed the settlers. On one occasion, two ships were requisitioned for their rice shipments to spare the population from famine. The French settlers also relied on fishing and hunting to survive. The African slaves, Malagasy Slaves and Indian settlers were very adept at using native resources such as wild plants and animals to survive. The use of imported rice to this day as the staple food of Mauritius was most probably set during those early days of French settlement. Bertrand François Mahé de Labourdonnais was appointed governor of the island in 1735 and he created free enterprise on the island that produced such livestock as chicken and took the initiative to introduce and cultivate cassava (manioc) from Brazil for use as a staple food when rice was not in plentiful supply. Cassava is also a staple food used by African slaves in their motherlands. They all came with their dietary preferences and cuisines that contributed to the Mauritian cuisine of today. Dishes such as quatre quatre manioc and bouillon brèdes in today's Mauritian cuisine originate from such times. It was European explorers and slaves ships that brought such products as chilli peppers and tomatoes, along with peanuts, maize and plantains into such places as Mauritius.

Governor Labourdonnais also brought in additional workers from India and slaves from Africa and Madagascar to work in plantations and newly setup sugar factories in Isle de France. It is reported that Governor Labourdonnais brought from Pondichery a number of artisans, especially joiners and masons to teach the crafts to the slaves. Fine pieces of furniture made by these Tamil craftsmen still exist, some of which are on exhibition at the Naval Museum in Mahebourg. Under French rule, the arrival of indigenous Indians of the Muslim faith from Pondicherry and Bengal brought Sunni Muslims into the island. They were referred to as "les matelots lascards" and allowed to settle in the area known today as Plaine Verte in Port Louis and constructed their first mosque on the island, to be known as the Camp des Lascars Mosque. Like members of other communities on the island, some of the earliest Chinese in Mauritius arrived involuntarily, having been 'shanghaied' from Sumatra in the 1740s to work in Mauritius in a scheme hatched by the French admiral Charles Hector, Comte d'Estaing; however, they soon went on strike to protest their kidnapping. Luckily for them, their refusal to work was not met by deadly force, but merely deportation back to Sumatra. In the 1780s, thousands of voluntary migrants set sail for Port Louis from Guangzhou on board British, French, and Danish ships; they found employment as blacksmiths, carpenters, cobblers, and tailors, and quickly formed a small Chinatown, the "Camp des Chinois" in Port Louis. The earliest migrants were largely Cantonese-speaking; but, later, Hakka-speaking Chinese from Meixian, further east in Canton (modern day Guangdong), came to dominate numerically. That was the beginning of Indian, Muslim and Chinese influence on Mauritian cuisine.

Governor Labourdonnais in conjunction with Pierre Poivre, introduced into Isle de France an impressive collection of plants, fruit trees, spices and vegetables. For example, on 27 June 1770, Pierre Poivre returned from an expedition and brought back 450 nutmeg trees, 75 clove trees, 10,000 nutmegs and a chestful of cloves. Rice was successfully grown and enjoyed by the Creole women (French women born in Isle de France), with curries prepared from locally grown produce, saffron and spices. The Indian influence on the French settlers had already begun. Seafood, beef, poultry, goat, pork (including wild pigs) and vegetables were in plentiful supply. The curries eaten with rice were very much preferred in French colonial households to plain French dishes with bread. Rice had already established itself as the preferred staple food of the island and curries a much popular choice. To this day, curry dishes are the most popular foods in Mauritian households.

Seafoods were in plentiful supply, with freshwater fish such as carp, lubin, cabots, mullets and large shrimps. Sea turtles, lobsters, crabs, oysters and whales were also eaten. Whilst the black slaves would not touch them, the Indians considered the wild bats found in the forests of Isle de France a delicacy. The Chinese on the other hand, caught the bambara (called boudins de mer) and consumed same as a delicacy with magical powers. The consumption of chillies, grown locally, had also made its appearance much to the delight of the whole population to add some more zest to the local dishes. The French ragouts were improved with the addition of chillies, herbs and other locally produced spices. Mauritian cuisine was born.

Water cress, water melons, cardamom, ginger, basil, pumpkin, eggplant, lemons, oranges, saffron, guava, papaya, badamier, avocado, jackfruit, tamarind, litchis, cinnamon, cloves, chillies, sugar cane, corn, rice, beef, wild pigs, goats, poultry, sheep, honey bees and many other produce had made their entry into Mauritian cuisine. This use of such a diversity of produce would be reinforced during the English administration.

The French also brought into Mauritius their savoir faire and cuisine. French influence is synonymous with art and architecture, legendary clothing designers, chic citizens, a beautiful language and incredible food. More, perhaps, than that of any other nation in the world, French food is regarded as a culinary pinnacle. From the simple sophistication of breakfast time croissants and brioches, to savoury pâtés and artisanal charcuterie, from silky sauces, airy omelettes, delicious gratins, succulent salmis, delicate crêpes, creamy hand-crafted cheeses, tarts, gateaux and baked crème brulée desserts, French cooking is masterful and like the French people themselves, stylish. The dinners and receptions held in Isle de France during the

French colonial days were as lavish as those held in Paris. This French sophistication was to make a huge imprint upon Mauritians for a long time to come.

The French settlers in Isle de France came from all parts of France and with them came the traditional recipes cooked at home. Whilst French cuisine can be lavish, the beauty of this cuisine is that local produce is used and the freshness of the ingredients is essential to get the best outcomes. As such, the French settlers instructed their slave servants to prepare French dishes and that was passed on from generation to generation. Until recently, maids in Mauritius were the best cooks and they could turn out delicious foods, learned from their masters. Very much of the so-called "Creole cuisine" is derived from French cuisine, influenced by Malagasy and African cuisines and adapted to local products. One of the very popular and well known Creole dish is the rougaille, that is very much derived from French Provencal cuisine with the spiciness of locally grown herbs, spices and chillies. Provencal cuisine was in turn very much influenced by Italian cuisine that included the tomato as a primary base ingredient. This rougaille sauce is now the foundation for many Mauritian dishes. French cuisine has now succinctly blended itself into Mauritian cuisine. For example, it is now very common and an accepted practice for French casserole dishes to be eaten with rice.

Oxtail with vegetables in red wine on rice (page 130)

Similarly, the trinity of Mauritian cuisine consists of garlic, ginger and onions. These three ingredients are almost always the ones which provide Mauritian cuisine with a special flavour. In addition, garlic, ginger and onions are very good for your health. This trinity of Mauritian cooking is almost always complemented with parsley and thyme (French cuisine) and coriander herbs (Indian cuisine). Garlic and onions are almost always an integral part of French cooking. Ginger is very much used in Chinese dishes. In Mauritius, all three are used simultaneously to bring this special mix of aromatic and flavoursome ingredients. French settlers also brought with them the discipline and techniques required to prepare the lavish French dishes such as the civets, salmis, gratins, bouillons, soups, their famous charcuterie and gateaux.

French cuisine has had a huge influence on Mauritian cuisine and it is a common misconception that French food is difficult to cook. It gave Creole cuisine a base structure from which it could grow. The secret is to learn the techniques from someone who knows.

Gateau Napolitaine, influenced by French patisserie (page 262)

Legend of the Pomme d'Amour

The appellation of tomatoes as pomme d'amour has its origins in France. In Marmande, France renowned for its production of tomatoes, the legend of the Pomme d'Amour has been passed down from generation to generation. Today, a statue of Ferline with the famous tomato stands proud in the garden of the Marmande town hall. Ferline was the daughter of a rich bourgeois of Marmande, beautiful and wise, decided not to marry to the disappointment of her father and numerous suitors. Peyrot Bory, a poor young man in Marmande was madly in love with Ferline. He dared not declare his love to Ferline and decided to leave his native Marmande and travel the world. Peyrot enlisted himself on a ship in Bordeaux and travelled the world for four years visiting French islands, Les Antilles, Nouvelle Grenade and South America.

Statue of Ferline in front of the Marmande Town Hall

He returned home to Marmande with some strange seedlings in his pockets. He sowed those same seeds in his family home garden. In spring, the seeds grew into plants that bore beautiful red fruits, smooth and round in shape. Every day, he would pick the most beautiful of those fruits, put them in a basket that he would place under the window of room where Ferline lived.

She caught him placing the fruits one day and asked: "Tell me my friend, the name of those delicious fruits that you bring to me every day!" He answered: "When I was in South America, the natives there called them tomatoes. I call them Ferline in your honour because these fruits are so beautiful like you." "All right" she said throwing herself into Peyrot's arms, "as from today, we'll call these fruits "Pomme d'Amour." This has become the legend of the "Pomme d'Amour."

It is to be noted that Mauritius is one of the very few places where the tomato is called pomme d'amour. It could well be that the early settlers in Isle de France came from the Provence region where the appellation pomme d'amour is well used to this day. It is also claimed that the aphrodisiac properties of the tomato led to its appellation as pomme d'amour in the Provence region. Many of the settlers during the early days of French settlement came from the Provence region.

Pomme d'amours à la Provencale recipe

Ingredients:

1. 4 firm large ripe tomatoes,
2. ½ cup bread crumbs from firm sourdough bread,
3. 1 large clove garlic finely crushed,
4. ½ cup finely chopped fresh parsley,
5. 3 to 4 tablespoons extra light olive oil,
6. Salt and pepper to taste.

Method:

1. Cut the tomatoes horizontally into halves. Using a small fork, gently remove the seeds and the membranes holding the seeds. Salt and pepper the inside of the tomatoes to taste. Place upside down on kitchen paper towel to allow the extracted water to drain out.
2. Mix the bread crumbs with the garlic, parsley, salt and pepper to taste. Whilst doing so, sprinkle with drops of the extra light olive oil and mix well. Divide the stuffing into 8 portions.
3. Set your oven to 200°C.
4. Pat the tomatoes dry with kitchen paper towel. Carefully put the portions of the parsley and bread crumb filling into and on top of the tomato halves. Place the tomato halves on a sheet of baking paper in a flat baking tray. Drizzle with the extra light olive oil without drenching the filling.
5. About 20 minutes before serving, oven bake in the middle level until the crumbs are lightly browned and the tomatoes are hot through but still hold their shape. Serve immediately.

English Settlement Influence on Mauritian Cuisine

After several battles, including the famous Battle of Grand Port, the British conquered Mauritius from the French on 3 December 1810 and the possession of Mauritius by the British was confirmed four years later by the Treaty of Paris (1814). They changed the name of the island back to Mauritius. Nothing much changed and the settlers were given lots of concessions. They would retain the laws and customs established under French rule. The French rendition agreement signed by the settlers who were land owners, stipulated that those who wished to migrate back to France could do so within a period of two years. Only a few left and the vast majority stayed. Many of my Aliphon ancestors who were land owners actually signed the rendition papers.

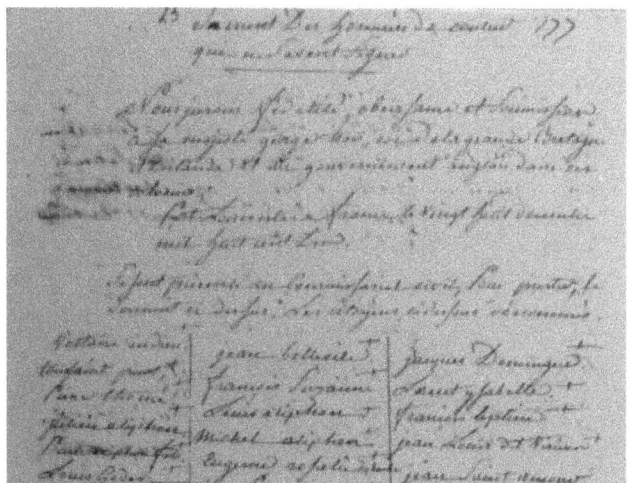

An example of the rendition papers, with the Aliphon signatures, exhibited at the museum l'Aventure du Sucre in Pamplemousses, Mauritius.

The aim of the British was not to settle in Mauritius but rather to control the island. In this context, the British did not have much influence on Mauritius cuisine and customs, except for the new labour force, including slaves they brought to the island.

The best description of Mauritian cuisine under British Rule in 1830 is narrated in an official report written by Charles Telfair, dated Jan 15, 1830 (Some Account of the State of Slavery at Mauritius since the British Occupation in 1810):

> *"It was deemed then by the British administration that "a mixture of animal and vegetable food seems to form a diet most conducive to health and strength. When animal food cannot be furnished in large quantity, the best substitute is a mixture of farinaceous and herbaceous products, with the addition of proper condiments, to stimulate the stomach and to secure general healthy action."*

There was a lot of wisdom in this approach and the Mauritian cuisine of today has much to be thankful for this decision. Some interesting and very relevant elements in the same 1830 Telfair report are worth mentioning. Carrots, celery and parsley were used in the preparation of soups. This is the same base vegetable stock used in French and Mauritian cuisine today. Ginger and saffron were used in soups and curries. Jackfruit was growing in abundance and very popular, with fruits weighing up to 30 lbs. Bananas were grown but not given as rations to the slaves. Mango trees were growing on every roadside, and on every estate but not given as rations to the slaves.

Guava plants were growing wild, giving fruits in abundance and their seeds propagated by birds through all the forests. Jambosa, roussaille and plums grew wild in all situations, but never given as rations to slaves. Bibasse was growing abundantly on many estates, but not given as rations to the slaves. Mason, custard apple (Atte) and coeur de boeuf were growing wild and producing an abundance of excellent and wholesome fruits.

Brèdes martin, brèdes malabar and brèdes de Flacq, with a choice from the following vegetables: margose, callebasse, giraumon, citrouille, pipengaille, bringèles or pomme d'amour were favourite dishes consumed by almost all the inhabitants of Mauritius, and frequently twice a day. I can remember some families in Mauritius who prepared a bouillon brèdes on a daily basis. Tamarin was used in curries and to make an acid drink with sugar. This drink was very popular among the slaves when at work. Chillies were growing wild on the estates, being propagated by the birds and used as a very wholesome condiment, used copiously by the slaves in their soups. All this is very similar to the current practices in Mauritian cuisine. Sagoo was imported from Singapore, but did not keep too well. It was also reported that the slaves on the way home from the fields were accustomed to cut and carry with them bundles of brèdes songe for their consumption. Most of these ingredients were either native to or introduced to Mauritius by the French under Governor Labourdonnais.

The abolition of slavery by the British in 1835, led to severe labour problems. Most of the 80,000 slaves that used to work in the plantation opted to leave. As a result the British turned to India to recruit workers on a contract basis (indentured labourers). Indentured labour began with Chinese, Malay, African and Malagasy labourers, but it was India that supplied much of the needed work force. Between 1835 and 1838, 24,000 Indian workers were imported to replace the slave workforce. In 1846, there were 56,200 Indians in a total population of 102,200. In 1861, the Indians were 192,600 more than half of a total population of 308,400.

The following information was read in the House of Commons in London, as part of a dispatch dated 27 May 1840 from Governor Sir William Nicolay to Lord John Russell. (Ref: Correspondence relative to the introduction of Indian labourers into Mauritius).

> *"The Indian labourers were subjected to much hardship, toiling the sugar cane fields and getting paid a pittance, with food rations and items of basic necessities being issued to them. Their daily rations consisted of rice, dhal or salt fish, ghee and salt. They basically survived on dhal and rice, with salt fish occasionally. Sometimes they were issued with curry powder, onions, beans, tamarinds and oil on special occasions."*

This combination has been the food consumed by poor members of the Indian community in Mauritius for a very long time. The black slave population or at least the slaves who were still working for their past masters after the abolition of slavery in 1835, were much better fed and treated.

From 1834 to 1922, 450,000 Indian workers came to Mauritius. Batches of immigrants came from Bihar, Uttar Pradesh, Orissa and other Hindi-speaking places. They were known as "Coolies" of whom Muslims constituted about 25%. The Tamils and Telegus were very cultured and greatly appreciated. This massive import of labour greatly modified the economic, cultural and political life of the island. French Mauritian cuisine suddenly had an influx of Indian, Tamil, Telegus, Chinese, Malay, African and Malagasy cuisines that started a hybridization and inter-culinary exchange of cuisines practiced by the respective cultures.

Indian Settlers influence on Mauritian Cuisine

The Indians from Bihar brought their cuisine to their new home in Mauritius. Predominantly, the food of Bihar is vegetarian. However, unlike Gujarat or some communities in southern India, non-vegetarian food is also quite acceptable even in traditional homes of Bihar. Traditional Bihar people did not eat eggs and chicken, though other types of birds and fowl were highly acceptable. As stated earlier, much of the food consumed by people in Bihar is vegetarian and very healthy. The staple food is "bhat, dhal, roti, tarkari (vegetables) and achar", prepared basically from rice, lentils, wheat flour, vegetables, and pickle. The Indian achar is prepared differently from the Malagasy achar. Traditionally, mustard oil and ghee (clarified butter) has been the popular cooking medium. "Khichdi" known in Mauritius as Kitcheree, a mix of rice and lentils, seasoned with spices, and served with several accompanying items like thick curd, chutney, pickles (more than 5000 varieties of pickles are known), papads, ghee and chokha (boiled mashed potatoes, seasoned with finely cut onions, green chillies) constitutes the lunch. In Mauritius, the mashed potatoes were replaced with rice and I have personally seen Indian labourers eat just rice seasoned with cut onions and chillies for lunch. Bihar people eat a mix of vegetable dishes prepared daily with each meal. Different type of stuffed parothas (in Mauritius called faratas) are also common.

Fish curry with tomato chatini on rice (page 234)

The most popular Bihari cuisine contribution to Mauritian cuisine would be the dhal puri, chatni, achar, dhals, curries and sweets such as ladoo. The original dhal puri in Bihar was made of salted wheat flour, which is filled with boiled-crushed gram-pulse that has been fried with special spices. In Mauritius, the refined dhal puri consists of boiled finely crushed dhal enclosed within a delicate flour pancake. The most famous chutney in Mauritius is the tomato, coriander leaves and chilli chatini.

Achars in Mauritius are made with a wide variety of vegetables and fruits. The most famous and popular achar in Mauritius is made with grated vegetables that is very popular in Madagascar, most probably introduced by Malay and Indonesian sailors or slaves who settled there.

In their native Bihar, Biharis are very fond of vegetables and cook them in different styles. As mustard is grown in abundance in Bihar, the mustard seed oil is the most preferred medium of cooking. Various spices are used to cook curries and make vegetables tasty. The curries are sometimes cooked in gravy or in its dry form. In its dry form the vegetable dish is called "bhujiya", and in curry form it is termed "tarkari". It is customary to have vegetables with rice during lunch and with rotis during dinner. Some vegetables like brinjal (eggplant), tomato and potato can be boiled or baked and mashed to make "chokha" or "bharta" after adding some spices, oil and salt. Mauritian cuisine has inherited most of Bihar cuisine brought in by the Bihari settlers. Chicken, mutton and dhal curries are all Bihari derived and now very popular in Mauritius.

Seven curries with tipuris and rice on banana leaf

Indian weddings are well known for their sumptuous foods. The wedding feast usually commences with appetisers, which are served before the main meal. Today, in Mauritius, it is well known that seven caris with tipuri pancakes will be served at the weddings. The main course meal contains by tradition, seven vegetable or dhal dishes (sept caris) eaten with tipuris (small fluffed up pancakes). After the primary meal, the guests are served with sweets to ease off the spicy and tingling tastes of the sept caris. All Mauritians have very happy memories of Indian weddings. An invitation to attend is an opportunity not to be missed.

Tamil and Telegu Settlers influence on Mauritian Cuisine

Tamils and Telegus from India also formed an important contingent of settlers to Mauritius. Tamil cuisine is famous for its deep belief that serving food to others is a service to humanity. My own experience with a Telegu family (Mulleegadoo) who lived next door to our home was that we were always receiving from them beautiful and very nice foods. That is very much part of the culture brought into Mauritian cuisine by these and the Muslim settlers in Mauritius.

Tamil cuisine has both non-vegetarian and vegetarian dishes, characterized by the use of rice, vegetables and lentils. Its distinct aroma and flavour is achieved by the blending of flavourings and spices, including curry leaves, mustard seeds, coriander, ginger, garlic, chilli, pepper, cinnamon, cloves, green cardamoms, cumin, nutmeg and other ingredients. Mostly used by the Tamils, rice has become the staple food of Mauritius. Curries especially fish and meat curries are now prepared the Tamil way in Mauritius, with masala (ground mix of spices). To this day, in the Port Louis Central Market, all sections except for the meat and fish sections are mostly occupied by Tamil stallholders.

On special occasions, traditional Tamil dishes in Mauritius are prepared in almost the same way as they were centuries ago - preparations that call for elaborate and leisurely cooking, and served in traditional style and ambience. The traditional way of eating a meal involves being seated on the floor, having the food served on a banana leaf, and using clean fingers of the right hand to transfer the food to the mouth. Vegetarian foods and meats will be served during Tamil marriage celebrations. Unlike the Indians, Tamils do not serve tipuris with sept caris at weddings. The sept caris are eaten with rice, followed by sago, appalams and vadai (sweet gateau piments) on the eve of the wedding. On the wedding day (known as Vindoo), meat curries are served with dhal, rason and goat offals, accompanied with rice. Chicken curry, cooked the Tamil way, is one of the favourite dishes that is served on important occasions by all Mauritians.

Telugu cuisine is native to the Telugu people from the states of Andhra Pradesh and Telangana in South India. It is also the cuisine of the Telegu-speaking population of Karnataka and Tamil Nadu with slight variations due to local influences. Generally known for its tangy, hot and spicy taste, Telegu cooking is very diverse due to the vast spread of the people and varied topological regions.

Millet-based breads (roti) and rice are the Telegu's predominant staple foods. Many of the curries (known as *koora*), snacks and sweets vary in the method of preparation and also differ in name. The Telegus are great users of red chilli, rice and spices, making Telegu food one of the richest and spiciest in the world. Vegetarian as well as meat and seafood feature prominently on the menus. Dhal, lentils, tomato and tamarind are largely used for cooking curries. Hence, the influence that curries in Mauritius can include crushed tomatoes. Spicy and hot varieties of pickles form an important part of Telegu cuisine and now Mauritian cuisine. Sweets and savouries form an important part of Telegu culture and are now very much part of the Mauritian culinary landscape. Made on festive and auspicious occasions, they are given to visiting relatives and are also made for evening snacks.

Muslim Settlers influence on Mauritian Cuisine

Post 1835, three distinctive groups of Muslims immigrants originating from the province of Gujerat settled on the island. The first group came to be known as Maiman merchants, hailing from the town of Kutch. The second group came from Hallai in the Indian Province of Kathiawar and were known as Hallaye merchants. Both were experts in the supply of cereals, mainly rice and dhal. The third group became known as Surtees and hailed mainly from the town of Surat and the surrounding towns of Rander and Bharuch. They specialised in the supply of textile products to the island.

The Muslims brought with them their rich artistic and gastronomic culture into Mauritian cuisine. Also known as Muglai cuisine, their lamb kebabs were laced with spices, the Indian rice pulaos cooked with meat were turned into wonderful bryanis. Lamb and meat roasts were flavoured with herbs, spices and seasonings. Plain Indian dishes were garnished with almonds, pistachios, cashews and raisins. Muslims also introduced leavened breads to Indian cuisine. Meats were marinated in yogurt and spices and also cooked in tandoors. However, both pork and beef were avoided to respect the traditions of Muslim and Indian cultures. Like the French who took great pride in their culinary savoir faire, Muslim cuisine also brought their panache and elegance to the table, with their foods often served in jade, silver and Chinese porcelain.

Muslim bryani dish (page 118)

Islamic cuisine is not well understood in Mauritius. This did not prevent all Mauritians from enjoying foods such as bryanis and poudine vermicelles in Muslim restaurants everywhere in Mauritius. The most well known is the Pakistan Hotel near Plaine Verte in Port Louis. Their doors are reported as never shut, except when cyclones class 4 warning is in force. The Pakistan Hotel is well known for its teas, sweets, bryanis and many other delicacies. I also recall when I was very young, we had gifts of gateau vermicelles and other sweets during the Ramadan period. The tradition of Iftaar (fast-breaking) must surely rank as one of the world's greatest culinary celebrations.

During the month of Ramadan, Muslims fast, pray and celebrate together while also trying to be thoughtful and generous to friends and family, but especially to the needy and poor. It is a month of warmth, compassion and generosity. Notwithstanding the intense spiritual values embodied by Ramadan, it is the popular tempo, the folklore and cultural traditions, marked by the vibrant atmosphere of Iftaar that mostly attract the attention of the outside public. This relationship between religion and food is an important contribution of Muslims in Mauritius to Mauritian culture and cuisine.

Travelling in towns and villages of Mauritius, it is a recurrent feature to come across halim and bryani dealers in street-corners. Halim is so well entrenched in the Mauritian tradition that it prominently features in the menu cards or display-boards side by side with boulette chinois and rasson. Overpowered by the spell of the spicy flavour and savoury taste that keeps the sense of gourmandise high, very few people pay attention to the origin of halim or ever care to know how it was introduced in Mauritius. Bryanis delicately prepared by specialist cooks are one of the most enjoyed foods in Mauritius. It is very popular now as a quick take away for most Mauritians to be enjoyed for all occasions. Muslim cuisine, more so than in other cuisines, is a reflection of the cooks, their love of the cuisine and individual attention to details.

Take away stall selling bryani in Rosehill

Chinese Settlers influence on Mauritian Cuisine

Between 1840 and 1843 alone, 3,000 Chinese contract workers arrived on the island; by 1850, the total resident Chinese population reached five thousand. By the 1860s, shops run by Sino-Mauritians could be found all over the island. They came from Guangzhou and brought with them their Cantonese cuisine. Guangzhou, the capital of Guangdong province, has long been a trading port and many imported foods and ingredients are used in Cantonese cuisine. Besides pork, beef and chicken, Cantonese cuisine incorporates almost all edible meats, including offal, chicken feet, duck's tongue, snakes, and snails. However, lamb and goat are rarely eaten, unlike the cuisines of northern or western China. Many cooking methods are used, with steaming and stir frying being the most favoured due to their convenience and rapidity. Other techniques include shallow frying, double steaming, braising, and deep frying. In Cantonese cuisine, a number of ingredients are used such as spring onion, sugar, salt, soy sauce, rice wine, cornstarch, vinegar, scallion oil, and sesame oil. This brought to Mauritius the Chinese component of Mauritian Cuisine, enjoyed by all Mauritians and visitors to Mauritius.

Even after the British takeover of the island, migration continued unabated. By mid-century, the total resident Chinese population reached 5,000. The earliest migrants were largely Cantonese speaking; but, later, Hakka-speaking Chinese from Meivian, further east in Canton (modern day Guangdong), came to dominate numerically; as in other overseas Chinese communities, rivalry between Hakka and Cantonese became a common feature of Chinese society.

Mauritian Chinese fried noodles (page 152)

By the 1860s, shops run by Sino-Mauritians could be found all over the island. Some members of the colonial government thought that further migration should be prohibited, but Governor

John Pope Hennessy recognising the role that Sino-Mauritians played in providing cheap goods to less well-off members of society, resisted the restrictionists' lobbying. These shops sold anything and everything on credit to the locals, and offered a 24 hour, seven days a week service. The Chinese settlers established restaurants and shops that would sell not only Chinese foods, but products, sweets and cakes consumed by all ethnic groups. Very often, a section of the shop would be selling alcoholic drinks where the local drinkers would meet after work sharing drinks with gajacks.

Chinese restaurants have been very much part of the Mauritian culinary landscape for centuries. Restaurants like Lai Min, ONU, Gros Pitit and Ciel Bleu Restaurants in Port Louis, Coin Ideal and Hollywood Restaurants in Rosehill, Rio Restaurant in Curepipe were the most well known. The Chinese restaurants in Mauritius, like Chinese restaurants worldwide, virtually standardized their dishes so that you knew what to expect whenever you order Chinese foods. The usual Chinese menu is available from most Mauritian Chinese restaurants and take-aways, such as fried rice, sweet and sour dishes, chilli prawns, pork or beef, stir fried vegetables, roast pork, spring rolls and dumplings. However, the up-market Chinese restaurants offer intricate dishes and lunches or dinners could last three to four hours without the same foods being consumed. I remember well the monthly rendez-vous at Ciel Bleu in Port Louis where Gerard Lefébure, Gol and Bonga Auleebux, Madeleine and Clancy Philippe and other friends would partake in elaborate lunches enjoying the delights of Chinese cuisine. Special treats such as crispy and flaky Hakien rolls which are very intricate to cook and contain delicacies such as lobster and prawns, would be specially ordered.

It is said that the Chinese will "eat anything that walks, flies or swims and turn it into a delicacy by proper seasoning and cooking." The cooking methods are as varied as the ingredients: stir fry, deep fry, roast, steam and broil (grill) – so long as the raw material is as fresh as possible and accompanied by the appropriate sauces and dips. Oyster sauce, chilli sauce, ground chillies and chopped chillies in soy sauce, fish sauce and sesame oil are common condiments to be found in Chinese cuisine. This dipping sauce and condiment habit has been adopted by all Mauritians and is an essential component of Mauritian cuisine. Snack foods prepared in other cuisines are almost always accompanied by a dipping sauce. Chinese cuisine in Mauritius is also home to roast pork, cured pork sausages, black beans and a staggering array of dim sum and pork preparations. Most Mauritian homes will cook at least one Chinese dish every week. Chinese fried rice and noodles have become essential components of the foods served on special occasions for all Mauritians, irrespective of culture. Even pork free or vegetable fried rice or noodles are specially prepared for non pork or non meat eating Mauritians.

Chinese weddings in Mauritius are very elaborate affairs. The Chinese wedding feast is loaded with foods symbolizing long life and prosperity. It is customary to serve eight courses, since eight is thought to be a lucky number. Appetizers will feature cold plates shaped like the dragon and the phoenix. In Chinese culture, the dragon and the phoenix symbolize the yin (the feminine side of our nature) and the yang (the masculine side of our nature) respectively. They are also associated with goodness and prosperity. The main courses commonly feature fowl that mate for life such as duck or geese. Peking duck is often served, since this is a red dish symbolising happiness. Chicken and duck will also be found on the banquet table - the two fowls represent a balance between the man and the woman in their new relationship. Sea cucumber may accompany vegetable dishes, since it is thought to symbolize harmony and a lack of conflict between the newly married couple.

Snacks and Gajacks

Snacks and gajacks are very much part of Mauritian cuisine. It is an established custom for delicious morsels and tasty appetisers to be served with drinks and whilst lunch or dinner is being prepared. In taverns in Mauritius, you can see gatherings of men enjoying their drinks with friends, inevitably enjoying the tasty servings prepared by the hosts. The tasty morsels of foods and bites are commonly referred to as gajacks. If the gajacks are nice, the drinking sessions will be prolonged til late. Delicacies are also served and some taverns and restaurants are known for their specialities. This practice has been continued by Mauritians in Australia when hosting, much to the delight of guests. The word gajak is used in northern India for a sweet made from nuts and sugar, that is cut into small bites for snacking. It is consumed to mark the end of winter, celebrate the birth of babies and the arrival of newly-wed brides in the family. How it came to be associated with tasty morsels of food in Mauritius to accompany drinks is a mystery.

Stir fried lamb morsels with vegetables gajack (page 61)

In the evenings or on occasions when family and friends are gathered together, it is expected that alcoholic drinks will be served with gajacks to offset the sharpness of the drinks. This also avoids drinking on an empty stomach. Sometimes, when no lunch or dinner is offered, the snacks and gajacks are more substantial and can replace a full meal.

Farata with beef and potato curry (pages 36 and 115)

Mauritian cuisine offers an incredible range of snacks and gajacks. Each component cuisine has its own spectrum of items that can be prepared in mins or elaborately put together. For example, the battered vegetables, meats and bread can be put together very quickly. Hakiens from Mauritian Chinese cuisine are very elaborate in their preparation. Very often, the special cooking techniques involved are well kept secrets. Similarly, Indian and Telegu expertise in making the huge inventory of snacks is jealously guarded. This expertise is passed on from generation to generation and kept in the family. Some restaurants and taverns have also developed a huge popularity for their snacks and gajacks. Many establishments in Port Louis, Beau Bassin, Rosehill and Curepipe have huge reputations for certain dishes. Hotel Pakistan in Port Louis stays open 24 hrs a day and offers the very best of Muslim cuisine. Patisserie Golden in Beau Bassin and Patisserie Sainte Thérèse in Curepipe were very popular for their patés. The snack sized noodles and fried rices of the smaller establishments in Beau Bassin and Rosehill do a brisk business selling quick lunches. La soupe Mama and bouillon boulettes in Port Louis are sold at street stalls. Many people have fond memories of late night snacks and bouillons after dances and night clubbing at Ghoul in Beau Bassin. This place stayed opened 24 hours a day. Dhal pouris are everywhere, very often these are exported for sale to Mauritian communities worldwide.

Onion Fritters
Bhajas

Ingredients (Make 15):
- 225 g of besan flour,
- 2 large onions finely sliced
- ½ teaspoon chilli powder,
- 1 teaspoon turmeric powder,
- 1 teaspoon baking powder,
- Salt to taste,
- ½ teaspoon cumin seeds coarsely crushed,
- 2 green chillies finely chopped,
- 2 tablespoons chopped coriander leaves,
- Vegetable oil for deep frying.

The same batter may be used with a variety of vegetables cut into bite sizes.

Method:
1. In a bowl, mix together the besan flour, chilli powder, turmeric, baking powder and salt to taste.
2. Add the coarsely crushed cumin seeds, sliced onions, chopped chillies and coriander leaves. Toss together well. Omit the onions if just making plain bhajas.
3. Very gradually add sufficient cold water to make a thick but still runny batter. Mix well together.
4. Heat oil in a wok or similar deep frying pan.
5. Drop 1 tablespoonful of the mixture into the hot oil and fry until golden brown. Leave enough space to turn the fritters. Drain well and serve hot. Goes well with chilli sauce.
6. Alternatively, dip vegetable pieces into batter for coating before frying in oil.

Boulettes Chouchou

Meatballs with Choko, Prawn and Pork (or Beef)

Ingredients (Make 20-25):
- 600 g grated chokoes (drained),
- 300 g minced pork (or beef),
- 200 g minced green prawns (shelled),
- 1 medium onion finely chopped,
- 3-4 tablespoons cornflour,
- 1-2 tablespoons light soy sauce,
- 1-2 tablespoons fish sauce,
- Salt to taste.

Method:
1. Shell and de-vein the prawns. Finely chop to a minced meat consistency. Put aside in fridge.
2. Peel the chokoes, cut into quarters lengthwise, trim away the centre bits. Coarsely grate and hand strain. Place in colander and allow excess water to drain.
3. Finely chop the medium onion. Mix with the minced pork (or beef) and minced prawn. Season with salt to taste. Add the light soy sauce and fish sauce. Mix well by hand. Add the grated chokoes and mix well into the pork (or beef) and prawn mixture. Gradually mix in the cornflour and hand mix well. Cover with cling wrap and put in fridge for 20 mins.
4. Meanwhile, prepare the steamer and put on simmer.
5. Using little quantities of the grated chokoes, pork (or beef) and prawn mix, make meatballs approximately 3 cm in diameter. Refer to photo above.
6. Place meatballs in steamer and simmer for 15-20 mins or until thoroughly cooked. Check by breaking one meatball in half to see if cooked inside.
7. Serve with hot chilli sauce.

Cheese Sticks
Batons de Fromage

Ingredients (Make 10-15):
- 1 cup white flour,
- ½ teaspoon baking powder,
- 1 cup grated cheddar cheese,
- ½ cup butter,
- 3 tablespoons ice water.

Optional:
- ½ cup grated cheddar cheese for sprinkling.

Method:
1. Preheat oven to 200°C. Sieve the white flour into a mixing bowl with the baking powder. Mix well.
2. Add 1 cup of grated cheese. Gradually blend in the butter until the mixture resembles coarse crumbs. Add water and mix well into a semi smooth pastry.
3. Roll pastry into sheets.
4. *Optional: If making thin twisted strips, sprinkle one side of the pastry sheets with ½ cup grated cheddar cheese. Gently press in by hand.*
5. Cut pastry sheets into 1 cm wide strips. The length can vary depending upon your preference. To make thin strips, gently twist the strips as shown in photo.
6. Bake on an ungreased baking sheet for 8-10 mins or until light golden brown. Keep an eye on the oven as the pastry can burn very quickly. Serve warm or cold.

Chilli Cakes
Gateaux Piments

Ingredients (Make 15-20):
- 250 g dholl (split peas),
- 2 or 3 green or red chillies (as few or as many as you like),
- 2 tablespoons chopped coriander leaves,
- 2 tablespoons finely chopped spring onions,
- Salt to taste,
- 1 teaspoon whole cumin seeds or ½ teaspoon powdered cumin,
- Vegetable oil for frying.

Method:
1. Wash dholl in running water. Allow to soak in water for at least 3-4 hours (preferably overnight).
2. Drain dholl thoroughly by placing in a sieve for a few mins. Blend to a combination of fine and not so fine consistency. The ground dholl should stick together when hand pressed.
3. Add all the other ingredients and mix well together. Add a little bit of water if necessary.
4. Heat up the oil over hot to medium heat. Shape mixture into small balls and deep fry in batches until golden brown. Make sure that the whole chilli cake is cooked. Lower heat if necessary to ensure thorough cooking.
5. Drain and place over several layers of kitchen paper towel to absorb the extra oil. Serve hot with fresh bread or eat as a snack.

Crêpes Salées
Pancakes

Ingredients (Make 5-10):
- 250 g sifted white flour,
- 3 eggs,
- 2 ½ cups (600 ml) milk or water,
- 2 tablespoons brandy,
- ½ teaspoon salt,
- 2 tablespoons melted butter.

Method:
1. Mix the flour with the eggs and enough milk to make a semi fluid batter. Add brandy and salt. Blend well. Leave to stand for 1 hour.
2. Heat some butter in a small pan, pour in 1 tablespoon of batter and cook quickly on one side, toss and brown the other side.
3. Serve with fillings and sauces of your choice.

Madeleine with a fan of her cuisine from Rome, Italy

Crêpes Douces
Crêpes Suzette
Pancakes

Ingredients (Make 5-10):
- 250 g sifted white flour,
- 75 g caster sugar,
- Pinch of salt,
- 6 eggs,
- ½ cup (125 ml) milk,
- 1 teaspoon vanilla sugar,
- 3 teaspoons brandy,
- 1 tablespoon butter.

Sauce Ingredients:
- 75 g butter,
- 75 g caster sugar,
- 3 tablespoons of your favourite liqueur,
- Juice from 1 tangerine,
- Sugar for sprinkling.

Method:
1. Mix the flour with sugar and salt. Gradually add eggs and milk. Beat well.
2. Add other ingredients. Blend together to a smooth batter. Leave to stand for 1 hour.
3. Heat some butter in a small pan, pour in 1 tablespoon batter and cook quickly on one side, toss and brown the other side.
4. Stack the pancakes on a warm to medium hot plate.
5. To make sauce, cream the butter, add the sugar and beat in well. Add the liqueur and tangerine juice.
6. To serve, place pancake on a plate, sprinkle with sugar. Pour about 1 tablespoon of sauce on to the centre of the pancake. Fold in quarters and serve very hot.

Dhall Pooris

Ingredients (Make 10-12):
- 500 g yellow split peas,
- 750 g white flour,
- 2 teaspoons ground cumin seeds,
- Turmeric powder,
- Salt to taste.

Method:
1. Boil the yellow split peas in water with a pinch of turmeric powder and salt to taste, until well cooked but not sticky. Strain and reserve the boiled water for pastry use later. Blend the yellow split peas well. The blend must be on the dry side rather than wet. Mix in the ground cumin seeds. Set aside.
2. Sift the flour with some salt to taste into a mixing bowl. Adding the warm reserved boiled water in small quantities, gradually work the paste until very soft but not sticky. Wrap in cling wrap and rest for 1 hour.
3. Mould the dough into 6 cm balls. Use your finger to make a hole into the centre of the dough balls. Carefully put one teaspoon of the yellow split peas mixture into the hole. Close by pushing in the sides. Toss the dough balls in flour and carefully roll out into thin circular pooris.
4. Heat up a flat saucepan large enough to hold the pooris. Brush the pan with oil and add the pooris. Cook on one side until slightly puffed up and flip on to the other side until just cooked. About half a minute in total. Do not overcook.
5. Serve hot with blended tomato or coriander chutneys.

Hint: Dhall pooris may be kept individually in layers separated by baking paper and frozen, placed in a plastic bag.
To use, allow to thaw, place in microwave between kitchen paper towels and warm up individually for thirty seconds.

Croquettes de Volaille
Chicken Pieces in Batter

Ingredients (Make 10-15):
- 125 g fresh chicken fillet,
- 2 teaspoons cornflour,
- 1 tablespoon fish sauce,
- Salt and pepper to taste,
- Vegetable oil for deep frying.

Batter:
- 125 g self raising flour,
- 2 eggs,
- 1 teaspoon salt,
- Water.

Method:
1. Cut chicken into 1 cm pieces.
2. Season with the fish sauce, salt and pepper. Set aside to absorb seasoning. Be careful not to add too much salt.
3. Beat up the 2 eggs and 1 tablespoon water.
4. Mix the self raising flour and salt. Gradually blend in the egg mixture. Add water in small quantities to obtain a thick batter.
5. Lightly coat the chicken pieces with cornflour. Drop into the batter. Mix well.
6. Heat oil in preparation for deep frying.
7. Spoon out each battered chicken piece and drop into the hot oil. Cook to a light golden brown colour. Reduce heat if browning too quickly.
8. Remove cooked croquettes, drain and serve hot with chilli sauce or sauce d'ail (garlic sauce).

James Coakes, Mauritian gajack gourmet.

Bringele Frire
Egg Plant Fritters
Piment Cari Frire
Chilli in Batter
Du Pain Frire
Bread Slices Fried in Batter

Ingredients:
- 200 g of besan (chickpea) flour,
- 1 tablespoon white flour,
- 1 tablespoon spring onion finely chopped,
- 1 teaspoon baking powder,
- ½ teaspoon crushed garlic,
- ½ teaspoon crushed ginger,
- Salt to taste,
- Oil for deep frying,
- 1 large round eggplant,
- Green piment cari,
- Bread slices (one day old),

Other variations:
- sliced potatoes or cauliflower florets.

Method:
1. Slice eggplant crosswise in ¼ - ½ cm slices. Cut the piment cari into halves lengthwise. Cut the bread slices into halves.
2. Sift besan and white flours together with the baking powder, into a mixing bowl.
3. Add the finely chopped spring onions, salt, crushed ginger and garlic. Mix with sufficient water to form a non-running batter that clings to the eggplant, bread slices and piment cari.
4. Heat oil over medium heat for deep frying.
5. Wash the eggplant slices in running water. Dry with kitchen paper towel and dip each slice into the batter coating evenly. Deep fry slices a few at a time so that the battered pieces are not touching. Fry to a light brown golden colour, turning over as required. Be careful as the besan batter can easily overcook.
6. Repeat same process with the bread slices and the piment cari.
7. Drain on kitchen paper towel and serve hot with chilli sauce or chatini pomme d'amour.

Faratas
Indian Bread (Paratha)

Ingredients (Make 10):
- 2 cups white flour,
- 3 tablespoons melted ghee or butter,
- 1 teaspoon salt,
- ½ cup + 2 tablespoons water.

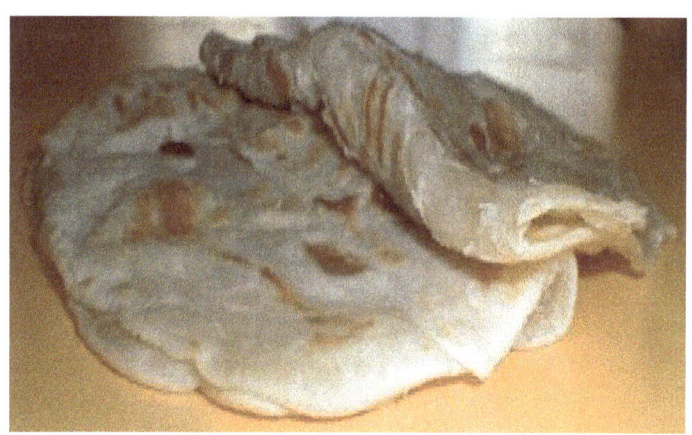

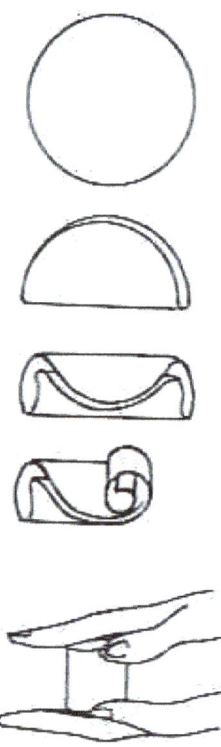

Method:
1. Sieve flour on to a flat surface. Add half the water, mix well and knead into a soft dough. Knead for a further 15 mins, gradually adding the remaining water, alternatively pressing and folding. Sprinkle with 1-2 tablespoons of water. Cover with a moist kitchen towel and set aside for 10 mins.
2. Divide the dough into 6 equal parts and shape into round balls. Roll into a flattened disc about 12 cms diameter. Refer to diagram on left.
3. Smear with a little melted ghee or butter and fold into a semi circle. Smear some more over the upper surface and fold a second time. Double fold it lengthwise. Press gently with your fingers and roll into a round circle making the edge thinner than the centre.
4. The secret is in the layering with a smear of ghee or butter in between the pastry sheets. The more layering, the flakier the farata will become.
5. Smear both sides of the farata with ghee or butter. Place on a hot griddle, cook for a few seconds turning over once.
6. Cook for a further few seconds until the farata is light golden brown on both sides.
7. Serve hot with curries.

Gateau Arouille
Taro Fritters

Ingredients (Make 15-20):
- 500 g taro peeled and grated,
- 2 tablespoons bread crumbs,
- ½ teaspoon sugar,
- 1 teaspoon freshly crushed ginger,
- 3-4 tablespoons cornflour,
- Salt to taste,
- Vegetable oil for frying.

Optional:
- 30 g bacon finely chopped and / or 2 spring onions finely chopped.

Method:
1. Combine grated taro and all the other ingredients in a mixing bowl.
2. Optional: *Fry the chopped bacon in 2 tablespoons of oil until crisp. Remove from pan and add to the combined ingredients.*
3. Add the finely chopped spring onions. Mix well together.
4. Take 1 rounded tablespoonful of the mixture, mould into a round shape. If necessary, dust with or add some more cornflour to get mixture to bind together.
5. Drop one by one into the oil and deep fry until golden brown. Reduce heat if browning too quickly.
6. Drain on kitchen paper towels and serve immediately. Season with chilli sauce to enhance flavour.

Paté Chaud with Minced Beef

"Patisserie St Therese / Patisserie Golden Style"

Ingredients (Make 15-20):
- Puff pastry 6-10 sheets,
- 500 g minced beef,
- 2 rashers bacon,
- 2 tablespoons dry sherry,
- 1 egg beaten,
- 1 medium onion finely chopped,
- 2 tablespoons vegetable oil,
- 1 teaspoon cornflour dissolved in small quantity of water,
- Milk to brush pastry,
- Salt and pepper to taste.

Method:
1. To make the filling, finely chop the onion. Add to the minced beef. Trim the bacon rashers of all fat and finely chop. Add to the minced beef together with 2 tablespoons of dry sherry. Mix well. Season with salt and pepper to taste. Be careful with the salt as the bacon is salty enough.
2. Heat 2 tablespoons of vegetable oil in a saucepan over medium high heat. Cook the minced beef and bacon mixture, stirring continually to ensure even cooking and to evaporate any moisture.
3. Just before removing from heat, stir in the cornflour with a small quantity of water to thicken the sauce. Cook for 1-2 mins. Remove from heat and allow to cool.
4. Meanwhile, preheat oven to 180°C.
5. To make each paté cut circular pieces 6 cm in diameter from the softened puff pastry. Set aside covered with a damp kitchen towel.
6. Add 1 whisked egg to the minced beef and bacon filling. Mix well together.
7. Put one circular piece of pastry on top of another taking care to brush the first piece with some water to ensure that the two pieces will stick together when cooked. Using a small spoon put some of the filling on the centre of the two round pastry pieces leaving a clear space around the perimeter.
8. Brush the outer clear space with some water. Place another round piece of puff pastry on top. Use the back of a fork to gently press the outer edge of all three layers together. Gently prick the top pastry round with a small fork. Place the finished paté on an oven tray lined with baking paper. Repeat with remaining pastry.
9. Brush with milk and cook in oven at mid position until the patés are light golden brown.

Pain Perdu
French Toast

Ingredients (Make 8):
- 8 slices white bread (baguettes),
- 125 g butter,
- 100 g granulated sugar,
- 250 ml milk,
- 4 eggs,
- 25 g vanilla sugar.

Method:
1. To clarify the butter, place in a small saucepan and cook slowly until a residue forms and sinks to the bottom. Remove from the heat and strain off the clarified butter on top for frying.
2. Bring the milk to the boil, with the sugar and vanilla sugar. Pour into a basin.
3. Beat the eggs well in another container.
4. Diagonally slice the baguette as shown in photo.
5. Slowly pour the clarified butter into a frying pan large enough to hold 4 slices of bread. Place over medium heat.
6. Quickly dip each slice of bread, first in the milk then in the beaten eggs, making sure both sides are covered. Fry one side then the other. It should take about 3-4 mins.
7. Remove the bread with a spatula and place on a serving dish. Gradually pour in the rest of the clarified butter and fry the remaining bread slices.
8. Serve immediately. Sprinkle the bread with sugar and serve with fruit purée or apricot jam. Ideal for breakfast.

Mauritian Prawn Hakien

Ingredients (Make 10-12):
- 400 g shelled green prawns,
- ½ cup finely sliced green cabbage,
- ½ cup finely grated carrot,
- ½ cup finely cut bamboo shoots 3-4 cm long,
- 1 cup white flour,
- 2 tablespoons vegetable oil for the pastry,
- 3-4 tablespoons cornflour,
- Salt and pepper to taste,
- Cold water,
- Oil for deep frying.

Optional:
- Substitute the prawn with fish or chicken.

Method:
1. Shell and de-vein the green prawns. Finely chop with a sharp and heavy knife so as not to mash the prawns. Transfer to a large bowl.
2. Add the green cabbage, bamboo shoots and carrots. Season lightly with salt and pepper. Mix well with your fingers.
3. Gradually add the cornflour to obtain a coherent mix. Use your hand to slightly compress the filling into self standing sausages, about 2-3 cm in diameter and 10 cm long. Thinly sprinkle flour on the kitchen bench. Roll each sausage in the flour.
4. Place on a non-stick surface and leave in the fridge uncovered for 30 mins to 1 hour.
5. Meanwhile prepare the batter. In a flat mixing bowl, wide enough to roll the sausage shaped pieces in the batter later, place 1 cup of sifted fine white flour with 1 teaspoon of salt. Add 2 tablespoons of vegetable oil. Gradually add the cold water in small steps using a wire whisk. Mix well in the same circular direction until the batter becomes aired up with some bubbles or air traps showing. Keep mixing / adding water until a semi liquid batter is obtained that will stick to the surface of the sausages.
6. Remove sausages from fridge. If shape has a flat bottom, gently reshape.
7. Heat up oil for deep frying over a medium to low heat. Frying pan must be large enough for the battered sausages to fry freely without sticking to each other.
8. When the oil is hot enough, take sausages one by one and carefully coat with the batter. Allow excess to drip off. Make sure that a uniformly coated batter is obtained. Obtain some assistance if possible. Slowly drop into the hot oil. Cook 2 or 3 at a time. Using a wooden spoon or tongs, make sure that the pieces don't stick to each other and turn over at regular intervals to ensure even cooking.

9. As soon as the battered pieces turn a slightly golden colour, remove from the frying pan and place on a wire drip tray.
10. Repeat with the other sausages, batter and fry as per above.
11. Add water in small quantities to the remaining batter until a thinner batter is obtained.
12. Repeat the batter and frying process, using the thinner batter and the already cooked pieces. This will build up a second crispy coating to the hakiens. Cook until a light golden crispy finish is obtained. Remove and place on a wire rack. Do not overcook. If the layered crispiness of the coating is not enough, repeat this last step again.
13. Enjoy with chilli or garlic sauce. Cut the hakiens at an angle with a sharp knife and serve as gajacks.

Very popular and flavoursome Mauritian hakien

Poulet Annabelle

Marinated Chicken Thigh Fillets

Ingredients (Serve 5):
- 1 kg chicken thigh fillets de-boned and skinned,
- 2 tablespoons fish sauce,
- 2 tablespoons light soy sauce,
- 2 tablespoons Worcestershire sauce (Lea and Perrins sauce),
- 100 ml dry white wine or dry sherry,
- Salt & pepper to taste,
- 4 tablespoons vegetable oil.

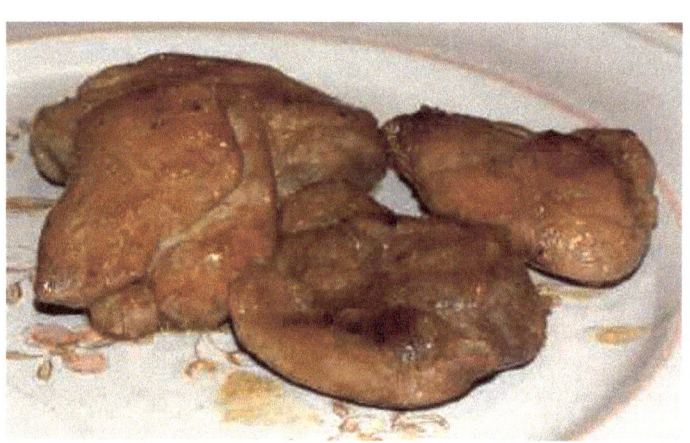

Method:
1. Skin the chicken thigh fillets, de-bone leaving the thigh fillet intact. Trim off any fat. Open up the thigh fillets and cut into two halves lengthwise. Season with salt and pepper to taste.
2. Mix the chicken thigh fillets with the fish sauce, light soy sauce, Worcestershire sauce and dry white wine (or dry sherry). Cover and marinate in refrigerator overnight (or for at least 4 hours at room temperature). Turn over the marinated pieces at least once.
3. Heat 4 tablespoons vegetable oil on high heat in a wok (or similar utensil) large enough to contain all the marinated chicken fillets. Carefully stir fry until light golden brown. Cover, reduce heat to medium high and simmer for 10-15 mins. Remove cover, gently stir the chicken fillets and simmer until sauce thickens to your preference.
4. Transfer to a warmed serving dish. Serve with salads or pastas.
5. Alternatively, cut the cooked chicken fillets into bite sizes and serve as a snack with drinks.
6. Enjoy. This dish is named after our granddaughter Annabelle - one of her favourite dishes.

Boulette Poisson
Fish Balls

Ingredients (Make 25):
- 450 g white fish fillets, skinned, boned and cubed,
- 3 spring onions chopped,
- 1 bacon fat rasher, with rind removed and chopped,
- 1 tablespoon Chinese white wine or dry sherry,
- 2 tablespoons light soy sauce,
- 1 egg white.

Method:
1. Put the cubed fish, spring onion pieces, bacon fat, rice wine, soy sauce and egg white in a food processor and process until smooth. With wetted hands or wearing wet plastic gloves, divide and form the blended mixture into about twenty five balls.
2. Steam the fish balls in batches in a lightly greased bamboo (or an ordinary) steamer for about 5-10 mins, until cooked through and firm to the touch. One trick for the fish balls not to stick is to place them on cabbage leaves or baling paper in the steamer.
3. Remove from the steamer and keep warm. Serve as an appetiser with sauce d'ail or in bouillon with chilli sauce.

Mashed Potatoes with Corned Beef

Ingredients (Serve 6):
- 325 g canned corned beef (use lean corned beef),
- 1.3 kg potatoes, suitable for mashing,
- 2 medium onions,
- 1-2 cups milk,
- 2 cloves garlic,
- 1 tablespoon finely chopped ginger,
- 400 g finely chopped canned tomatoes,
- 150 g butter,
- Breadcrumbs for topping,
- 125 g freshly grated cheddar,
- 125 g freshly grated parmesan cheese,
- ½ cup extra light olive oil,
- 1 cup water,
- 2 tablespoons vegetable oil,
- 4 tablespoons fresh parsley,
- Salt and pepper to taste.

Optional:
- Sliced red chillies according to taste.

Method:
1. Peel the potatoes and immerse in a container of cold water (add a little lemon juice to acidulate) to stop the potatoes from turning brown. Cut into quarters. Put the potato pieces in a covered microwave proof oven dish. Add 1 cup of water. Cover and cook on high in 10-15 mins intervals until cooked and soft enough for mashing.
2. Remove potatoes from oven dish and mash immediately to a uniform and smooth consistency. If still firm, microwave in steps of 5 mins until tender.
3. Add 1 cup milk and 150 g butter, half of the finely chopped onions and half of the finely crushed garlic. Mix well into the mashed potatoes. Add the freshly grated cheddar cheese.
4. Mix well together and blend into the mashed potatoes and other ingredients. Add half of the finely chopped parsley and mix well into the mashed potatoes. Add salt and pepper to taste and mix well together.
5. Over a medium to high heat, place 2 tablespoons of vegetable oil in a saucepan large enough to contain the ingredients, and allow to sizzle. Add the remaining finely chopped onions, finely crushed garlic and ginger. Stir in and allow the ingredients to cook until the onions become transparent but not burning.

6. Add the finely crushed canned tomatoes, finely chopped parsley and mix well together. Optional: *add some finely chopped red chillies to your taste.* Cover and reduce heat to medium low. Allow to cook until the tomato sauce is well blended. Add salt and pepper to taste. Stir and check at intervals to make sure that the tomato sauce does not burn and that the sauce remains semi liquid. Add a little hot water to maintain the semi liquid sauce consistency or if watery, uncover pan and allow excess water to evaporate.
7. Set oven to 150°C.
8. Cut the corned beef into small cubes and gently incorporate into the well blended tomato sauce. Cover and simmer for 2-3 mins. Do not overcook and melt the corned beef. Remove from stove and set aside.
9. In an oven tray, large and deep enough to contain 2 layers of corned beef in tomato sauce and 3 layers of mashed potatoes, spread evenly one third of the mashed potato at the bottom of the tray. Spread half of the corned beef in tomato mixture onto the mashed potato layer. Spread gently so as not to disturb the mashed potato layer underneath. Add half of the remaining mashed potato as the next layer. Repeat with the remaining corned beef in tomato sauce mixture. Complete with the remaining mashed potato mixture and spread evenly without disturbing the lower layers.
10. Sprinkle a thin layer of breadcrumbs on top followed by a thin layer of freshly grated parmesan cheese. Drizzle with extra light olive oil.
11. Place tray on lower shelf of oven. Allow to bake for 20-30 mins or until the layers start to bubble and the parmesan/breadcrumb layer turns into a light golden brown topping. If necessary, place under grill to finish off the light golden layer to your preference. Do not overgrill. However, monitor closely and be very careful not to burn the topping.
12. Remove from oven and allow to cool down on a suitable surface for 15-20 mins. This will allow the layers to bond together and make it easier to serve without the layers falling apart or squashing down.
13. Using a flat spatula, loosen the sides and cut into the layers vertically to obtain suitable serve portions.
14. Enjoy with fresh crusty sour dough bread and a fresh lettuce salad.

Croque Monsieur

Ingredients (Make 2):
- 4 slices of white bread,
- 60 g butter,
- 100 ml milk,
- 1 tablespoon plain white flour,
- 3 slices Gruyère cheese,
- grated nutmeg,
- 2 tablespoons Dijon mustard,
- 2 slices of ham,
- Salad garnish.

Method:
1. Semi melt the butter in the microwave.
2. Spread one side of each slice of white bread with some of the melted butter.
3. Place bread slice buttered side up, under a low heat grill and toast to a light golden colour. Do not allow the bread slices to burn. Remove from the grill.
4. Place the remaining butter into a small saucepan and sift in the plain white flour. Whisk together and cook for a minute, then gradually whisk in the milk. Whisk to a smooth paste and simmer under low heat until thickened. Take off the heat and stir in one slice of the Gruyère broken into small pieces. Whisk together until the mixture is well blended into a good Béchamel sauce. Grate in a little nutmeg and stir into the sauce. Put aside.
5. Spread the Dijon mustard on the non toasted side of two bread slices. Place the ham slices on the Dijon mustard followed by the Gruyère cheese slices. Grill under low heat with the cheese slices uppermost. Allow the cheese to melt. Remove from the grill and top with the remaining two bread slices, toasted side uppermost. Press well into the melted cheese. Top with the white Béchamel sauce from step 4.
6. Put the sandwiches on an oven tray. Grill for about five mins or until golden and bubbling.
7. Remove from oven and serve immediately.

Croque Madame

Ingredients (Make 2):
- 4 slices of white bread,
- 60 g butter,
- 100 ml milk,
- 1 tablespoon plain white flour,
- 3 slices Gruyère cheese,
- grated nutmeg,
- 2 tablespoons Dijon mustard,
- 2 slices of ham,
- 2 eggs
- Salad garnish.

Method:
1. Semi melt the butter in the microwave.
2. Spread one side of each slice of white bread with some of the melted butter.
3. Place bread slice buttered side up, under a low heat grill and toast to a light golden colour. Do not allow the bread slices to burn. Remove from the grill.
4. Place the remaining butter into a small saucepan and sift in the plain white flour. Whisk together and cook for a minute, then gradually whisk in the milk. Whisk to a smooth paste and simmer under low heat until thickened. Remove from the heat and stir in one slice of the Gruyère broken into small pieces. Whisk together until the mixture is well blended into a good Béchamel sauce. Grate in a little nutmeg and stir into the sauce. Put aside.
5. Spread the Dijon mustard on the non toasted side of two bread slices. Place the ham slices on the Dijon mustard followed with the Gruyère cheese slices. Grill under low heat with the cheese slices uppermost. Allow the cheese to melt. Remove from the grill and top with the remaining two bread slices, toasted side uppermost. Press well into the melted cheese.
6. Fry the two eggs. Top the sandwiches from step 5 with a fried egg each. Spread the Béchamel sauce from 4 on top of the eggs and toast.
7. Put the sandwiches on to an oven tray. Grill for about 5 mins or until golden and bubbling.
8. Remove from oven and serve immediately.

Salted Peanuts

Pistaches Salées
Recipe by Guito Aliphon

Ingredients:
- 1 kg shelled peanuts (small),
- 1-2 cups fine grained sea salt,
- Pink food colouring,
- Cold water.

Method:
1. Wash shelled peanuts carefully without bruising. Use the smaller variety as these are easier to salt and cook. Drain the wash water and soak in cold water for 20 mins (or until the peanuts have absorbed some water). The soak time will depend upon the freshness of the peanuts. Vary soaking time accordingly.
2. Drain all water and carefully rinse to wash out all impurities. Do not bruise or dislodge the thin skin. After rinsing the peanuts should stay moist.
3. Wear a pair of gloves and gradually sprinkle the ~~nuts~~ with the fine sea salt. Mix carefully without bruising, taking care not to add excess salt as this will give a sharp salty taste.
4. With gloved hands, add a few drops of the pink food colouring and gently mix in to obtain a uniform colour. Gloves prevent your hands from being stained pink. Again, be careful not to bruise the peanuts.
5. Spread a layer of coloured peanuts on a flat ovenproof plate. Place in the microwave and cook on high for 2 mins 30 seconds. Using a wooden spoon, loosen the peanuts. Return to microwave and cook on high for another 2 mins 30 seconds. Again carefully loosen the peanuts and cook for another 2 mins or until they start spluttering.
6. Allow to cool. Taste to check and adjust cooking time accordingly. Do not cook for long periods without monitoring, this could lead to the peanuts turning black.
7. Remove cooked peanuts from the microwave and spread on a flat oven metal plate to cool. Loosen any clusters. Repeat with the remainder of the peanuts in batches. Allow them to cool down and dry overnight in an open container to eliminate any remaining moisture.
8. Store in an airtight container. Will keep for a month.

Soya Eggs

Ingredients (Make 8 or 16):
- 4 eggs,
- 4 tablespoons soy sauce,
- 5 tablespoons water,
- 1 teaspoon sugar,
- 1 teaspoon sesame oil.

Note - *Soya eggs are good for hors d'oeuvre.*

Method:
1. Boil eggs for 5 mins, soak in cold water until eggs have cooled down. Remove shells.
2. Heat soy sauce, water, sugar, and sesame oil. Put eggs into mixture, gently stir cook for 5 mins over low heat or until the eggs have taken a bit of colour.
3. Remove from heat and leave the eggs in this mixture for 30 mins.
4. Turn eggs in mixture often until evenly coloured. Remove from sauce. Allow excess sauce to drain. Cut each egg into two or four pieces.
5. Place on a dish, garnish and serve.

Cotelettes de Poulet

Chicken Cutlets

Ingredients (Make 4):
- 4 chicken drumsticks,
- 50 g yoghurt,
- 2 tablespoons chopped coriander leaves,
- cooking oil,
- 1 large onion finely chopped,
- 1 teaspoon crushed ginger,
- 60 g flour,
- 2 large eggs beaten with a dash of salt,
- Bread crumbs enough to coat cutlets.

Method:
1. Carefully remove all skin from chicken drumsticks. With the blunt edge of a big knife and starting at the smaller end of the drumstick, clear flesh from as close as possible to bone, and gently push towards the big end of drumstick. Keep chicken meat in one piece. Leave last 1 cm of chicken flesh connected to the bone.
2. Mix the yoghurt, coriander, chopped onions and crushed ginger together. Marinate the chicken pieces in mixture for at least 2 hours.
3. Remove chicken pieces and shape into flat cutlets as in picture. Coat with flour, then beaten eggs, and finally with a thin layer of breadcrumbs. Press breadcrumbs onto cutlets with fingers.
4. Heat oil in a frying pan over medium heat until it starts to sizzle. Carefully place cutlets and fry one by one until cooked on both sides. Turn cutlets over to cook both sides until light golden brown. Be careful not to overcook.
5. Place cutlets on a grill in an oven tray. Heat oven to 180°C and place cutlets in middle position for 30 mins or until cooked on the inside. Check at regular intervals to make sure that the cutlets do not overcook on the surface.
6. Serve with potato chips.

Char Siu

Barbecue Pork

Ingredients (Serve 4):
- 900 g fillet of pork,
- 225 g Hoi Sin sauce,
- 2 tablespoons Shao Hsing rice wine or brandy,
- 1 teaspoon sesame oil,
- 3 tablespoons honey.

Method:
1. Cut the pork into strips about 20 cms by 4 cms.
2. Marinate with the Hoi Sin sauce, wine and sesame oil in a shallow dish under cover for at least 12 hours. Optional: add a little red colouring.
3. Place a baking pan filled with about 3 cups boiling water at the bottom of a preheated 220°C oven. Remove the pork strips from the marinade and drain (reserve the marinade). Place the meat flat on a greased wire rack and roast on the mid shelf of the oven for 15-20 mins, allowing the juices to drip into the pan of water. Baste with the marinade, reduce the oven temperature to 180°C and continue roasting for a further 20-25 mins.
4. Remove the meat from the oven and brush with the honey (thinned down with a little water); return the meat to the oven and cook for another 4-5 mins to crisp the outside a little and give it a rich colour.
5. When the meat is cool, slice across the grain just before serving; this preserves the flavour and moist texture. Bring the marinade to a boil with the drippings and water in the baking pan; simmer gently for a few mins and strain into the jug to serve with the meat.
6. For health conscious persons, serve with hot chilli sauce instead of this gravy.

Prawn Dumplings

Ingredients (Make 10-15):
- 500 g shelled & de-veined prawns,
- 2 tablespoons finely chopped bamboo shoots,
- 1 tablespoon finely chopped spring onions (white part only),
- 2 tablespoons vegetable oil,
- 3 teaspoons light soy sauce,
- 2 tablespoons dry sherry,
- 2 teaspoons white sugar,
- ½ teaspoon salt,
- 2 teaspoons sesame oil,
- Vegetable oil as required for oiling,
- 4 teaspoons tapioca starch.

Wrapper:
- 1 ½ cups wheat starch, plus extra for kneading,
- 2 tablespoons tapioca starch,
- 1 cup boiling water,
- 1 tablespoon vegetable oil,
- ¼ teaspoon salt.

Method:
1. *Make Wrapper Dough*:
   In a bowl, combine the wheat starch, tapioca starch and salt. Stir slowly into 1 cup of boiling water. Add the oil and when cooled down, use your hands to knead the dough, until it is smooth and shiny. Cover bowl with cling wrap and rest for 30 mins.
2. *Make Dumplings:*
   Finely mince the prawns and add in all the other ingredients for the filling. Mix together in one direction until it almost feels elastic. Cover with cling wrap, set aside and place in refrigerator for 2 hours. This will allow the flavours to blend.
3. Coat a paper towel with some vegetable oil. Use to oil your working board and the broad side of a Chinese cleaver.
4. Make sure to keep the dough from Step 1 covered with a moist kitchen towel so it does not dry up. Break off 1 teaspoon of the dough, roll into a ball. Flatten it with the palm of the hand. Place flattened dough on oiled board. Then, use the oiled broad side of the cleaver to press it down to form a circle about 7 cms in diameter.
5. Add a heaped teaspoon of filling in the middle of the wrapper, spreading it evenly but not touching the edges.

6. Carefully pleat the front side of the dumpling dough. Use your thumb and forefinger to form the pleats in the dough. Bring the back side forward, pleat and seal with the front pleat. Pinch the edges closed. Pleat the sides in a similar way and bring together at the top. Traditionally, there are about 7 pleats per dumpling. Use an even number to make it easier, like 4 pleats.
7. Cover the dumplings with a moist kitchen towel, whilst preparing the remainder of the dumplings.
8. Prepare a steamer. Steam the dumplings in batches on an oiled plate until well cooked and looking very translucent, but not falling apart. About 10-15 mins. Do not over steam and monitor at regular intervals, making sure there is always water in the steamer. Carefully remove and place on a non stick surface to serve. I use baking paper both in the steamer and on the serving dish.
9. Serve when still hot with a chilli sauce or any other sauce of your preference.

Prawn dumplings showing the pleats

Sticky Chicken Wings

Marinated Chicken Wings

Ingredients (Make 15-20):
- 1 kg chicken wings,
- ½ cup honey,
- ½ cup light soy sauce,
- Juice of 1 lemon,
- 1 teaspoon crushed ginger,
- 2 teaspoons crushed garlic.

Method:
1. With a sharp knife, cut off the wing tips and separate the whole chicken wing at the joint into two pieces. Remove any traces of feather and undesirable bits.
2. In a large bowl, mix the honey, light soy sauce, lemon juice, crushed garlic and ginger.
3. Add the chicken wing pieces to the marinade, cover and allow to marinade in the fridge for at least one hour. Overnight is best. Turn chicken pieces around at least once or twice.
4. Heat up oven at 190°C. Place chicken pieces on a grill in an oven tray. Baste with remaining marinade. Place tray in mid position in the oven. Cook for 1 hour or until the chicken pieces are cooked and the marinade has turned into a sticky glaze. Rotate chicken pieces in the tray once or twice during the cooking. Monitor at regular intervals to avoid overcooking.
5. Remove chicken pieces from oven. Transfer to a warmed serving dish and serve immediately, with either a chilli or garlic sauce.

Beef and Chicken Meatballs

Ingredients (Makes 15-20):
- 500 g minced beef,
- 1 chicken fillet (medium),
- 1 small onion finely chopped,
- 2 tablespoons finely chopped parsley,
- 50 ml dry sherry,
- 2 egg yolks,
- Breadcrumbs for coating,
- Vegetable oil for frying,
- Salt and pepper to taste.

Method:
1. Boil chicken fillet in water with ½ teaspoon of salt until just cooked and opaque. Remove from water and allow to cool down. Mince chicken with a sharp knife.
2. Season the minced beef with salt and pepper to taste and mix well together. Add the minced chicken, chopped parsley, chopped onions, sherry and 2 egg yolks to the minced beef and mix well together.
3. Pick a small quantity of the minced beef and chicken mixture at a time and form small meat balls. Coat the meat balls with the breadcrumbs and set aside. The meat balls (shaped as shown in photo) can also be flattened.
4. Deep fry in vegetable oil over medium low heat until rich golden brown. Be careful not to overcook. Check the fried meat balls after the first ones are cooked. Reduce heat and cook for longer if the meat inside is not thoroughly cooked.
5. Serve as a gajack (appetiser snack) with chilli sauce.

Mini Spring Rolls

Ingredients (Make 24):
- 500 g pork mince,
- 250 g prawn meat,
- 6 carrots medium size,
- ½ medium size onion,
- 50 g dried bean fine thread noodles,
- 30 g dried black fungus mushrooms,
- 2 dozens mini spring rolls wrappers ready made (alternatively use dried wrappers soaked in water),
- Egg white to seal wrappers.

Seasoning:
- 1 tablespoon sesame oil,
- 1 tablespoon vegetable oil,
- 1 teaspoon salt,
- 1 teaspoon black pepper.

Optional:
- Chillies to taste.

Method:
1. Chop the prawn meat into very small pieces without mashing it.
2. Soak the black fungus mushrooms in warm water until soft.
3. Chop the onion into very small pieces.
4. Grate the carrot into fine slivers.
5. Soak the dried bean thread noodles in warm water until soft. Then cut into small 1 cm lengths.
6. Strain all the water from the black fungus mushrooms and chop into very small pieces.
7. Mix all the above ingredients together. Cover and rest the mixture for 5-10 mins.
8. Spread one tablespoon of the mixture uniformly along one edge of the spring roll wrapper, allowing some space at each end for folding in. Roll up the wrapper as tightly as possible and at midway, tuck in the sides and continue rolling. Seal up the last flap with egg white. Continue filling the remaining wrappers in the same way, lay on a plate. Cover with a plastic wrap until ready to cook. Any leftover filling can be frozen for future use.
9. Heat enough oil to cover the spring rolls while frying in batches. Deep fry the rolls for 5 to 6 mins or until crisp and golden brown. Drain on kitchen paper towel.
10. Serve with the seasoning mixture with lettuce leaves.

Samoosas

Ingredients (Make 25):
- Rectangular samoosa pastry sheets (25),
- 1 medium onion,
- ½ cup frozen green peas,
- 200 g potatoes,
- 1 cup finely chopped coriander leaves,
- ½ tablespoon crushed chillies (optional),
- ½ tablespoon crushed ginger,
- ½ tablespoon dry mango powder,
- ½ tablespoon garam masala powder,
- Juice of ¼ lemon,
- Salt to taste,
- ½ teaspoon mustard seeds,
- 4 curry leaves – finely chopped,
- 1 tablespoon vegetable oil.
- Vegetable oil for deep frying,
- Flour and water paste for sealing.

Method:
1. Boil potatoes in salt water until just soft. Allow to cool, remove skin and break with a fork into small ½ cm pieces. Lightly season with salt.
2. Put 2 cups of water in a pan and allow to boil. Using a strainer, quickly blanch the frozen peas for 30 seconds and drop into very cold water.
3. Sauté mustard seeds in 1 tablespoon oil. When the seeds stop spluttering, add the chopped onion, curry leaves, coriander leaves, garam masala, dry mango powder and crushed ginger. Stir fry for 1 minute or until you can smell the fragrance of the ingredients. Remove from heat.
4. In a large container, mix the sauté ingredients with the potato pieces. Add the lemon juice. When mixed, gently add the blanched green peas. Taste and season with salt if necessary.
5. Take one rectangle of pastry. Place a spoonful of filling at one end. Refer to photo. Make the first diagonal fold, then the second diagonal fold.
6. Hold firmly with one hand, wrap the remaining length of the pastry sheet around the samoosa. Use the flour and water paste for sealing. Do not leave any gaps.
7. Deep fry the samoosas in hot oil until they are a beautiful golden hue. Drain on kitchen paper.
8. Enjoy with chilli sauce.

Battered Zucchini Flowers

Ingredients (Make 15):
- 15 zucchini flowers,
- 200 g cheddar cheese,
- 75 g mozzarella cheese,
- 1 tablespoon fresh cream,
- 3 tablespoons finely chopped parsley,
- 100 g white flour,
- 1 teaspoon baking powder,
- 1 egg yolk,
- 2 tablespoons of light olive oil,
- 150 ml of milk,
- Salt and pepper to taste,
- Vegetable oil,
- Salt to taste.

Method:
1. Clean the zucchini flowers of any impurities. With a sharp knife, cut stems off except for 1 cm. Carefully open the flowers and remove the pistils. Put aside.
2. Grate the cheddar and mozzarella cheeses and mix with 3 tablespoons of finely chopped parsley. Add 1 tablespoon of the fresh cream and mix well. Add salt and pepper to taste.
3. Beat up the mixture to a uniform creamy consistency. Be careful not to add too much salt and pepper as the batter will also contain salt and pepper.
4. Carefully open the zucchini flowers and using a small spoon, put the cheese, parsley and fresh cream mixture into the zucchini. Do not overfill, close the petals and pass the stuffed flowers through the batter. Put aside.
5. Add 1 teaspoon of baking powder to the white flour. Add a small amount of salt and pepper to taste. Mix well and gradually incorporate the milk and 2 tablespoons of the light olive oil. Add the egg yolk and mix well. The consistency of the batter should be runny but thick enough to stay on the zucchini flower.
6. Heat up sufficient vegetable oil in a deep frying pan to immerse the battered zucchini flowers into the oil for deep frying. Use low to medium heat. Carefully hold the zucchini flowers one at a time and pass through the batter, rotating to obtain a uniform coating around the zucchini flower. Place into the hot oil and allow the batter to fry to a light golden colour. Only deep fry two flowers at a time to prevent them sticking to each other. With a pair of tongs carefully rotate the stuffed flowers for even cooking.
7. Remove the flowers from the frying pan, allow the surplus oil to drip back into the frying pan and place on a tray with kitchen paper to soak away any excess oil.

Salmon Patties

Croquettes de Saumon

Ingredients (Make 8-10):
- 415 g of canned red salmon,
- 500 g potatoes,
- 1 teaspoon finely grated lemon rind,
- 1 small onion finely chopped,
- 3 tablespoons milk,
- 2 tablespoons chopped parsley,
- 1 egg white,
- Breadcrumbs for coating,
- Oil for frying.

Method:
1. Peel and cube the potatoes. Put the cubed potatoes in a microwave safe container. Pour in the liquid from the canned salmon, cover and cook the potatoes in the microwave on high for 10-15 mins or until the potato cubes are cooked and ready for mashing.
2. Allow to cool. Mash the potato cubes to a smooth consistency.
3. Finely flake the red salmon into small pieces. Not too big, not too small.
4. Combine the mashed potatoes with the milk, grated lemon rind, chopped parsley, finely chopped onion and the egg white. Mix well together. Add the red salmon pieces and combine well without mashing the salmon. Shape mixture into 8 patties and coat with the breadcrumbs. Refrigerate for 30 mins to let them set.
5. Grill or pan fry until golden brown and heated through. Brush off excess breadcrumbs before frying in pan.
6. Serve with chilli sauce.

Ti Pooris
Unleavened pancakes

Ingredients
(Make 10-15):
- 500 g white flour,
- 2 tablespoons vegetable oil or ghee (vary quantity depending upon pan diameter),
- 200 ml water,
- Vegetable oil or ghee for frying,
- Salt to taste.

Method:
1. Blend the flour with the vegetable oil or melted ghee. Add water gradually and work into dough until a uniform consistency is obtained.
2. Wrap up dough in cling wrap and allow to rest for 30 mins.
3. Break dough into small pieces and roll into dough balls. Size of each ball can be at your own discretion. Flatten each dough ball with a rolling pin to ¼ cm thick. Do not sprinkle with dry flour.
4. Heat oil or ghee in a flat saucepan over medium heat. Add enough oil to cover whole surface of pan. Place each poori into pan and allow to cook one at a time. Move poori in oil and as soon as poori expands, turn over and immediately remove from pan. Poori must stay white in colour. Drain and place on absorbent kitchen paper.
5. Serve with potato curry, or any other.
6. Enjoy. Close your eyes and see yourself eating pooris with 'sept caris'.

Lamb Gajack

Ingredients (Serve 4):
- 500 g lean lamb (can substitute with other meats),
- 2 medium onions,
- 3 green chillies (long variety),
- 2 tablespoons dry sherry,
- 3 tablespoons oyster sauce,
- 1 teaspoon sesame oil,
- Chinese brèdes (greens),
- 3 tablespoons vegetable oil,
- 1 teaspoon cornflour,
- Salt and pepper to taste.

Photo: Kerwin Mohun

Method:
1. Cut the lamb into bite size pieces. Season with 2 tablespoons sherry, salt and pepper. Cover and rest for at least 30 mins.
2. Finely slice the onions. Wash the Chinese greens. Preferably use greens with tender stalks. Cut into bite size pieces.
3. Remove stems from the long green chillies and slice lengthwise into thin strips.
4. In a wok or a frying pan, heat up 3 tablespoons oil over high heat.
5. Stir fry the lamb pieces until cooked and golden brown. Stir at intervals. Add the sliced onions and stir fry with the lamb pieces until transparent. Stir in the oyster sauce. Cook for 3 mins. Stir at intervals to prevent the ingredients from burning.
6. Add the sliced green chillies, followed by Chinese greens. Stir fry quickly until just cooked, but still crisp. Sprinkle with 1 teaspoon sesame oil.
7. Quickly, mix 1 teaspoon cornflour into a little cold water. Stir into the ingredients and allow sauce to thicken.
8. Serve immediately. Eat with fresh crispy bread. Enjoy as gajack soulards.

Mines Bouilli
"Mines Tounis" Vegetarian Noodles

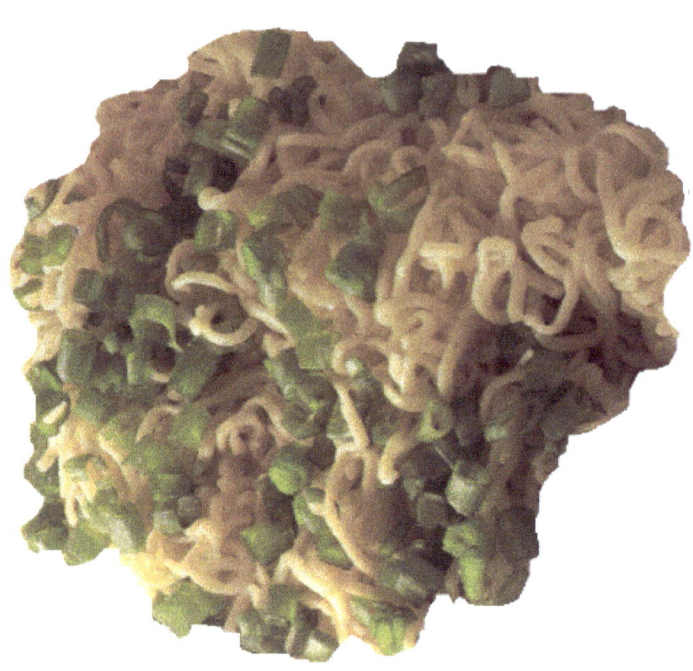

Ingredients (Serve 4):
- 450 g Chinese noodles,
- 2 tablespoons finely chopped spring onions,
- 1 tablespoon finely chopped garlic,
- 1 tablespoon white sugar,
- 1 teaspoon chilli sauce or as much as you can take,
- freshly ground pepper to taste,
- 2 tablespoons soy sauce,
- 3 tablespoons sesame paste,
- 1 tablespoon sesame oil,
- 2 tablespoons vinegar.

Optional:
- Chilli sauce.

Method:
1. Mix well together all the ingredients, except for the noodles, garlic and spring onions. Add pepper to taste. Divide the mixture and put into four separate noodle bowls.
2. Boil the noodles for 10-15 mins or according to instructions on the packet. Drain and while still steaming hot, divide into four portions and place on top of the ingredients already in the bowls. Sprinkle with the finely chopped spring onions and the finely chopped garlic.
3. Each person can then toss the noodles with the mixture at the bottom of the bowls and the seasoning together. Can also drizzle with chilli sauce to your preference.
4. This dish is extremely good as a snack and very satisfying, just like the 'mines tounis' we used to have in the Chinese restaurants in Port Louis, Beau Bassin, Rosehill and Curepipe.

Soups and Bouillons

Soups and bouillons have a special place in Mauritian cuisine. After celebrations when one has overeaten to the point when "la bouche pas bon" (mouth is not feeling too good), a nice bouillon or soup comes in handy. Similarly, when one has had a night out after night clubbing or gambling at the casino, a good bouillon or soup can fill you up and give you renewed energy.

Most Mauritians would know the street stall soups and bouillons in Port Louis Chinatown. La Soupe Mama was very well known and appreciated by many after a night out at the L'Amicale de Port Louis when it was operating in Port Louis Chinatown. Street stalls in Port Louis are still seen selling soups, bouillons and noodles, for a quick meal on the run.

Bouillon de tec tec (pipis) (page 72)

Mauritian cuisine has inherited soups and bouillons from French, Indian, Tamil, Telegu, Chinese, African, Malagasy and Chinese cuisines. The most popular and very tasty ones include tomato soup, prawn and oyster bisque, bouillon crabes, bouillon tec tec, bouillon brèdes, bouillon mee foon, rasson, halim, soupe mamma and moulouctani.

Bouillons crabes are very reminiscent of luscious bouillons in Chinese restaurants. The flavour and taste of this bouillon could never be reproduced at home. The simple reason was that in Chinese restaurants almost all trimmings from other preparations were added to the stock pot. Hence the taste of their bouillons crabes is always very special.

Bouillons brèdes are very popular in Mauritius and are of Magalasy origin. Poor people who are finding it very hard to feed the family almost always resort to a bouillon brèdes plus an appetizer with rice. Brèdes are cheap and many would have these growing in their backyards, by the roadside in rural areas or within sugar cane fields. Having a brède mouroum tree in the backyard meant that the family could always be fed either from the leaves or using the seed pods (batons mouroum) with dholl in curries. With a little rice, the family was fed. Many refer to bouillons brèdes as food for "dimoune misere" (poor people). This could not be further from the truth.

Bouillon brèdes cresson with vindaye poisson (pages 66 and 238)

The combination of a bouillon brèdes with a rougaille is a dish that Mauritians enjoy most. Flight attendants for Air Mauritius agree that after being away for long periods, the dish that they all yearn for on their return home would be a bouillon brèdes with a rougaille or vindaye on rice. Bouillons brèdes are also very appropriate as a re-conditioner food that would cleanse the mouth and digestive system after a day's feasting and over indulging in drinks and other festive foods. In addition, bouillons brèdes are low in fat, high in dietary fibre, and rich in folic acid, vitamin C, potassium and magnesium, as well as containing a host of phytochemicals, such as lutein, beta-cryptoxanthin, zeaxanthin, and beta-carotene. It is claimed that a daily serving of green leafy vegetables, lowered the risk of cardiovascular disease by 11 percent. In Reunion Island, it has become customary for one daily serving of a bouillon brèdes to be included as part of the dinner menu. Many families in Mauritius are now following suit.

Oyster and Prawn Bisque

Ingredients (Serve 4-6):
- 100 g green prawn meat,
- 1 dozen oysters,
- 500 ml fresh milk,
- 1 cup fish stock,
- ½ cup finely sliced celery,
- ½ cup finely sliced carrot,
- 2 shallots finely sliced,
- 1 ½ tablespoons white flour,
- 1 teaspoon finely grated lemon peel,
- 1 tablespoon fresh natural yoghurt,
- Salt and pepper to taste.

This oyster and prawn bisque adds a touch of class to any meal. It has a delicate seafood flavour with a velvety sauce. Goes well with crusty French baguette as an entrée.

Method:
1. Clean oysters and carefully remove meat from shells in one piece. Remove any grit from the oysters. Put aside.
2. De-vein the prawn meat and wash, dry with kitchen paper towel and cut into small pieces (or to your preference). Set aside.
3. In a heavy saucepan, add 400 ml of milk, the fish stock, finely sliced celery, carrots and shallots. Simmer over medium heat until all vegetables have softened. Reduce heat to low.
4. Put the white flour in a separate bowl and carefully blend in the remaining milk. Slowly add the milk and flour mixture to the cooked vegetables, stirring constantly for uniform blending. Continue to stir and cook until mixture thickens and becomes bubbly. Remove from heat and allow to cool.
5. Using a blender, purée the mixture in three batches. Return the purée to saucepan on medium high heat. Add some hot water or more chicken stock if purée is too thick. When mixture starts to bubble, add the prawn pieces and simmer until prawns are slightly cooked. Add the oysters, lemon rind, salt and pepper to taste.
6. Simmer for two more mins or until heated through. Adjust the bisque consistency by adding some more chicken stock or hot water and simmer for a little bit longer. Pour into a soup tureen and fold in the yoghurt.
7. Decorate with a sprig of your favourite herb.
8. Enjoy. Delightful as a seafood entrée.

Bouillon Brèdes (1)

Ingredients (Serve 2-4):
- Watercress or Chinese greens (Choy Sum),
- 1 medium onion finely sliced,
- 1 teaspoon crushed garlic,
- 1 teaspoon crushed ginger,
- 2 tablespoons vegetable oil,
- 3 cups water or more as desired,
- Salt to taste.

Method:
1. Clean greens (brèdes) and cut into 7-10 cm long pieces.
2. Heat oil in deep saucepan to simmering point. Add the sliced onions, crushed ginger and garlic. Cook until the onion slices become transparent.
3. Add three to four cups of water (quantity can vary according to taste). Bring to boil. Season with salt to taste.
4. Add the greens and cook for a few mins only, until just cooked to retain their bright green colour. Be careful not to overcook.
5. Remove from heat and serve hot.
6. Eat with a fish vindaille, a rougaille, steak on rice or as an accompaniment to cari poule and rice.
7. Enjoy.

Bouillon Crabes

Ingredients (Serve 4):
- 4 medium blue swimmer crabs (or any other suitable variety such as sand crabs),
- 1 medium onion coarsely chopped,
- 1 tablespoon chopped thyme leaves,
- 2 cups chicken stock,
- 1 cup water,
- 425 g can finely crushed tomatoes,
- 1 teaspoon freshly crushed garlic,
- 1 teaspoon freshly crushed ginger,
- 1 tablespoon finely chopped coriander roots and stem,
- 1 tablespoon finely chopped coriander leaves,
- 3 tablespoons vegetable oil,
- Salt and pepper to taste.

Optional:
- 4 finely chopped red chillies.

Method:
1. Clean up crabs and break/cut into serve pieces. Crack the claws to make it easy for eating the meat within. Keep the crab swimmers in a separate dish.
2. Season the crab pieces with salt and pepper to taste.
3. Add oil to a deep saucepan and heat to simmering point. Add the chopped onions, thyme, ginger and garlic. Cook until the chopped onions become transparent.
4. Add the crushed tomatoes. Mix well and increase heat to high. Simmer until the sauce is well blended and the tomatoes cooked. Stir at intervals to prevent burning.
5. Add the chopped coriander roots and stem, *chopped red chillies if desired* and 1 cup hot water. Mix well and simmer again until the sauce is well blended.
6. Add the chicken stock, adding some more hot water if desired to increase quantity of bouillon.
7. 10-15 mins before serving, add the crab pieces and simmer until the crab pieces turn red. Taste the bouillon and season again with salt and pepper if necessary.
8. Eat with rice and chatini pomme d'amour.

Bouillon Brèdes (2)

Watercress, Martin, Chou Chou or Giraumon

Ingredients (Serve 4):
- 1 bunch watercress (or brèdes martin, chou chou or giraumon),
- 1 red onion halved then finely sliced,
- 1 tablespoon crushed ginger,
- 1 tablespoon crushed garlic,
- 2 tablespoons vegetable oil,
- 2-4 cups of water,
- Salt to taste.

When meals have to be put together for the family, the bouillon brèdes is a life saver. It is cheap to make and goes well with accompaniments like a good rougaille or an achar. I have known poor families to eat a bouillon brèdes, with fried potato slices on rice.

Method:
1. Pick the young shoots from the watercress (or brèdes martin, chou chou or giraumon). Cut into small lengths. Do not use the thick stalks. Wash in cold water and set aside.
2. In a deep saucepan, gently fry the sliced onions, crushed ginger and garlic in the vegetable oil, until the onions become transparent. Add water to the cooked onions (quantity can vary depending upon your preference). Over medium heat, allow the water to boil for 5-10 mins. Season bouillon with salt to your preference.
3. Put the young shoots in a serving bowl and pour the hot bouillon over the greens and serve immediately.
4. Serve on rice with rougailles, steaks or fried beef strips, accompanied with a chatini pomme d'amour.

Beef Bouillon

Ingredients (Serve 4):
- 500 g bite size beef cubes,
- 400 g canned whole peeled tomatoes,
- 4 cups chicken stock,
- Lettuce or watercress,
- 1 medium onion finely chopped,
- 2 tablespoons chopped coriander leaves,
- 2 tablespoons vegetable oil,
- 1 tablespoon crushed garlic,
- 1 tablespoon crushed ginger,
- Salt and pepper to taste.

Method:
1. Season beef cubes with salt and pepper to taste. Place in refrigerator until required. Finely blend the canned whole peeled tomatoes. Put aside.
2. Clean lettuce and coarsely cut 5-6 leaves lengthwise into 3 cm strips. If using watercress, clean and cut into bite size sprigs (avoid the tough stems). Set aside.
3. Heat 2 tablespoons of vegetable oil in a deep saucepan. Add the finely chopped onion, crushed ginger and garlic.
4. Stir fry over medium high heat until the onion pieces become transparent. Add the blended tomatoes and mix well. Cover and simmer over medium heat for 20-30 mins or until the tomatoes are well cooked and the sauce is well blended. You may add some hot water to prevent sauce from becoming too thick. Stir at frequent intervals to prevent the sauce from burning.
5. Add the chicken or vegetable stock and stir into the mixture. Cover and simmer over medium to high heat for 15-20 mins or until the tomato sauce and chicken / vegetable stock are well blended. Season with salt and pepper to taste. If not serving immediately, you can pause the cooking and re-start 10-15 mins before serving.
6. With the bouillon simmering, add the beef cubes. Simmer again under cover over medium high heat for 10-15 mins or until beef pieces are cooked. Place the cut lettuce in a serving bowl large enough to contain the bouillon. Add the bouillon and cooked beef cubes to the lettuce. Allow to rest for 5 mins. Serve on rice.

Bouillon Mee Foon

Ingredients (Serve 4):
- 1 leftover chicken carcass,
- 10 dried mushrooms (soaked overnight),
- 1 chicken fillet,
- 10 medium green prawns,
- 1 tablespoon peanut oil,
- 1 baby choy sum green,
- 5 spring onions (white stems only),
- 140 g sliced bamboo shoots,
- 250 g rice vermicelli,
- 2 tablespoons fish sauce,
- Salt and pepper to taste.

Method:
1. Boil chicken carcass in 3 litres of water, with 1 teaspoon salt for 30 - 45 mins. Discard chicken carcass and remove any remaining chicken bones. Strain the stock and set aside.
2. Shell and de-vein prawns. Cut prawns in half. Season lightly with salt and pepper. Set aside.
3. Cut the bamboo shoot slices into bite size pieces. Cut the spring onions (white part only) into 2 cm pieces. Cut the chicken fillet into bite size pieces. Set aside.
4. Place the chicken stock into a deep saucepan and simmer over medium low heat.
5. Drain the soaked dried mushrooms. Gently hand squeeze to remove excess water. Cut into bite size strips.
6. Put the chicken, mushroom and bamboo shoot pieces into a bowl. Season with fish sauce, salt and pepper to taste if necessary. Mix well.
7. Transfer the chicken, mushroom and bamboo shoot mixture into the simmering chicken stock. Mix well. Reduce heat to medium low.
8. Cover and simmer for 30 mins. Taste and season with more salt if necessary. If you are adding soy sauce later, do not add too much salt.
9. While the bouillon is simmering, soak the rice vermicelli in warm water for 10-15 mins. Clean the choy sum green and cut into bite size pieces. Drain the rice vermicelli and put into the bouillon. When the rice vermicelli is cooked, add the choy sum, spring onion pieces and the prawns. Simmer for 2-3 mins. Remove from heat.
10. Serve in individual bowls. It is recommended to warm the bowls prior to serving. Make sure that ingredients are evenly distributed.
11. Season with light soy sauce / red chilli sauce to taste.

Bouillon Poisson

Ingredients (Serve 4):
- 1 kg whole fish (cleaned and scaled),
- 2 medium onions finely chopped,
- 1 can (450 g) finely crushed tomatoes,
- Peanut oil to fry fish slices,
- Cornflour,
- 1 tablespoon freshly crushed ginger,
- 1 tablespoon freshly crushed garlic,
- 1 tablespoon chopped thyme,
- 2 tablespoon chopped coriander leaves,
- 3 lemon slices,
- 3 curry leaves,
- Salt and pepper to taste.

Optional:
- 10 small and tender okras with stems removed.

Method:
1. Clean the fish and cut into serve slices. Season with salt and pepper to taste. Lightly sprinkle with cornflour all round. Remove excess.
2. Deep fry fish slices and fish head(s) to a light golden brown colour.
3. Remove from pan and set aside.
4. Add 3 tablespoons oil into a deep saucepan and heat to simmering point. Add chopped onions, thyme, 1 tablespoon coriander leaves, curry leaves, crushed ginger and garlic. Stir and cook until onions become transparent.
5. Add finely crushed tomatoes. Mix well and simmer for 15 mins or until sauce is cooked and well blended. Add some hot water to adjust the sauce consistency and to prevent it from drying up.
6. Add fish head and mix well with the sauce. Cover and simmer for 10 mins. Add hot water in sufficient quantity to obtain a bouillon to your liking. Add the lemon slices, cover and simmer for 20 mins. Taste and season with salt and pepper.
7. Optional: *Add the okras (lalos) into the bouillon and simmer until the okras are cooked.*
8. Add the fried fish slices and carefully stir the bouillon without breaking the okras and fish slices. Simmer for another 5 mins.
9. Carefully remove the fish pieces and okras, place into a deep serving dish. Pour the bouillon into the dish over the fish and okras. Sprinkle with the finely chopped coriander leaves.
10. Serve on a bed of rice, with a chutney prepared from tomato, onion, coriander and chilli.

Bouillon Tec Tec

Ingredients (Serve 6):
- 1 kg live pipis,
- 2 tablespoons vegetable oil,
- 450 g can crushed tomatoes,
- 1 teaspoon crushed garlic,
- 1 teaspoon crushed ginger,
- 1 medium size onion finely chopped,
- 1 tablespoon chopped thyme,
- 3 cups water,
- 2 cups chicken stock,
- 3 tablespoons chopped coriander leaves,
- Salt and pepper to taste.

Optional:
- Red chillies finely chopped.

Method:
1. Wash pipis. Dissolve 1 tablespoon of salt in 3 litres of water at room temperature. Soak pipis in salt water for 2 hours or preferably overnight.
2. Pour out salt water. Rinse pipis and immediately place in 3 litres of warm water to make pipis open.
3. Carefully clean and scrub pipis, de-vein and remove intestinal tubes. Leave meat attached to shells.
4. Heat 2 tablespoons of vegetable oil in deep saucepan over medium heat. Add chopped onions, chopped thyme, garlic and ginger. Stir fry until onions become transparent. Add crushed tomatoes, mix, cover the saucepan and simmer until a thick well blended sauce is formed. Stir at intervals and add a little hot water if necessary to prevent the sauce from burning.
5. Add chicken stock and 2 cups of water (or more if more bouillon is required). Add half of chopped coriander leaves, *chillies*, salt and pepper to taste. Simmer for half an hour.
6. Add pipis and simmer for 15 to 20 mins.
7. Transfer from saucepan into warm soup bowls. Sprinkle with chopped coriander.

Chicken Mulligatawny

Ingredients (Serve 6):
- 1 kg chicken with bones cut into bite size pieces,
- 2 cups dry dholl peas,
- 1 teaspoon chopped thyme,
- 1 medium onion chopped,
- 1 tablespoon crushed garlic,
- 1 tablespoon crushed ginger,
- 1 tablespoon crushed cumin seeds,
- 2 tablespoons turmeric powder,
- 2 tablespoons tamarind paste (dissolved in ½ cup of hot water),
- 6 curry leaves,
- 2 tablespoons chopped coriander leaves,
- Salt and pepper to taste.

Dholl is the Mauritian spelling of dhal or dal.

Method:
1. Boil dholl peas in four cups of water until tender and crushable between 2 fingers. Remove from pan and set aside. If necessary add more water to avoid burning the dholl. Set aside in saucepan and keep the water.
2. Season the bite size chicken pieces with salt and pepper. Set aside for 30 mins.
3. Add oil to a deep frying pan. Over medium high heat, fry the seasoned chicken pieces until light golden brown. Add the chopped onion, garlic and ginger. Stir well. Then add the curry leaves, chopped thyme, crushed cumin seeds and half of the chopped coriander. Mix and simmer for 2 to 3 mins.
4. Add the cooked dholl peas with water, to the fried chicken pieces. Mix well and simmer for 4 to 5 mins.
5. Add the turmeric and the dissolved tamarind paste and stir well. Adjust soup with hot water if necessary to maintain a liquid consistency. Not too watery and not too thick. Boil for 20 to 30 mins or until the dholl is cooked to your preference.. Season to taste with salt and pepper.
6. Pour into serving casserole dish and add remaining chopped coriander leaves on top.
7. Serve with rice, accompanied with tomato or coconut chutney.

Chicken and Sweet Corn Soup

Ingredients (Serve 6):
- 375 g fresh or tinned sweetcorn kernels,
- 1 litre chicken stock,
- 3 spring onions, thinly sliced,
- 1cm piece ginger, peeled and grated,
- 1 large chicken breast skinned,
- 1 tablespoon cornflour mixed with 2 tablespoons water,
- 1 egg white beaten with 1 teaspoon water,
- Sesame oil,
- Salt and pepper to taste.

Method:
1. Puree half the sweetcorn with 1 cup of the stock in a food processor or blender. Set aside.
2. Pour the remaining stock into a saucepan, add the ginger and bring to a simmer. Poach the chicken breast until cooked through, approximately 8-10 mins. Remove the chicken breast and shred into stringy bits.
3. Add the spring onions, pureed sweetcorn, remaining sweetcorn and shredded chicken to the stock in the saucepan. Heat until simmering. Season to taste with salt and pepper.
4. Take the saucepan off the heat and blend in the cornflour mixture stirring quickly. Return to the heat and simmer for 10 mins.
5. Take the saucepan off the heat again and add the egg white while stirring. Continue to stir until the egg white sets in threads. Serve in separate bowls.
6. Drizzle a little sesame oil over each serving and garnish with spring onions.
7. Perfect as an entrée for all meals.

Halim Soup

Ingredients (Serve 6):
- 3 tablespoons oil,
- 3 small onions finely sliced,
- 750 g goat meat,
- 3 cardamons,
- 90 g black lentils or dholl,
- 60 g coarsely ground wheat,
- ½ teaspoon turmeric powder,
- 1 teaspoon chilli powder (reduce or increase according to taste),
- 1 tablespoon ground cumin roasted,
- 3 tablespoons of chopped coriander,
- 3 tablespoons of chopped mint leaves,
- 3 tablespoons of chopped shallots,
- 3 tablespoons of chopped green chillies,
- Water,
- Salt and pepper to taste.

Spices for grinding (finely crush together):
- 2 small onions,
- 4 medium cloves garlic,
- ½ teaspoon finely sliced ginger,
- Small piece cinnamon,
- ½ teaspoon whole black peppercorns.

Method:
1. Cut the meat into bite size pieces. Season with salt and pepper. Set aside. Soak the lentils or dholl.
2. Grind the spices as listed.
3. Heat oil in saucepan over medium to high heat. Brown the sliced onions, drain and place on kitchen paper.
4. In the same oil add the bite size meat pieces. Cook until light golden. Stir at intervals.
5. Add ground spices and stir fry for 10-15 mins or until cooked and integrated.
6. Transfer mixture to a pressure cooker with the washed lentils or dholl and coarsely ground wheat, the other powdered ingredients, fried onions and the cumin. Add one litre of hot water. Mix well, close pressure cooker and pressure cook until the meat and lentils or dholl are tender. Taste soup and season with salt if necessary.
7. Add chopped coriander and mint leaves. Simmer uncovered for ten mins. Add water if soup is too thick or reduce according to your preference.
8. Serve immediately in small bowls sprinkled with chopped shallots and chillies.
9. Eat with bread or rice.

Hot and Sour Soup

Ingredients (Serve 6):
- 100 g boneless pork, shredded,
- 1.2 litres chicken stock,
- 125 g carrot shredded and parboiled,
- 125 g dried Chinese mushrooms, soaked in warm water and shredded,
- 125 g canned bamboo shoots shredded,
- 125 g ham, shredded,
- 3 eggs, beaten,
- 1 spring onion chopped,
- 4 teaspoons cornflour,
- 1 teaspoon salt,
- 2 tablespoons soy sauce,
- ½ teaspoon pepper,
- 2 tablespoons vinegar,
- 4 ½ tablespoons water.

Method:
1. Sprinkle shredded pork with pinch of salt and pepper and 1 teaspoon cornflour.
2. Bring chicken stock to boil. Add shredded pork, carrot, mushrooms, bamboo shoots, chopped spring onion and ham. Stir well into the stock.
3. Cook for 2 mins or until pork is cooked. Add mixture of soy sauce, pepper and vinegar, remaining cornflour and water. Stir for a few seconds until soup thickens.
4. Slowly pour in beaten eggs in a fine thread, stirring gently in a circular manner.
5. Add salt and pepper to taste.
6. Optional: A few drops of Tabasco sauce.

Rasson Soup

Ingredients (Serve 8):
- 3 litres water,
- 1 teaspoon crushed garlic,
- 2 dried chillies (adjust quantity to taste),
- 8 curry leaves (cari poulet),
- 3 to 4 tablespoons tamarind paste,
- 200 g dholl,
- 2 teaspoons chopped parsley,
- 1 tablespoon chopped coriander leaves,
- 200 g can crushed tomatoes
- ½ tablespoon chopped thyme,
- 3 curry (cari poulet) leaves,
- 1 or 2 cloves,
- 1 tablespoon crushed cumin seeds,
- 1 teaspoon turmeric powder,
- 1 teaspoon crushed black pepper,
- 4 tablespoons oil,
- 2 chopped onions,
- Salt to taste.

Optional:
- 500 g of taro leaves (brèdes songes),
- Other ingredients such as prawns, chicken bones, crabs at stage 4 to add more taste to the rasson.

Method:
1. Boil the dholl in half litre (500 ml) of water with a little salt and the turmeric powder. Boil until dholl is very tender and crushable between two fingers. Strain cooked dholl and keep liquid in a container. Crush the dholl into a creamy consistency. Blend the crushed tomatoes and set aside.
2. Optional (if available): *Boil the taro leaves in half litre (500 ml) of water until a purée is obtained. Crush and blend well. Set aside.*
3. Heat oil, fry chopped onions for 1 minute. Add the dholl liquid, *the taro leaves purée*, the crushed tomatoes and the tamarind paste. Cook for 5 mins. Add half litre (500 ml) of water and all remaining ingredients, including the crushed cooked dholl. Stir well to mix and blend the ingredients.
4. Reduce heat and simmer to a bouillon for 15 mins. Add remainder of water (1.5 litres) and allow to simmer again for 1 hour. Season with salt to taste.
5. Serve hot and enjoy. Sprinkle with chopped coriander and some curry leaves.

Soupe Mama

Ingredients (Serve 4-6):
- 125 g long or short grain rice,
- 1 litre chicken stock,
- 250 g firm white fish fillet,
- 2 tablespoons light soy sauce,
- 1 tablespoon dry sherry,
- 2 teaspoons cornflour,
- 2 tablespoons finely chopped spring onion,
- 1 tablespoon finely shredded fresh ginger,
- 1 teaspoon sesame oil,
- Salt and pepper to taste.

Optional:
- 1 egg per person,
- fried crispy noodles,
- finely crushed red or green chillies.
- Substitute fish stock for the chicken stock.

Method:
1. Wash and rinse the rice only once to retain the rice starch. Place in a saucepan large enough to hold the stock and ingredients. Add the chicken stock and bring to the boil. Simmer until the rice is thoroughly cooked and the soup thickens to a purée consistency. Alternatively, cook same in a pressure cooker for 30 mins.
2. While the soup is cooking, cut the fish fillet into small thin slices or shreds. Marinate in soy sauce, dry sherry, cornflour, spring onions and ginger. Add to soup and mix well without crushing the fish.
3. Serve immediately, topped with optional *fried egg, a sprinkle of fried crispy noodles to add crunchiness and/or finely crushed red or green chillies.*
4. Enjoy. Close your eyes and see yourself at Hotel Mama in Quartier Chinois, Route Royale, Port Louis, Mauritius.

Tomato Soup

Ingredients (Serve 4):
- 8 red ripe tomatoes (medium size),
- 1 cucumber,
- 4 sprigs fresh basil,
- Juice from 1 lemon,
- Salt and pepper to taste.

Method:
1. Wash the tomatoes and immerse in boiling water for 1 minute.
2. Remove and submerge immediately in cold water. Peel off the skin, cut the tomatoes in halves and discard the seeds.
3. Peel the cucumber and cut into small 2 cm pieces.
4. Blend the tomatoes and cucumber pieces together. Add the lemon juice. Season with salt and pepper to taste.
5. Pour the mixture into individual bowls and place in the refrigerator for 30-40 mins.
6. Sprinkle with chopped basil leaves.
7. Serve cold.

Tomato Soup
Alternative Recipe

Ingredients (Serve 4-6):
- 750 g red ripe tomatoes,
- 3 tablespoons extra virgin olive oil,
- 1 tablespoon crushed garlic,
- 1 tablespoon tomato paste,
- 1 litre vegetable stock,
- 4 tablespoons chopped fresh basil leaves,
- French baguette,
- Salt and pepper to taste.

Optional:
- Use canned crushed tomatoes instead of fresh tomatoes and tomato paste.
- Use light olive oil if the extra virgin oil is too strong.

Method:
1. Wash the tomatoes and immerse in boiling water for 1 minute.
2. Remove and submerge immediately in cold water. Peel off the skin, cut the tomatoes in halves and discard the seeds. Finely chop.
3. Heat 1 tablespoon of extra virgin olive oil in a large saucepan over medium heat. Add the crushed garlic, chopped tomatoes and tomato paste. Reduce heat to medium low. Simmer, stirring occasionally for 10-15 mins or until reduced and thickened.
4. Add the vegetable stock and mix well. Increase heat and bring to boil. ~~Allow to~~ simmer for 2-3 mins stirring occasionally. Reduce heat to medium. Stir in the chopped fresh basil leaves and 2 tablespoons of extra virgin olive oil. Simmer for 5 mins. Season with salt and pepper to taste.
5. Adjust the sauce by adding hot water or allowing the soup to simmer and reduce to suit your preference.
6. Serve hot.
7. Drop a slice of French baguette into the soup when serving.

Bouillon & Fried Wan Tan

Ingredients (Serve 4-6):
- 24 egg wan tan frozen wrappers,
- 175 g pork coarsely chopped,
- 75 g peeled green prawns coarsely chopped,
- 600 ml chicken stock,
- 1 teaspoon sugar,
- 1 tablespoon dry sherry,
- 1 tablespoon light soy sauce,
- 2 tablespoons finely chopped spring onions half for garnishing,
- ½ teaspoon freshly crushed ginger,
- ½ teaspoon sesame oil,
- 1 tablespoon light soy sauce for serving,
- Salt and pepper to taste.

Alternatively, deep fry the wan tans until light golden.

Method:
1. Allow the wan tan wrappers to defrost and soften.
2. Prepare the filling first. Combine the coarsely chopped pork and prawns together with the sugar, dry sherry, 1 tablespoon light soy sauce, 1 tablespoon chopped spring onions, ginger and sesame oil. Manually blend well together to form a smooth mixture. Allow to stand for 25-30 mins.
3. Drop a heaped tablespoon of filling in the centre of the wan tan wrapper leaving the perimeter clear. Moisten all 4 edges with water and pull the top corner down to the bottom, folding the wrapper over the filling to make a triangle. Press edges firmly to make a seal. Bring left and right corners together above the filling. Overlap the tips of these corners, moisten with water and press together. Repeat with the remaining wrappers.
4. Bring the chicken stock to the boil. Carefully drop in the filled wan tans one by one and simmer for 7-8 mins. Add more light soy sauce, salt and pepper to taste.
5. Serve in individual bowls and garnish with the remaining finely chopped spring onions.

Watercress Soup

Ingredients (Serve 4-6):
- 1 watercress bunch,
- 4 medium potatoes,
- 1 medium onion finely chopped,
- 2 tablespoons butter,
- 1 teaspoon vegetable oil,
- 1 cup grated cheddar cheese,
- 2 egg yolks,
- 1 cup milk,
- 1 litre water,
- Salt and pepper to taste,
- Sprig of watercress for serving.

Optional:
- Fresh cream.
- Fresh crispy bread.

Method:
1. Peel the potatoes and cut in halves. Keep immersed in cold water to prevent discoloration. Wash the watercress and remove any soil and stringy bits, including roots. Cut the watercress in 2 cm lengths. Finely chop the onion. Grate the cheddar cheese. Set aside.
2. In 1 litre of water, boil the potato halves and the watercress until the potatoes are cooked. Test with a fork for tenderness. Remove from heat. Drain but keep the water for use later.
3. In a deep saucepan over medium high heat, add two tablespoons butter and 1 teaspoon vegetable oil. Heat until the butter starts sizzling. Cook the finely chopped onion until transparent.
4. Add the cooked potato and watercress. Stir well into the butter / oil mixture. Allow to cook for 2-3 mins. Stir constantly to avoid burning.
5. Meanwhile, mix the two egg yolks into the milk.
6. Add the saved boiled water to the potato and watercress. Stir well. Allow to simmer for 5 - 10 mins. Remove from heat. Add the grated cheese, egg yolks / milk mixture. Mix well. Add salt and pepper to taste.
7. Blend the mixture in batches until smooth.
8. Serve hot with a swirl of fresh cream (optional) and a sprig of watercress, with fresh crispy bread.
9. Enjoy as an entrée for a formal dinner or just on its own.

Oxtail Soup

Ingredients (Serve 4-6):
- 2 kg oxtails, cut into 2 cm thick pieces,
- ½ teaspoon red wine vinegar,
- ½ cup all-purpose flour,
- 2 teaspoons crushed mustard seeds,
- ¼ cup vegetable oil,
- 1 cup red wine,
- 1 onion finely chopped,
- 2 cloves crushed garlic,
- 1 tablespoon tomato paste,
- 3 carrots, sliced 1 cm thick,
- 3 ribs celery sliced 1 cm thick,
- 2 leeks, trimmed, cut in half lengthwise, sliced 1 cm thick,
- 2 bay leaves,
- 4 sprigs thyme,
- 5 cups low salt beef stock,
- 2 tablespoons chopped fresh parsley,
- Salt and pepper to taste.

This is the oxtail soup that Madeleine used to prepare traditionally every Saturday night. I had one of these the night when she captured my heart.

Method:
1. Place oxtail pieces in a large bowl and cover with cold water. Add vinegar, cover bowl and refrigerate for at least 4 hours or overnight. Drain and pat dry.
2. Place a rack in the lower third of oven and preheat to 180ºC.
3. In a large container, mix flour, crushed mustard seeds, 1 teaspoon salt and ½ teaspoon pepper. Heat 2 tablespoons oil in a large pot over medium-high heat. Working in batches, toss oxtail pieces in flour mixture, shake off excess and brown on all sides in pot, turning with tongs. Do not overcrowd the pan. Remove to a plate, repeat with remaining pieces, adding more oil to pan as needed.
4. Pour wine into pan and cook for 3 mins, stirring to scrape up browned bits from bottom. Add onions and garlic and cook for 2 mins, stirring occasionally. Stir in tomato paste; cook for 1 minute.
5. Return meat to pan and add carrots, celery, leeks, bay leaves and thyme. Season with salt and pepper. Pour in beef stock and bring to a boil over high heat. Cover pot and place in oven. Cook until meat is very tender when pierced with the tip of a knife, about 3 hours.
6. Remove oxtail pieces to a plate to cool. Discard bay leaves and thyme sprigs. Skim fat off top of stew in pot. Pick meat off bones and return to pot; discard bones and gristle. Re-warm stew over medium heat, stirring occasionally. Season with salt and pepper, if desired, and stir in parsley.

Typical street food stall serving soups and bouillons in Port Louis

Condiments, Sauces, Chutneys and Pickles

Condiments, sauces, chutneys and pickles are very much part of the Mauritian way of life. The different cuisines making up Mauritian cuisine have a wide variety of accompaniments that complement the flavours of the dishes. Over time, through a process of trial and error, Mauritians have learned which accompaniment goes with which food. The beauty of this process is that Indian pickles are eaten with French dishes and similarly, Chinese dishes are eaten with Tamil pickles and chutneys. These combinations have produced particularly savoury results. The palate just gets titillated with a wide spectrum of flavours for which Mauritian cuisine is renowned.

Tomato, coriander, onion and chilli chatini (page 108)

However, the discipline and the purity of the various cuisines are respected. For example, Mauritians have huge respect for mayonnaise and sauces like Béchamel sauce that are still prepared the French way. Similarly, the traditional spices such as mustard seeds and turmeric powder are used in achars and vindaloo dishes. No Mauritian meals would be complete without the appropriate condiments, sauces, chutneys and pickles accompanying the various dishes being served. The recipes herewith would provide you with more than enough accompaniments to make good dishes taste brilliant and make a lasting impression on your guests. Several combinations such as coconut mint chutney with bouillon poisson (fish bouillon) and green mango chutney or vegetable achar with curries are very well known. These accompaniments are also very healthy when compared with commercial sugar laden sauces such as such tomato ketchups and the like.

Achar
Vegetable Pickle

Ingredients:
- 200 g finely sliced cabbage,
- 200 g carrots cut into matchsticks,
- 200 g French/haricot beans finely sliced lengthwise,
- ½ medium cauliflower, separated into small pieces,
- 3 tablespoons black mustard seeds,
- 2 tablespoons crushed garlic,
- 1 tablespoon turmeric powder,
- 5 tablespoons of vegetable oil (preferably mustard oil),
- 2 large onions finely sliced,
- 2 tablespoons white vinegar,
- Salt to taste.

Optional:
- Sliced green chillies according to taste.

Method:
1. Drop vegetables (*and green chillies*) in hot boiling salted water and blanch for two mins until slightly cooked but still crisp.
2. Remove from water, drain and immediately put in very cold water. Drain and set aside.
3. Blend mustard seeds, turmeric powder with garlic and a little water.
4. Heat vegetable oil in a wok or large saucepan to simmering, stir fry the sliced onions until transparent. Add the blended mustard, turmeric and garlic in water paste. Stir fry for one minute or until well blended.
5. Add the blanched vegetables, mix well until well coated. Season with salt to taste. Stir the ingredients to distribute the salt. Remove from heat.
6. Allow to cool and stir in the vinegar.
7. Place in dry glass jars with lids and store in refrigerator. Will keep for a month.
8. Enjoy as an appetiser or in white bread rolls.

Clancy Philippe making achar at Les Deux Petits Pois in Fougax Barrineuf, Midi Pyrenees

Achar Bilimbi

Bilimbi Pickle

Ingredients:
- 500 g of bilimbi longues sliced into halves lengthwise,
- 3 tablespoons salt,
- 2 teaspoons fenugreek seeds,
- 3 tablespoons mustard seeds,
- 2 garlic cloves crushed,
- 4 dried red chillies finely chopped,
- 2 tablespoons turmeric powder,
- 3 tablespoons white vinegar,
- 4 tablespoons vegetable oil.

Method:
1. Spread sliced bilimbis on a flat non-metallic container and uniformly sprinkle with salt. Ensure that all slices have been salted. Place in a food dehydrator or the sun (half or full day depending on the temperature) and allow to dehydrate. When dry, gently hand-strain any remaining water and salt from the dehydrated slices. Place in another non metallic container.
2. In a deep and thick bottomed saucepan on low heat, slightly roast the fenugreek seeds for 2-3 mins. Remove seeds from saucepan and slightly crush. Crush the mustard seeds, garlic and red chillies together using a pestle and mortar to form a paste, adding a little water if necessary.
3. In another container mix the vinegar, turmeric powder with the crushed fenugreek, mustard seeds, garlic and red chilli paste. Stir well together into a uniform paste. Add a little bit of water if necessary.
4. In the same saucepan, heat up vegetable oil on medium low. Add the spicy ingredients from step 3. Stir well and allow the ingredients to blend and cook, until you can smell the aroma of the spices. Add the strained bilimbi slices into the mixture, stir well together and cook until the bilimbi slices are well coated.
5. Remove saucepan from heat and allow to cool. Store in dry sealed glass jars. Cover the pickle with a thin layer of vegetable oil. Keep in fridge for up to 4 weeks.

Peanut Coriander Chutney

Ingredients:

- 5 tablespoons shelled and roasted peanuts,
- 2 ¼ cups fresh green coriander, finely chopped,
- 6-7 hot green chillies, finely chopped,
- ½ cm piece of fresh ginger, peeled and finely chopped,
- ½ teaspoon salt,
- ¼ teaspoon sugar,
- 1 tablespoon fresh lemon or lime juice.

Method:
1. Remove all skins from the roasted peanuts. Grind to a coarse powder in a clean coffee grinder.
2. Put the coriander, chillies, ginger, salt, sugar and lime juice into an electric blender. Add 50 ml (4 tablespoons) water. Blend to a fine paste.
3. Keep in a dry sealed glass container. The chutney will keep for at least 2 days in a refrigerator.
4. Serve with dhal pouris or on du pain frire.

Coriander Leaves Chutney

Ingredients:
- 1 cup chopped coriander leaves,
- 2 medium size garlic cloves,
- 2 medium size ripe tomatoes,
- Green chillies to taste (as much as you can take),
- Salt to taste.

Method:
1. Clean and wash the coriander leaves. Remove any roots and finely chop. Finely crush the garlic to a smooth paste.
2. Cut the tomatoes into quarters. Finely chop with a sharp knife.
3. Blend all the ingredients together (except the salt) to a fine paste.
4. Season with salt to taste just before serving.
5. Serve with rice and curry or with dhal pooris.
6. Will keep in the fridge for a few days in a sealed container.
7. Ideally eaten with dhal pouris.

Coconut & Mint Chutney

Ingredients:

- Fresh coconut flesh from ½ coconut (alternatively use dehydrated grated coconut - 125 g),
- 1 tablespoon fresh tamarind paste,
- Juice and skin from ½ medium lemon,
- 1 tablespoon vegetable oil,
- Salt to taste,
- 3-5 small green chillies,
- ½ cup mint leaves,
- 2 cloves garlic.

Method:

1. Grate the white coconut flesh taking care not to include the brown outer skin. Roast the grated coconut flesh in a heavy saucepan with 1 tablespoon vegetable oil until light brown.
2. Dilute the tamarind paste with a little water to make liquid. Juice the lemon and add to the tamarind paste. Remove the seeds from the lemon and chop into small pieces for blending.
3. Remove stalks from the green chillies and thinly slice for blending. Wash the mint leaves to remove any soil and grit. Coarsely chop for blending. Crush the garlic to a smooth paste.
4. Blend the grated coconut with all the other ingredients to a fine paste. Some water may be added to obtain paste consistency.
5. Serve with rice and curry or with bouillon brèdes.
6. Will keep in fridge for a few days.

Cucumber Salad

Grated or Sliced

Ingredients:

- 1 continental or Lebanese cucumber,
- 1 small onion finely sliced,
- 1 tablespoon white vinegar,
- 3 red or green chillies *(or more to taste),*
- 1 tablespoon light olive oil,
- Salt and pepper to taste.

Photo 1

Photo 2

Method:

1. Peel skin off cucumber.
2. If using a continental cucumber, coarsely grate the fleshy part into a serving dish. Refer to photo 1. Avoid grating the centre part containing the seeds.
3. If using a Lebanese cucumber, cut into halves lengthwise. Remove seeds in centre part. Finely slice halves as shown in photo 2.
4. Finely slice the chillies and onion. Place in a salad mixing bowl, add 1 tablespoon white vinegar and 1 tablespoon light olive oil. Add salt and pepper to taste. Mix well.
5. Add the grated or sliced cucumber. Gently mix well together.
6. Serve as an appetiser with curries and bouillons. To be consumed fresh.

Pickled Mangoes

Ingredients:
- 2-3 large size green mangoes,
- 3 tablespoons chilli powder,
- 1 teaspoon turmeric powder,
- 1 teaspoon roasted methi (fenugreek) powder,
- 3 tablespoons mustard oil,
- 1 teaspoons mustard seeds,
- 2 tablespoons salt.

Optional:
- 1 teaspoon asafoetida.

Method:
1. Rinse the mangoes well, then stone and cut into the desired sizes. Do not peel.
2. Put the green mango pieces, skins and flesh, into a large glass or metallic mixing bowl that can withstand hot oil.
3. Add the chilli powder, roasted methi powder, turmeric powder, asaefotida and salt. Mix gently without crushing.
4. Heat 3 tablespoons mustard oil in a saucepan over medium heat. Add the mustard seeds. When the seeds start to splutter, remove oil from heat and pour over the green mango pieces. Mix well with the other ingredients. Allow to cool.
5. Leave in a closed glass jar at room temperature overnight. Afterwards, keep in the fridge for immediate use. Better still, place in the fridge, and allow the pickle to mature for at least one month. It will be tastier.
6. Using a dry spoon, serve as an appetiser with bouillons brèdes, curries or fricassées.

Mango Kutcha

Ingredients:

- 2 green or semi ripe mangoes,
- 4 sliced red chillies,
- 1 tablespoon turmeric,
- 50 ml white vinegar,
- 1 medium onion finely sliced,
- 50 ml mustard oil,
- 2 tablespoons crushed mustard seeds,
- 1 tablespoon crushed ginger,
- 1 tablespoon crushed garlic,
- Salt to taste.

Traditionally, the mango is crushed using a pestle and mortar. Kutcha means crushed.

Method:

1. Wash the mangoes. Using a sharp knife, remove the green skin. Coarsely grate the mango flesh into a bowl.
2. Blend the turmeric powder into the vinegar to make a paste. Thinly slice the chillies and onion. Crush the mustard seeds.
3. Over medium heat, put the mustard oil in a large saucepan. Stir fry the crushed ginger, garlic and sliced red chillies. Cook for 1 minute. Add the vinegar and turmeric mixture. Mix well. Add the finely sliced onions and cook for 2-3 mins.
4. Add the grated mango to the fried mixture. Add the crushed mustard seeds. Mix well and cook for 2-3 mins. Season with salt to taste.
5. Serve hot or allow the kutcha to cool down. Recommended as an accompaniment for dhal pouris.
6. To be consumed fresh.

Curry Powder
Curry Powder No.1 (hot)

Ingredients:
- 10 dried red chillies (vary quantity to taste),
- 6 tablespoons coriander seeds,
- 4 tablespoons cumin seeds,
- 2 teaspoons fenugreek seeds,
- 2 teaspoons black mustard seeds,
- 2 teaspoons black peppercorns,
- 1 tablespoon ground turmeric,
- 1 teaspoon ground ginger.

Additional:
- 4 fresh curry leaves.

Method:
1. Remove stalks from the dried red chillies. Heat up a heavy frying pan (cast iron carail is best). Using medium heat, dry fry the chillies, coriander, cumin, fenugreek, mustard seeds and black peppercorns until a rich aroma is developed. Stir constantly to even roast and avoid burning the ingredients.
2. Allow to cool. Grind the spices in a coffee grinder or use a pestle and mortar. Stir in the ginger and turmeric. Mix well together.
3. This curry powder will keep well in closed jars or tins for at least 6 months. Use instead of commercial ones.
4. When cooking a curry, add 4 fresh curry leaves to the powder.

Curry Powder
Curry Powder No.2 (mild)

Ingredients:
- 6 tablespoons coriander seeds,
- 3 tablespoons cumin seeds,
- 1 tablespoon fennel seeds,
- 1 teaspoon fenugreek seeds,
- 5 cm piece of cinnamon stick,
- 1 teaspoon cloves,
- 8 green cardamoms,
- 6 dried curry leaves,
- 1-2 teaspoons chilli powder (vary quantity for mildness).

Method:
1. Heat up a heavy frying pan (cast iron carail is best). Using medium heat, individually dry fry or roast the coriander, cumin, fennel and fenugreek as they roast in several stages. Remove and put aside. Then, dry fry or roast the cinnamon stick, cloves and green cardamoms together until they give off a spicy aroma.
2. Extract the seeds from the cardamom pods. Using a coffee grinder or a pestle and mortar, grind all the ingredients with the dried curry leaves and chilli powder until a fine curry powder is obtained. Mix well together.
3. Use this rich curry powder with fish, poultry, meat or vegetables.
4. This curry powder will keep well in closed jars or tins for at least 6 months. Use instead of commercial ones.

Curry Paste

Ingredients:
- 6 teaspoons black cumin seeds,
- 1 ½ teaspoon turmeric,
- 1 teaspoon crushed mustard seeds,
- ¼ cup coriander seeds,
- ½ teaspoon cracked black peppercorns,
- 5 hot red chillies (or to taste) crushed,
- 1-2 teaspoon(s) freshly crushed garlic,
- 1-2 teaspoon(s) freshly crushed ginger,
- 3-4 tablespoons white vinegar.

Method:
1. Finely grind the black cumin seeds and coriander seeds in a coffee grinder or in a pestle and mortar. Set aside.
2. Combine the ground coriander and cumin seeds with the turmeric, mustard seeds, cracked black peppercorns, salt, crushed chillies, garlic and ginger. Mix well together and gradually add the white vinegar to form a semi-moist smooth paste.
3. Use for meat curry dishes, instead of curry powder. Better to prepare and use freshly made.
4. This curry paste will keep for a week in the fridge, not recommended for freezing.

Curry Sauce

Ingredients:
for 8 main course dishes
- 900 g onions,
- 50 g fresh ginger,
- 50 g fresh garlic,
- 1 litre water,
- 1 teaspoon salt,
- 225 g canned crushed tomatoes,
- 5 tablespoons vegetable oil,
- 1 teaspoon tomato paste,
- 1 tablespoon turmeric,
- 1 teaspoon paprika.

Method:
1. Finely slice the onions.
2. Peel and chop the ginger and garlic. Put the ginger and garlic in a blender with 1 cup of the water and blend until smooth.
3. Using a large heavy bottomed saucepan, add the onions, the blended garlic and ginger with 3 cups of the water. Add the salt and bring to the boil. Turn down the heat to very low. Cover and simmer for 40-45 mins. Allow to cool.
4. Pour about half the boiled onion mixture in a blender and blend until very smooth. Pour the blended onion into a clean bowl and repeat with the remaining half of the boiled onion mixture.
5. Pour the canned crushed tomatoes into the blender and blend to a smooth mixture.
6. In a clean saucepan, add the vegetable oil, tomato paste, turmeric and paprika. Add the blended tomatoes and bring to the boil, stirring at intervals, for about 10 mins.
7. Add the onion mixture to the saucepan and bring to the boil again. Reduce the heat and allow sauce to simmer. Skim the froth that rises to the surface. Keep simmering and skimming for 20-25 mins, stirring at intervals to prevent the mixture from burning.
8. Use immediately or allow to cool and keep in refrigerator for up to 5 days.
9. Mixture can be frozen and stored in serve quantities.
10. This forms the base of all restaurant curries. Can be prepared in advance and used to cook quick curries in a matter of mins.
11. Use with meats, seafoods, vegetables and other ingredients to make delicious curries.

Chilli Paste

Ingredients:
- 250 g green or red chillies with stems removed,
- 3 medium onions peeled and quartered,
- 2 tablespoons freshly crushed ginger,
- 2 tablespoons white vinegar,
- 5 tablespoons of vegetable oil.

Method:
1. Blend to a smooth paste the chillies, crushed ginger and the onions. Put in a bowl and mix well with the white vinegar. If necessary, add a little vinegar to assist the blending.
2. Heat 5 tablespoons vegetable oil in a deep thick bottomed saucepan. Add the chilli paste. Stir into the oil. Simmer for 3-5 mins, stirring at intervals to prevent the paste from burning.
3. The secret is to allow all the moisture within the paste to evaporate without overcooking the chilli paste.
4. Allow to cool and put in clean jars. Top up with vegetable oil. Can be stored in the freezer for up to 6 months and individually thaw before use. Alternatively, keep in the refrigerator for up to 3-4 weeks.
5. Use with all meals.

Roche Cari Curry Paste

Ingredients:
- 3 tablespoons coriander seeds,
- 2 tablespoons cumin seeds,
- 2 tablespoons ground turmeric,
- 3 cm cinnamon stick,
- 1 teaspoon cloves,
- Seeds from 5 black (or green) cardamom pods,
- 1 teaspoon fenugreek seeds,
- 1 teaspoon black pepper seeds,
- Seeds from 4 star aniseed pods (or 1 teaspoon fennel seeds),
- 1 teaspoon black mustard seeds,
- 1 teaspoon smoked chilli powder,
- 3 dry red chillies,
- 10 curry leaves,
- 3 tablespoons chopped coriander leaves,
- 2 cm piece of ginger finely chopped without skin,
- 2 medium garlic cloves crushed,
- 1 medium size onion finely chopped.

Use gloves to avoid the turmeric from colouring your fingers.

Method:
1. In a dry heavy saucepan, under mild heat slowly dry roast (stir continuously to prevent burning) the following ingredients: coriander seeds, cumin seeds, cloves, seeds from cardamom pods, fenugreek seeds, black pepper seeds, seeds from star aniseed pods and black mustard seeds. Roast until you can smell the fragrance of these ingredients. Do not allow to burn. This will bring out the aromatic oils from the spices. Allow to cool down.
2. Shortcut: To save time and effort, use a coffee grinder to grind to a coarse consistency the dry roasted ingredients: coriander seeds, cumin seeds, cloves, seeds from cardamom pods, fenugreek seeds, black pepper seeds, seeds from star aniseed pods and black mustard seeds. Also grind the cinnamon stick with the dry roasted ingredients. This can be done in batches.
3. Coarsely chop the coriander leaves, onion and curry leaves. Coarsely crush the ginger and garlic. Chop the dry red chillies into 1 cm lengths pieces. In a large bowl, add these ingredients to the ground roasted seeds and cinnamon stick from the coffee grinder, together with the turmeric and smoked chilli powder. Mix well together using a spoon.

4. In small batches, use a roche cari or alternatively use a large stone pestle and mortar to blend together the mixed ingredients. With a roche cari, use forward and backward movements to crush the ingredients. If using a mortar and pestle, use a circular motion to gradually bring together the crushed ingredients. Use a spoon to push down the ingredients. Add the rest to the crushed ingredients in the mortar in small batches. Add small quantities of cold water to assist in the blending process. When the curry paste starts forming, use vertical pounding movements from the side down to further crush the curry paste. Slowly but surely, the ingredients will come together to produce the famous roche cari paste (or at least its equivalent) as shown in the photo.
5. Continue crushing to the desired consistency, using circular and vertical movements. There should be enough curry paste for at least two curry dishes. Use instead of curry powder.
6.   Better to use freshly prepared. Can be kept in the fridge for a week. Enjoy.

Devi Amrita Persand crushing spices on the roche cari

Mauritian Mayonnaise

Ingredients:
- 2 large egg yolks,
- 1 teaspoon Dijon mustard,
- 1 teaspoon crushed garlic,
- 1 teaspoon salt,
- ½ teaspoon ground black pepper,
- 275 ml vegetable oil.

Optional:
- White vinegar.

Should the mixture break down, restart with one egg yolk. Then gradually add the broken down mixture instead of oil. It will blend in just as well.

Homemade mayonnaise is very different from the tasteless commercial ones. Make it once and you will never buy bottled mayonnaise from the supermarket.

Method:
1. Place the egg yolks in a large container.
2. Add the crushed garlic, mustard, pepper and salt. Beat up the mixture with an electric blender or hand whisk.
3. Add a few drops of oil. Continue beating. Add a few more drops of oil. Blend again. The mixture will gradually begin to thicken. Add some more oil in very small quantities and blend again. Repeat.
4. If the mixture appears to thicken too much, add a little white vinegar to thin the mixture.
5. Repeat the oil addition and blending until all the oil is used up.
6. If necessary, season with salt and pepper to taste.

Béchamel Sauce

Ingredients:
- 500 ml homogenised milk,
- 1 bay leaf,
- 1 thick slice of onion,
- 3 tablespoons butter,
- 6 tablespoons flour,
- Grated nutmeg.

The original Béchamel sauce owes its name to the Marquis of Béchamel. It was originally prepared by adding large quantities of fresh cream to a thick velouté.

Method:
1. Gently heat milk with 1 bay leaf and 1 thick slice of onion in a saucepan. Remove from heat just as the milk boils, cover the saucepan and set aside for at least 30 mins.
2. Strain the milk and discard the flavouring ingredients.
3. Melt 3 tablespoons of butter over a low heat in a heavy bottomed saucepan. Add 6 tablespoons of flour and stir briskly until the mixture is smoothly blended without allowing it to change colour.
4. Gradually stir in the milk and bring to the boil, beating well with a whisk to prevent any lumps forming. Use a stick blender if necessary to break up any lumps. Season with salt and pepper.
5. Simmer the sauce gently for 3-5 mins, stirring from time to time. Remove from heat as soon as sauce starts to stiffen. Use to coat other foods when still warm and flowing. Eat immediately.

Mazavaroo
Chilli Paste With Dry Prawns

Note: Avoid dried small prawns (chevrettes) that have been artificially coloured.

Ingredients:
- 125 g red chillies,
- 125 g small dried prawns (or fresh chevrettes),
- 1 small onion finely chopped,
- 1 tablespoon crushed ginger,
- 2 tablespoons vinegar,
- Juice from 1 lemon,
- 8 tablespoons vegetable oil,
- Salt to taste.

Caution:
Open all windows when cooking, as the chilli prawn mazavaroo mix will emanate a very strong aroma when cooked.

Method:
1. De-stem the red chillies and roughly chop.
2. If dried prawns are used, soak in hot water until they soften. Remove any loose shells or impurities. Strain all water from the prawns. Alternatively, use small cooked prawns. In the latter case, clean and de-vein the prawns as much as possible.
3. Using a food processor, blend small quantities of the chopped red chillies, prawns, crushed ginger and finely chopped onion into a smooth but gritty paste.
4. A little hot water, vinegar or lemon juice may be added to the mix, to assist in the blending. Repeat until all the ingredients are blended together.
5. In an open casserole saucepan (a wok is ideal), over high heat add 8 tablespoons of vegetable oil. Allow the oil to heat up until very hot but not burning. Stir in the mazavaroo paste and stir fry to cook. Stir constantly to avoid burning the paste. Season to taste with salt. Allow the moisture to evaporate, then cook for another minute. Remove from heat and allow to cool.
6. Store in small glass jars in fridge or freezer. Use within a week if kept in fridge. If frozen, defrost in microwave for 1 minute and use within one week.

Pickled Chillies

Ingredients:
- Fresh green chillies,
- Salt equivalent to a third of the chilli quantity,
- White vinegar,
- Clean glass jars with screw tops.

Be careful. Do not rub your eyes or any other sensitive parts of your body with your chilli stained fingers. It will burn like fire.

Method:
1. Obtain fresh green chillies. The small to medium ones are the best. Wash thoroughly and allow to drip dry in a colander. Destalk the chillies by carefully removing the stems.
   Sterilise clear glass jars (including the covers) by washing in boiling water. Allow to dry completely.
2. Stack the chillies carefully in the glass jars, in layers until two thirds full.
3. Pour the salt into the jar. Tap the glass jars at intervals to allow the salt to get in between the chillies. Fill the top third of the jar with salt.
4. Pour white vinegar into the glass jar in small quantities until completely filled.
5. Carefully put on the screw tops. If the jar tops are metallic, use plastic wraps in between the contents and the metallic cover. This will stop the metallic cover from rusting and tainting the chillies.
6. Place the jars in a sunny location for at least a week to allow the chillies to macerate and pickle well. The longer it is allowed to mature, the better. Will keep for months.

Garlic Sauce

Ingredients:
- 1 tablespoon finely crushed garlic cloves,
- 50 ml of hot water,
- 100 ml of white vinegar,
- 100 ml of cold water,
- 1 tablespoon honey,
- 1 tablespoon finely chopped spring onions,
- ½ teaspoon salt.

Method:
1. Mix honey in 50 ml of hot water until well dissolved.
2. Add vinegar followed by crushed garlic. Mix thoroughly until well blended.
3. Add 100 ml of cold water, salt and finely chopped spring onions.
4. Mix well. Leave to stand for one hour at least before serving.
5. Can be put in closed jars and stored in fridge. Use within 2-3 weeks. Goes very well with Chinese fried rice. Better prepared fresh and allowed to mature in the fridge overnight before use.

Sweet and Sour Sauce

Ingredients:
- ½ cup sugar,
- ½ cup vinegar,
- 4-5 tablespoons light soy sauce,
- 1 tablespoon dark soy sauce,
- 2 tablespoons sherry,
- 1½ tablespoons cornflour blended with ½ cup cold water.

In China, traditionally the sweet and sour sauces are made from mixing sugar or honey with a sour liquid such as rice vinegar, soy sauce, and spices such as ginger and cloves.

Method:
1. Combine sugar, vinegar, light soy sauce, dark soy sauce and sherry. Mix well together.
2. Bring to boil over low heat and stir in the blended cornflour to thicken.
3. Remove from heat as soon as the sauce starts to thicken. Continue to stir for 30 seconds.
4. This sauce can be used for all sweet and sour sauce dishes.
5. Better prepared fresh for immediate use.

Tomato Chutney
Chatini Pomme d'Amour

Ingredients:
- 6 ripe tomatoes (medium size),
- 2 green chillies chopped,
- 1 teaspoon chopped coriander leaves,
- 1 medium onion finely sliced,
- ½ teaspoon vegetable oil,
- Salt to taste.

Method:
1. Remove stem eyes from tomatoes. Finely chop with a sharp heavy knife.
2. Finely chop chillies and add to the chopped tomatoes.
3. Add the finely sliced onion and finely chopped coriander leaves. Mix well with the chopped tomatoes and chillies. Sprinkle with a dribble of vegetable oil. Mix well.
4. Cover and allow to rest.
5. Just before serving, add salt and thoroughly mix the chutney.
6. Can be used as an accompaniment for many dishes and is better prepared fresh. If prepared too long in advance, it can become watery.

Chatini Peau de Pipengaille
Luffa Peel Chutney

Ingredients:
- Outer skin from 1 kg of pipengaille (*luffa acutangula*),
- 1 medium onion finely chopped,
- 1 tablespoon finely crushed ginger,
- 2 tablespoons finely crushed garlic,
- green chillies to taste,
- 1 green kaffir lime,
- 1 branch of caripoulet leaves or 2 kaffir lime leaves,
- 2 (or 3) tablespoons vegetable oil,
- Salt to taste,
- Water to boil pipengaille skin.

Optional:
- 50 g dried prawns.

Method:
1. If dried prawns are included, soak overnight in water at room temperature.
2. Carefully cut your pipengaille into 15 cm lengths. Using a very sharp knife, slice off and remove only the green pipengaille peels.
3. Boil the peels in plenty of water, with the crushed garlic and the caripoulet or kaffir lime leaves. Allow to simmer until the peels have softened and suitable for blending.
4. Drain the pipengaille peels and put aside on kitchen paper towel. If using dried prawns, drain the soaked prawns. Hand press gently to remove all excess water.
5. Put 1 tablespoon of vegetable oil in a small saucepan over medium high heat, gently fry the soaked prawns to a light golden colour. Make sure not to overcook or burn. Remove from saucepan, drain and set aside.
6. In batches, place the boiled pipengaille peels, finely chopped onions, remaining garlic, crushed ginger, *fried prawns if desired*, quartered kaffir lime and green chillies in a blender. Blend well to a fine and uniform paste. Set aside.
7. In a saucepan large enough to contain the blended ingredients, heat 2 tablespoons vegetable oil over medium to high heat. When hot, add the blended ingredients, gently stir fry the mixture until cooked and all free moisture allowed to evaporate. Be careful not to overcook or burn the ingredients. Stir at intervals to prevent the paste from burning. Season with salt to taste.
8. Store in fridge and use within 1 week.

Star Fruit Pickle
Achar de Caramboles

Ingredients:
- 5 caramboles (star fruits)
- 2 tablespoons black mustard seeds,
- 2 tablespoons crushed garlic,
- 1 tablespoon turmeric powder,
- Optional: sliced green chillies according to taste,
- Juice of 1 lemon (to preserve carambole and green chilli colour),
- 5 tablespoons of vegetable oil (preferably mustard oil),
- 1 large onion finely sliced,
- 2 tablespoons white vinegar,
- Salt to taste.

Method:
1. Clean carambole fruits. Slice off any unsightly bits. Slice and cut into serve size pieces. Refer to photo. Remove all seeds and attached piths. If using green chillies, slice into serve size pieces. Remove seeds and attached piths.
2. Drop carambole and chilli pieces in boiling salted water, with the juice of one lemon added. Bring back to the boil and blanch for 30 seconds, until slightly cooked but still crisp.
3. Remove from boiling water, immerse immediately in cold water to cool down the carambole and chilli slices, drain and set aside.
4. Blend the mustard seeds, turmeric powder and crushed garlic with a little water.
5. Heat 5 tablespoons vegetable oil over medium high heat. Stir fry the sliced onion until transparent. Add the mustard seed, turmeric and garlic paste. Stir fry for one minute or until the paste is well blended.
6. Add the carambole slices and green chillies, stir fry with the paste until well coated. Cook for two mins. Remove from heat and set aside.
7. Allow to cool and stir in the vinegar. Season with salt to taste. Place in dry jars and store in fridge for up to two weeks.

Dried Octopus Salad

Chatini Ourite Sec

Ingredients:
- 350 g dried octopus,
- 3 medium ripe red tomatoes finely chopped,
- 1 large onion finely sliced,
- 2 tablespoons chopped coriander leaves,
- 2 tablespoons fresh lemon juice,
- 1 tablespoon light olive oil,
- Salt and pepper to taste.

Optional:
- Chopped green or chillies.

Method:
1. Cut the dried octopus in lengths to fit into a deep and heavy saucepan. Soak the octopus in water overnight and leave at room temperature. Cover the container to avoid the dried octopus aroma from permeating through the house.
2. Boil the dried octopus for about 30-45 mins or until the texture is very soft and suitable for eating. Test with a small knife or small skewer. Remove from boiling water and allow to cool. With a very sharp knife slice into half cm pieces. Set aside.
3. Some people like to quickly stir fry the boiled octopus pieces in a hot non-stick wok to impart a slightly grilled flavour and texture. Alternatively, heat up a non stick wok and stir fry the boiled octopus pieces without the oil. Do this very quickly and remove the octopus pieces immediately to stop burning this precious ingredient. Transfer to a large bowl.
4. Optional: *Slice the green or red chillies thinly.*
5. Mix the tomatoes, onions, coriander leaves and chillies (if used) with the octopus pieces in the large bowl. Add salt and pepper to taste. Sprinkle with the lemon juice and the light olive oil. Mix well together, without crushing the ingredients. Leave overnight in fridge to allow the octopus flavor to permeate the other ingredients.
6. Enjoy as an accompaniment to other main courses with rice. Just delicious. People crave for the unique flavor of dried octopus. Eat within 2 days. Store in fridge.

Chatini Bringeles
Eggplant Chatini

Ingredients:
- 3 medium eggplants
- 1 large onion finely sliced,
- 1 tablespoons chopped green chillies,
- 2 tablespoons vinegar,
- 1 tablespoon light olive oil,
- Salt to taste.

This is considered by Mauritians to be the equivalent of vegetable caviar.

Method:
1. Grill the eggplants over a bbq or charcoal fire, until the skin starts to burn and the inside flesh is cooked. Turn the eggplants around to ensure even grilling.
2. Remove from fire and allow to cool down.
3. Carefully slice open the eggplants with a sharp knife. With a spoon, scrape out the cooked eggplant flesh. Chop the flesh to a smooth texture. Set aside.
4. In your serving bowl, mix the finely sliced onion with the chopped green chillies, vinegar and light olive oil. Add the cooked eggplant flesh and incorporate with the seasonings.
5. Serve as an appetizer with curries or on cracker biscuits as gajack.

Main Courses, including Fricassées, Curries, Rougailles, Vindaloos, Stir Fries, Noodles, Gratins and Etouffées

Mauritian cuisine is rich with beautiful foods that anyone can cook with incredible results. Invariably, anyone who tastes our cuisine for the first time finds that their taste buds are entering a new culinary adventure. The multiplicity of ingredients sourced from French, Indian, Telegu, Chinese, African, Creole and Muslim cuisines constitutes a unique culinary canvas.

Mauritian pilau (page 133)

You will find yourself eating within the same meal, dishes and preparations from the various cuisines. It is not uncommon for foods from various cuisines to be served at the same sitting. It did not take long for French settlers to forfeit their French main courses eaten with bread, for various curries eaten with rice. Similarly, many French based dishes are eaten with rice in Mauritius. Various combinations have emerged through time to become favourite choices with lovers of Mauritian cuisine. Once tasted, your palate will be craving for those dishes all the time. Vindaloos are eaten with lentils or dhalls on rice. Our very popular chatini pomme d'amour with coriander leaves and chillies will be a welcome addition to any meal. Many families irrespective of what is being prepared for dinner, also include a bowl of lentils or a bouillon brèdes to increase the appetite. An appetizer like "chatini coco la menthe" is a must with fish or any other bouillons. Curries are very popular and very often eaten as part of the weekly menu.

Mauritians have a huge list of main course meals and standalone eats from which to choose. In practice, it is not impossible to eat a different dish each day for the whole year. This diversity of ingredients and cooking styles make Mauritian cuisine one of the healthiest in the world. A medical report published in "The Lancet" has confirmed this claim. The following main courses and standalone eats will take you through a culinary journey that you, your family and guests will enjoy. If you practice long enough, you will soon start preparing incredible dishes that will make people, who have already sampled them, crave for another dinner invitation at your place.

Beef Curry

Ingredients (Serve 4):
- 1kg beef cubed,
- 1 medium onion,
- 400 g canned finely crushed tomatoes,
- 1 tablespoon crushed garlic,
- 1 tablespoon crushed ginger,
- 1 tablespoon chopped thyme leaves,
- 2 tablespoons vegetable oil,
- 4-6 curry leaves (cari poulet),
- 2 tablespoons chopped coriander leaves,
- 3 tablespoons curry powder (hot or mild depending on your preference).

Method:
1. Cut beef into 1-2 cm cubes or bite size pieces, depending on your preference. Season beef pieces with salt and pepper to taste. Set aside.
2. Finely chop the medium onion.
3. Over medium high heat, add 2 tablespoons of vegetable oil in a deep saucepan. Stir fry the crushed garlic, ginger, chopped thyme leaves, crushed curry leaves and finely chopped onion, until the onion pieces become transparent.
4. Stir in the finely crushed tomatoes, add 1 tablespoon of coarsely chopped coriander leaves. Mix well together.
5. Simmer for 10-15 mins or until the crushed tomatoes are cooked and the sauce is well blended. Add a little hot water if necessary to maintain sauce consistency and to prevent it from drying out. Mix well and stir continually to prevent sauce from burning.
6. Stir 3 tablespoons of curry powder into the sauce. Mix well and simmer for a further 5 mins. Add a little hot water if necessary to maintain sauce consistency. The sauce should be thick and creamy, but not too liquid and not too thick.
7. Add and stir in the beef cubes. Add ½-1 cup of hot water and mix well. Reduce heat to medium-low. Cover and simmer for 25-30 mins or until the beef pieces are cooked. Adjust the sauce with a little hot water if necessary to maintain the sauce consistency to your preference.
8. If a dry curry is preferred, do not add too much water but make sure that the sauce is liquid enough to prevent it from burning. Hot water, a little at a time can be added until the sauce is adjusted to your preference. Garnish with 1 tablespoon of coarsely chopped coriander leaves.

Beef and Potato Curry

Ingredients (Serve 4):
- 1 kg beef (silverside),
- 500 g potatoes,
- 400 g can finely crushed tomatoes,
- 1 medium onion finely chopped,
- 4 level tablespoons curry powder hot or mild depending upon your preference,
- 5-10 curry leaves,
- 1 cup hot water,
- 1 tablespoon crushed garlic,
- 1 tablespoon crushed ginger,
- 1 tablespoon thyme finely chopped,
- 2 tablespoons chopped coriander leaves,
- 1 tablespoon chopped coriander leaves for garnishing,
- Salt and pepper to taste.

Method:
1. Peel potatoes and cut into bite size cubes (1-2 cm). Immerse immediately in cold water to prevent oxidation and set aside.
2. Cut beef into bite size cubes (1-2 cm). Season with salt and pepper. Set aside.
3. Add 3 tablespoons of vegetable oil in a deep thick bottom saucepan over medium/high heat. Add the beef cubes and stir at intervals until cooked through. If the beef turns watery, simmer until the liquid evaporates.
4. Add the chopped onions, crushed garlic and ginger. Stir in and cook until the onion pieces become transparent. Add the finely chopped tomatoes and mix well. Simmer until the sauce is well blended.
5. Stir in 2 tablespoons of the chopped coriander leaves. Add 4 tablespoons of curry powder. Mix well. Cook for 10 mins. Add some hot water if the sauce thickens.
6. Drain off the water from the cubed potato pieces. Add to the saucepan and mix well together without crushing the potatoes. Cook for 2 mins. Add the curry leaves followed by 1 cup of hot water to form the sauce. Adjust the sauce by adding a little more hot water if necessary to maintain consistency and to suit your preference. Taste sauce and season with salt if required. Stir at intervals.
7. Cover and allow to simmer under medium heat for about 20 mins or until the potato cubes and meat are cooked to your preference. Check sauce at intervals and if too liquid, uncover and allow sauce to reduce. Serve with faratas or rice.

Beef with Mushrooms in Red Wine

Ingredients (Serve 4):
- 1 kg beef cubes-bite size,
- 500 g fresh mushrooms,
- ¼ cup dry sherry,
- 400 g canned crushed tomatoes,
- 1 medium onion,
- 1 cup dry red wine,
- 2 tablespoons chopped thyme,
- 2 tablespoons chopped fresh parsley,
- 2 tablespoons vegetable oil,
- 1 tablespoon crushed garlic,
- 1 tablespoon crushed ginger,
- 5 cloves whole,
- Salt and pepper to taste,
- 2 tablespoons vegetable oil.

Method:
1. Marinate beef cubes in the dry sherry with the cloves, salt and pepper. Allow 30 mins.
2. Lightly blend the crushed tomatoes in a food processor or with a blender. Be careful not to over-blend and liquefy the tomatoes. Finely chop one medium onion.
3. In a large saucepan heat 2 tablespoons of vegetable oil over medium high heat. Stir fry the finely chopped onion, chopped thyme, crushed garlic and ginger until the onion pieces are cooked and become transparent.
4. Add the blended tomatoes. Stir, cover and allow to simmer over medium heat for 15-20 mins, or until the tomatoes are cooked and well blended.
5. Stir at regular intervals to prevent the sauce from burning or sticking to the saucepan. Add a little hot water if the sauce dries up. Taste and if necessary add salt and pepper to your preference. Add the beef cubes and mix well with the sauce. Cover and simmer for 2-3 mins. Add ½ cup of dry red wine. Mix well, cover and allow the beef cubes to simmer slowly over low heat. Stir at intervals to prevent the meat cubes from burning.
6. Add a little hot water to maintain the sauce if it thickens. Cook for 25-30 mins or until the beef cubes are cooked and tender. Be careful not to add too much water as the mushroom slices will release water when cooked.
7. Meanwhile, clean and pat dry the mushrooms with kitchen paper towel. Slice the mushrooms into thick bite size slices. When the beef cubes are cooked, add the sliced mushrooms to the beef and sauce. Mix well.
8. Be careful not to break the mushroom slices or the cooked beef cubes. Simmer over low heat for 15-20 mins or until the mushroom slices are cooked. Halfway through, stir in ½ cup of dry red wine. Do not overcook. If the sauce is too watery, thicken the sauce by dissolving 1 teaspoon of cornflour in ¼ cup of cold water. Add the cornflour mixture to the saucepan and gently mix into the sauce. Simmer for another 3-4 mins.
9. Transfer to a warmed serving dish. Sprinkle with the chopped parsley.

Madeleine Philippe with grandchildren Annabelle, Brandon and Joshua

Beef Bryani
Easy Method

Ingredients (Serve 6):
- 500 g onions,
- 500 g lean beef,
- 1 tablespoon chopped garlic,
- 1 tablespoon chopped ginger,
- 125 ml vegetable oil,
- 1 teaspoon black cumin seeds,
- 1 cup plain yoghurt,
- 1 tablespoon salt,
- 1 teaspoon garam masala,
- 1 bay leaf,
- 60 ml single cream,
- 2 tablespoons chopped coriander.

For the rice:
- 315 g long-grain basmati rice,
- ½ teaspoon black cumin seeds,
- 2 green cardamom pods,
- 2 cloves,
- 1 small piece stick cinnamon, broken up,
- 1 teaspoon salt,
- 2 tablespoons vegetable oil,
- ½ teaspoon saffron threads in 2 tablespoons warm milk.

Method:
1. Rinse the rice under cold water until the water runs clear. Put the rice in a bowl and cover with water. Leave to soak for 30 mins. Set aside.
2. Slice 250 g of the onions, set aside and finely chop the remainder. Cut the beef into bite size cubes and season with salt. Set aside.
3. Put the garlic and ginger in a mortar and use the pestle to make a smooth paste.
4. Heat 60 ml oil in a thick bottomed saucepan or flameproof casserole over a medium heat and fry the sliced onions for about 10 mins, stirring occasionally, until golden brown and crisp. Use a slotted spoon to transfer the onions to kitchen paper. Set aside.
5. In the same oil over a high heat, stir-fry the black cumin seeds, garlic, ginger paste and chopped onions until the onions are transparent.
6. Add the beef and continue stir-frying until all the pieces look opaque and slightly fried. Cover the pan, lower the heat and simmer for about 5 mins or until the beef is just cooked and the sauce well blended. Stir at intervals to prevent the ingredients from burning.

7. Stir in 250 ml water, the yoghurt, salt, garam masala and bay leaf. Cover the pan again and bring to the boil. Lower the heat and simmer for about 45 mins until all the liquid is absorbed and the meat is tender. If all the liquid is absorbed before the meat is tender, stir in a little more water and continue simmering. If the meat is tender before all the liquid is absorbed, remove the meat pieces and cook the mixture, uncovered, over a high heat, stirring occasionally to evaporate excess water until a creamy consistency is obtained. Then return the meat to the saucepan.
8. Remove saucepan with all the ingredients from the heat and stir in the cream, crisp onions and chopped fresh coriander. Set aside.
9. Drain the rice. Heat two tablespoons oil in another thick bottomed saucepan or flameproof casserole over a high heat and add the cumin seeds, cardamom pods, cloves and cinnamon.
10. When the seeds splutter, add the drained rice, stirring to coat each grain in oil. Stir in 750 ml water and bring to the boil. Cover the pan, lower the heat and simmer for about 8 mins until all the liquid is absorbed and grains are just cooked and almost tender.
11. Meanwhile, soak the saffron threads in the warm milk.
12. Set the oven to 150°C.
13. Put half the beef mixture in an ovenproof dish or pan, large enough to contain the rice and all the other ingredients. Top with half the rice, then layer with the remaining beef mixture, followed with the remaining rice. Spoon the saffron and milk over the top. Cover with aluminium foil and bake for 30 mins. Serve by spooning out the layered ingredients.
14. Goes well with a vinegar and chilli seasoned cucumber or carrot salad.

Enjoying bryani during a Mauritian Picnic

Beef Bryani
Traditional Method

Ingredients (Serve 8):
- 2 kg tender cut of beef (or any other meat),
- 2 kg long grained basmati rice,
- 1 kg potatoes,
- 500 g finely sliced onions,
- 1 tablespoons crushed garlic,
- 1 tablespoons crushed ginger,
- 4 cups natural yoghurt,
- 250 ml vegetable oil,
- 250 g butter,
- ½ cup mint leaves,
- 5 cloves,
- 1 tablespoon cracked black pepper,
- 2 green cardamom pods,
- 10 curry leaves,
- ½ teaspoon black cumin seeds,
- 1 small cinnamon stick,
- 2 teaspoons salt or to taste,
- 1 teaspoon garam masala,
- 100 ml single cream,
- 2 tablespoons chopped coriander,
- 1 teaspoon saffron threads,
- 6 eggs.

Method:
1. Finely chop the coriander and mint leaves. Set aside. Blend the cumin and cardamom seeds, garam masala, together with the cinnamon. Set aside.
2. Cut the meat in bite size pieces. Add salt to the meat and thoroughly mix with all the spices and herbs. Melt the butter in a separate container and add to the meat. Add the yoghurt, cream and mix well. Allow to marinate for 1-2 hours in a cool place. Note: If it is a tough cut of meat, it would be advisable to half cook the meat in the butter before adding the rest of the ingredients.
3. Boil the eggs. Allow to cool in cold water. Remove shells and set aside. Cut into halves
4. Peel and quarter the potatoes. To avoid the potatoes tainting, immediately place in cold water after peeling.
5. Fry the onion slices in the vegetable oil until just light golden. Remove from oil and set aside. Pat dry the quartered potatoes and fry until light golden. Remove from oil and set aside. Lightly season with salt.
6. Cook the rice in boiling water for 5-6 mins or until the rice is two thirds cooked. Drain and set aside. Fluff up the rice grains so that the grains do not stick together.
7. Soak the saffron threads in 350 ml of warm water.

8. Choose a thick bottomed cooking pot with a tight fitting lid large enough to contain all the ingredients. In Mauritius, a semi moist flour dough is used to form a seal between the cover and the pot. See photo. A large rice cooker is the best option. Place a thin layer of the partly cooked rice at the bottom of the pot. Cover with half the meat, spice, potatoes and fried onions. Add the six halves of the boiled eggs. Cover with a layer of half the partly cooked rice. Repeat with another layer of meat, spices, potatoes, eggs and onions. Cover with rest of the partly cooked rice.
9. Sprinkle the rice with the saffron threads and water. Cover the cooking pot and cook over low heat for 60-90 mins or until the rice and meat are fully cooked. Add some more hot water if necessary to cook the rice to your preferred consistency. The secret is to have the rice, meat and potatoes cooked to perfection. Not always easy to achieve.
10. Serve carefully and avoid crushing the potatoes and eggs. Some chefs use a cup saucer to serve the bryani.
11. Enjoy. Serve with a carrot or cucumber salad.

Bryani pot sealed with moist flour dough

Chicken Curry with Optional Prawns

Ingredients (Serve 6):
- 1.8 kg chicken,
- 1 medium onion,
- 1 tablespoon crushed garlic,
- 1 tablespoon crushed ginger,
- 1 teaspoon chopped thyme leaves,
- 2 tablespoons coarsely chopped coriander leaves,
- 400 g finely crushed tomatoes - canned tomatoes recommended,
- 4-5 curry leaves kaffir lime leaves can also be used,
- 3 level tablespoons curry powder (hot or mild),
- 3 tablespoons vegetable oil,
- Salt and pepper to taste.

Optional:
- 500 g shelled green prawns.

Method:
1. Skin chicken, remove fat and cut into serve pieces. Carefully remove any loose bone pieces. Season with salt and pepper to taste. Set aside.
2. If eaten with faratas, de-bone the chicken and cut into bite size pieces.
3. Finely chop onion. Optional: Shell prawns and remove dorsal veins. Leave prawns whole but remove heads.
4. Heat 3 tablespoons of vegetable oil in a thick bottomed saucepan over medium high heat. When oil is hot, add the crushed garlic and ginger, together with the thyme leaves. Stir fry until the onion pieces are cooked and become transparent.
5. Stir in the crushed tomatoes. Cook for 5-10 mins or until the tomatoes are cooked and the sauce is well blended. Add ½ cup of hot water if necessary to maintain the sauce in a semi liquid state. Stir at intervals to prevent sauce from burning.
6. Stir in 3 tablespoons of curry powder and 1 tablespoon of coarsely chopped coriander leaves. Mix well and simmer for 5-10 mins or until the sauce is cooked and well blended. Stir constantly to prevent sauce from burning. It should become creamy and come clean off the saucepan when stirred. Add a little hot water if necessary to maintain sauce in semi liquid state. Mix well.
7. Add the chicken pieces and mix well with the sauce. Simmer for 2-3 mins. Stir at intervals to prevent the sauce and chicken from burning. Add ½ cup hot water and mix well into sauce. Cover and allow to simmer over low heat for 25-45 mins or until chicken pieces are cooked.

8. The cooking time will depend upon the chicken meat texture. Check and continue to stir at intervals to prevent burning, stirring gently to avoid crushing the chicken. Add a little hot water if necessary to maintain sauce. To thicken the sauce remove cover and simmer to allow the water to evaporate.
9. Optional: If prawns are added to your curry, add the shelled and de-veined prawns when the chicken pieces are just cooked, then simmer for 5 mins more or until the prawns turn red and are just cooked. Do not overcook.
10. Gently mix well together and transfer to a warmed serving dish. Garnish with 1 tablespoon of coarsely chopped coriander leaves.
11. Serve on rice with a tomato chutney. This chicken curry with or without the prawns can also be eaten with faratas.

Clancy Philippe promoting Mauritian cuisine on Radio One, Mauritius

Chicken Curry with Prawns

Alternative Recipe using Turmeric and Other Spices

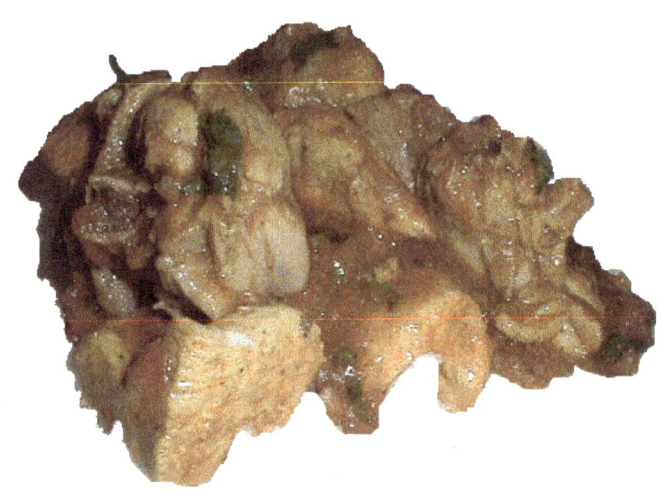

Ingredients (Serve 4):
- 1 kg chicken,
- 250 g prawns,
- 1 large onion,
- 3-4 chopped tomatoes (or use 400 g crushed tomatoes in cans),
- 5 curry leaves,
- chopped coriander leaves,
- 1 tablespoon coriander powder (crush coriander seeds in your coffee blender),
- 1 level tablespoon turmeric powder,
- ½ teaspoon chilli powder (or use chopped green chillies- as much as you can take),
- ¼ teaspoon cinnamon powder,
- 1 tablespoon crushed ginger,
- 1 tablespoon crushed garlic,
- Vegetable oil,
- Salt and pepper.

Method:
1. Cut chicken into bite size pieces. Season with salt and pepper. Allow to rest. De-vein and shell prawns. Season with salt and pepper. Set aside. Finely chop the onion and set aside.
2. Mix together powdered ingredients and make into a paste with some water. Fold in the crushed garlic and ginger. Set aside.
3. Gently stir fry the chicken pieces in vegetable oil until it turns light golden. Remove from frying pan, drain over kitchen paper towel and set aside.
4. Fry prawns (do not overcook) in the same oil. Remove from pan as soon as the prawns turn red, drain and set aside.
5. Place 3 tablespoons of the same oil in a large saucepan. Over medium heat, fry the finely chopped onion until just cooked and transparent. Add curry paste from step 2 and stir fry until the spices are cooked, and the mixture leaves the side of the pan when stirred.
6. Add the crushed tomatoes and curry leaves. Mix well, cover, cook over medium heat until the sauce thickens and the crushed tomatoes are cooked.
7. Stir at intervals to make sure that the sauce does not stick to the pan. Taste and season with salt if necessary.
8. Add the chicken and prawns to the sauce with ½ cup of water (or enough to keep the sauce in a slightly watery consistency). Mix well, cover and simmer until the chicken pieces are cooked and tender. If the sauce thickens too much, add a little more hot water. It the sauce is too watery, uncover pot and allow sauce to evaporate and thicken.
9. Remove from heat and garnish with chopped coriander leaves. Serve hot on rice.

Bouillon Malgache

Beef Bouillon with Lettuce or Watercress

Ingredients (Serve 4):
- 500 g beef cubes-bite size,
- 400 g canned whole peeled tomatoes,
- 4 cups chicken or vegetable stock,
- Iceberg lettuce or watercress,
- 1 medium onion finely chopped,
- 2 tablespoons chopped coriander leaves,
- 2 tablespoons vegetable oil,
- 1 tablespoon crushed garlic,
- 1 tablespoon crushed ginger,
- Salt and pepper to taste.

Method:
1. Season beef cubes with salt and pepper to taste. Place in refrigerator until required. Finely blend the canned whole peeled tomatoes in a food processor or blender until well blended but not liquefied. Set aside.
2. Clean lettuce and coarsely cut 5-6 leaves into 3 cm wide strips. If using watercress, clean and cut into bite size sprigs (avoid the tough stems). Quantity can be adjusted later.
3. In a deep saucepan, add 2 tablespoons of vegetable oil. Over medium high heat cook the finely chopped onion, crushed ginger and garlic in 2 tablespoons of vegetable oil. When the onion pieces become transparent, add the blended tomatoes and mix well.
4. Cover and allow to simmer over medium heat for 20-30 mins or until the tomatoes are well cooked and the sauce is well blended. If necessary, add some hot water to prevent sauce from becoming too thick. Stir at frequent intervals to prevent the sauce from burning.
5. Stir in the chicken or vegetable stock. Cover and simmer over medium high heat for 15-20 mins or until the stock and tomato sauce are well blended. Season with salt and pepper to taste.
6. Just before serving, add the beef cubes and simmer under cover over medium high heat for 10-15 mins or until the beef cubes are cooked. Do not overcook.
7. Place the cut lettuce leaves / watercress sprigs in a serving bowl. Pour over the bouillon and cooked beef cubes. Allow to rest for 5 mins.
8. Serve on rice. Enjoy with an appetiser such as chatini pomme d'amour or achar.

Choko and Pork Curry
Cari Chou Chou et Porc

Ingredients (Serve 4):
- 1 kg pork spare ribs or pork fillet
  (*can also use beef or lamb meat cubes*),
- 4 medium size chokoes (chou chou),
- 425 g canned finely chopped tomatoes,
- 1 medium onion,
- 6 level tablespoons curry powder (hot or mild depending upon your preference),
- 1 teaspoon crushed garlic,
- 1 teaspoon crushed ginger,
- 1 sprig thyme,
- 4 cari poulet leaves - or bay leaves,
- 2 tablespoons coriander leaves,
- 2 tablespoons vegetable oil,
- Salt and pepper to taste.

Method:
1. Cut pork spare ribs into bite sizes. Season with salt and pepper. Alternatively, use beef or lamb. Peel the chokoes and cut into 2 cm cubes. Finely slice the onion and finely chop the thyme leaves. Coarsely chop the coriander leaves. Set aside.
2. Into a deep, thick bottomed saucepan on high heat, add 2 tablespoons of vegetable oil.
3. Add the pork spare rib pieces and stir fry until a light golden colour. Stir continually to ensure even cooking and to prevent the meat from sticking to the saucepan.
4. Add the crushed garlic, crushed ginger and finely sliced onion. Mix well with the meat. Cook until the finely sliced onions become transparent. Add the finely crushed tomatoes, curry leaves, 1 tablespoon coriander leaves and the chopped thyme leaves. Mix well. Cover and simmer until the tomatoes are well cooked and the sauce well blended.
5. Stir continually to ensure even cooking and to prevent the sauce from burning. Add some hot water if necessary to maintain the sauce consistency. Or if the sauce is too liquid, uncover and simmer to allow the sauce to reduce.
6. Add the curry powder and mix well. Stir in the pork spare rib pieces. Add the choko pieces. Mix well. Cover and allow to simmer for 10-15 mins or until the pork and choko pieces are well cooked. Stir at intervals to stop the sauce from burning.
7. If the sauce dries up, gently stir in some hot water without crushing the choko pieces or the pork.
8. Make sure that the curry sauce is well blended and the pork pieces are cooked. The choko pieces should be tender but still firm without being crushed.
9. Taste the sauce and season with salt and pepper to your preference. Serve to a warmed dish and garnish with 1 tablespoon of coarsely chopped coriander leaves.

Curry Janot Delaitre

Pork Spare Ribs in Rich Curry Sauce

Ingredients (Serve 2):
- 500 g pork spare ribs *(can also use pork, lamb or beef meat cubes)*,
- 6 teaspoons black cumin seeds,
- 1 ½ teaspoon turmeric,
- 1 teaspoon mustard seeds,
- ¼ cup coriander seeds,
- ½ teaspoon cracked black peppercorns,
- 5 hot red chillies crushed,
- 1 tablespoon freshly crushed garlic,
- 1 tablespoon freshly crushed ginger,
- 3-4 tablespoons white vinegar,
- 2-3 tablespoons peanut oil,
- 1-2 medium onions finely chopped,
- ½ cup tomato paste,
- 1 cup beef stock,
- Salt to taste.

Method:
1. Cut the spare ribs into serve length pieces (4-5 cms) with a sharp knife. Alternatively cut the pork, lamb or beef into 2-3 cm cubes.
2. Finely grind the black cumin, mustard, cracked peppercorn and coriander seeds in a coffee grinder or in a mortar and pestle. Combine with the turmeric, salt, crushed chillies, garlic and ginger. Mix well together and gradually add the white vinegar to form a semi-moist smooth paste.
3. Heat up a large casserole pan or a wok over high heat. Add the peanut oil and coat the pan uniformly with the oil.
4. Cook the onions until soft and transparent. Add the curry paste and mix well with the onions. Stir fry for 2-3 mins or until thoroughly cooked. Stir constantly to avoid burning the paste
5. Add the spare ribs or meat pieces and mix well to coat the spare ribs and meat pieces uniformly. Cook for 5-8 mins or until the coated spare ribs or meat pieces are semi-cooked and start frying.
6. Stir the mixture at regular intervals to prevent burning. Add the tomato paste and beef stock. Mix well together. Cover and allow to simmer for one hour or until the meat is thoroughly cooked or the sauce is reduced to your preferred consistency.
7. Carefully stir the mixture at intervals to prevent burning. Add some hot water if necessary to prevent the meat from burning and/or keep the curry sauce creamy and moist. If the sauce is too liquid, remove cover and simmer to allow the sauce to thicken.
8. Serve hot on rice with a tomato chutney.

Civet de Lièvre (ou Lapin)

Hare or Rabbit in Red Wine

Ingredients (Serve 4):
- 3 cups (750 ml) dry red wine,
- 3 tablespoons cognac,
- 1 onion sliced,
- 1 medium carrot peeled and sliced,
- 2 cloves garlic, peeled and quartered,
- 1 sprig thyme,
- 1 bay leaf,
- 1 sprig rosemary,
- 1 teaspoon coarsely ground pepper,
- 1 hare (or rabbit) (2 kg) cut into 9-10 serving pieces,
- 250 g streaky bacon,
- 3 tablespoons vegetable oil,
- 18 small pickling onions,
- 250 g button mushrooms,
- 1 tablespoon plain flour,
- Salt and freshly ground pepper.

Method:
1. Pour the wine and cognac into a bowl. Add the sliced onion, carrot, garlic, 1 teaspoon freshly ground pepper, thyme and rosemary. Mix well together. Add the hare (rabbit) pieces to this marinade, turn around to coat uniformly. Cover and marinate for 12 hours in the fridge, turning over the pieces at regular intervals.
2. Remove meat from marinade and pat dry. Strain the marinade, discarding the herbs and other ingredients and set aside.
3. Cut the bacon into match sticks, removing the rind.
4. Heat the oil in a heavy based pot (4 litres) and lightly brown the meat for about 10 mins. Add the bacon and pickling onions.
5. Stir fry for a further 5 mins until the meat is well browned. Sprinkle with flour and stir fry for 1 minute.
6. Pour the marinade into the pot and bring to the boil. Cover and cook for 2 hours over low heat, stirring occasionally. Season with salt and pepper.
7. Meanwhile, trim and wash the mushrooms, pat dry and cut into quarters. Stir them into the pot after two hours. Cook with the mushrooms for 30 mins more.
8. Remove the hare (rabbit) pieces from the pot with a slotted spoon and place on a warm serving dish. Keep warm.
9. Pour the sauce immediately over the pieces of hare (rabbit) in the serving plate. If sauce is too thick, try adding a little hot water and simmer for a few mins. If too thin uncover pot and simmer to allow sauce to thicken.
10. Serve immediately. Eat with fresh pain baguette as a starter course.
11. Just beautiful and a real treat on special occasions.

Goyaves de Chine seller at Rosehill bus interchange

Oxtail in Red Wine with Carrots

Queue de Boeuf au Vin Rouge

Ingredients (Serve 4):
- 1 kg oxtail, cut into serve pieces,
- 1 medium size onion,
- 1 cup red wine,
- 1 cup water,
- 450 g finely chopped canned tomatoes,
- 1 teaspoon fennel seeds,
- 2 bay (kaffir lime) leaves,
- 3 sprigs parsley leaves,
- 2 medium garlic cloves,
- 5-6 medium carrots,
- 1 tablespoon corn flour,
- 4 tablespoons vegetable oil,
- Salt and pepper to taste.

Optional:
- 2 sliced red chillies.

Method:
1. With a sharp knife, remove all fatty bits from the oxtail pieces. Set aside.
2. Finely chop the parsley and set aside. Finely crush the garlic cloves and set aside. With a potato peeler, peel the carrots. Cut off the end bits and cut into bite pieces or to your preference. Finely chop the onion and set aside.
3. In a large heavy bottomed saucepan, add 4 tablespoons of the vegetable oil. Put in some of the oxtail pieces and fry on all sides until golden brown. Remove and place on a wire rack to drain. Repeat with the remaining oxtail pieces.
4. Drain oil from the saucepan, except for two tablespoons. Heat on medium high until the oil starts simmering. Fry the finely chopped onion pieces until they start to caramelise, but not burning. Reduce heat to low. Add the red wine, water, finely crushed garlic, fennel seeds, finely chopped tomatoes, *sliced red chillies if used*, carrot pieces, finely chopped parsley and bay or kaffir lime leaves. Mix well together. Add the browned oxtail pieces. Gently mix well together. Cover the saucepan.
5. Over low heat, allow the oxtail pieces in the sauce to simmer for 2-3 hours. Using a slow cooker gives better control of the cooking and produces better results.
6. Check at regular intervals to ensure that nothing is sticking to the bottom of the saucepan. Carefully move the ingredients around to ensure even cooking. This is very necessary if a saucepan is used. Watch the progress at close intervals.
7. If the sauce dries up, add a little hot water or red wine to prevent the ingredients from burning. Test the oxtail pieces to ensure that these are thoroughly cooked and tender, falling off the bone. Add salt and pepper to taste.
8. If the sauce is too liquid, dissolve one teaspoon of cornflour in a little cold water. Add to the ingredients and gently mix well together. Allow to simmer and the sauce to thicken. Use some more cornflour in a little cold water, if the sauce does not thicken enough.
9. Serve garnished with finely chopped parsley. Eat with bread or rice.

Bol Deviré
Upside Down Bowl

Ingredients (Serve 4):
- 500 g boneless chicken,
- 500 g cooked rice,
- 10 Chinese Shiitake dried mushrooms (soaked overnight),
- 1 bunch Chinese greens (e.g. bok choy),
- 2 Chinese sausages,
- 2 tablespoons oyster sauce,
- 4 eggs,
- 1 tablespoon fish sauce,
- 2 tablespoons light soy sauce,
- 3 tablespoons oil,
- 1 tablespoon crushed ginger,
- 1 tablespoon crushed garlic,
- 1 teaspoon cornflour,
- Salt to taste.

Method:
1. Cut chicken into bite size pieces. Season with 1 tablespoon fish sauce and 1 tablespoon light soy sauce. Marinate for 20 mins. Set aside.
2. Meanwhile, cook the rice to your liking and keep warm. Cut Chinese sausages diagonally into thin slices.
3. Wash and cut the Chinese greens into bite size strips. Remove soaked 'dried mushrooms' from water and wash well in running cold water. Strain all absorbed water by squeezing in your hand. Cut into thin bite size strips.
4. Add 3 tablespoons oil to a wok and stir fry the crushed garlic and ginger until just cooked. Add the chicken pieces and stir fry until cooked to a light golden colour.
5. Add the mushroom strips to the chicken. Stir in and cook for 3 mins or until the mushrooms are cooked. Season with 1 tablespoon soy sauce and 2 tablespoons oyster sauce. Stir in the sliced Chinese sausages. Mix well stirring continually to avoid the food burning. Add the sliced Chinese greens. Stir in without crushing the ingredients.
6. Dissolve 1 teaspoon cornflour in a small quantity of cold water. Pour over chicken mixture. Stir well and when sauce thickens, remove from heat, cover and keep warm.
7. In a separate pan fry the four eggs one by one in a little oil to your liking. Place a fried egg in an inverted position in each of the four soup bowls. Put some of the chicken mixture on top of the eggs, followed by the greens. Fill the bowls to the top with the warm rice.
8. Cover each bowl with an inverted plate. Hold plate firmly to the bowl. Invert bowl contents on to the plate. Remove bowl. Decorate with coriander leaves. Serve hot with tomato and coriander chutney.

Cassoulet by Chef Jean Claude Rodriguez of Chateau Saint Martin, Carcassonne

Pilau
Mauritian Style Pilaf

Ingredients (Serve 6):
- 300 g beef cubes,
- 300 g chicken pieces,
- 300 g continental sausages,
- 600 g basmati rice,
- 4 cups (1000 ml) water,
- 1 medium onion chopped,
- 1 teaspoon garlic crushed,
- 1 teaspoon ginger crushed,
- 2 tablespoons chopped coriander leaves,
- 2 tablespoons chopped thyme,
- 7 cloves,
- 4 tablespoons vegetable oil,
- 1 teaspoon whole black pepper,
- ¼ cup turmeric,
- 4 curry leaves (or kaffir lime leaves),
- Salt and pepper to taste.

Method:
1. Cut the beef and chicken into bite size portions according to your own preference. Keep separate. Season with salt and pepper to taste. Set aside.
2. Prick the sausages with a tooth pick. Place in a microwave safe covered container and cook in the microwave under high for 8-10 mins. Allow to cool and cut into bite size portions. Alternatively, fry the sausages. Set aside.
3. Heat the oil in a deep frying pan to simmering point. Fry the chicken pieces until cooked thoroughly and golden brown. Remove from the pan. Allow oil to drain by placing on kitchen paper towel.
4. Fry the beef pieces until golden brown in the same oil. If necessary, add a little more oil. Add the chopped onions, crushed garlic and ginger. Fry until the onions become transparent. Add the chicken pieces, turmeric, curry leaves, chopped coriander, chopped thyme, cloves and whole black pepper. Mix well and remove pan from heat. If necessary, season with salt to taste.
5. Wash rice in running water several times until water runs clear. Drain and cook in rice cooker with 4 cups (1000 ml) of water. When rice is half cooked, open rice cooker and add in all the ingredients, including the sausage pieces. Carefully mix. Close lid and finish cooking.
6. Immediately open rice cooker. Some of the chicken, beef and sausage pieces will have floated to the top. Taking great care, mix all the ingredients to obtain a uniform mix. Close lid and rest for 10-20 mins before serving.

Poulet aux Champignons
Chicken with Mushrooms

Ingredients (Serve 6):
- 1.2 kg chicken,
- 600 g fresh button mushrooms,
- 150 g tomato paste,
- 1 tablespoon crushed garlic,
- 1 large onion finely chopped,
- 3 tablespoons vegetable oil,
- 2 tablespoons chopped parsley,
- ½ cup dry sherry,
- ½ cup dry red wine,
- 6 cloves,
- Salt and pepper to taste.

Method:
1. Cut the chicken into bite size pieces and mix with the garlic, onions, sherry, 1 tablespoon chopped parsley, cloves, salt and pepper. Allow to marinate for 30 mins or preferably overnight in the fridge.
2. Clean the mushrooms and cut into ½ cm thick slices. Heat oil in a deep saucepan to simmering point. Add the marinated chicken pieces and marinade into the pan. Stir thoroughly and cook until the chicken pieces are a golden brown colour. Be careful not to overcook.
3. Stir in the tomato paste. Mix thoroughly and add ½ cup of hot water. Mix well, cover and simmer for 10 mins. Add ¼ cup of red wine and simmer for a further 5 mins. If necessary, add a little hot water to avoid the sauce from drying up.
4. Add the sliced mushrooms and carefully mix with the chicken pieces and sauce. Avoid crushing the chicken or sliced mushrooms. Add ¼ cup of red wine. Simmer over low heat for 15 mins or until mushroom pieces are thoroughly cooked. Keep saucepan covered or uncovered, depending upon your preferred sauce consistency. Uncover to thicken sauce. Cover and add a little hot water to make sauce liquid. If necessary, season with salt and pepper to taste.
5. Transfer chicken, mushrooms and sauce into a serving dish. Sprinkle with 1 tablespoon of finely chopped parsley.
6. Serve on a bed of rice with a lettuce salad or with achar de legumes.

Rougaille Boudin

Black Pudding in Tomato Sauce

Ingredients (Serve 2):
- 500 g black pudding,
- 1 medium onion finely chopped,
- 1 tablespoon chopped thyme,
- 1 teaspoon crushed garlic,
- 1 teaspoon crushed ginger,
- 400 g can of crushed tomatoes,
- 1 tablespoon chopped parsley,
- Half cup of water,
- Salt and pepper to taste,
- ½ cup of vegetable oil.

Method:
1. Cut black pudding into 2 cm long pieces.
2. Heat up ½ cup of oil in a deep frying pan. When oil is ready, fry black pudding pieces in batches until crusty on the outside, but moist inside without burning. Take care not to break the pieces.
3. Remove the black pudding, drain surplus oil and place on kitchen paper towel.
4. Discard all oil in frying pan except for two tablespoonfuls. Heat over medium heat. Add ginger, garlic, onion and thyme. Mix well and stir fry until chopped onion pieces become transparent.
5. Add the crushed tomatoes. Mix well, cover and simmer for 10-15 mins. Stir occasionally until sauce is well blended and cooked, scraping bottom of pan with a wooden spoon at intervals to prevent sauce from burning. Add salt and pepper to taste.
6. Stir in half cup of hot water and simmer uncovered on low for 2-3 mins. Gently stir the fried black pudding pieces into the sauce without breaking. Allow to simmer for five more mins or until sauce thickens to your preference.
7. Remove black pudding pieces gently and carefully place in serving dish. Pour the sauce on top. Sprinkle with the chopped parsley.
8. Serve hot and eat with bouillon brèdes, rice and red (or black) lentils or better still with rice and fricassée giraumon (pumpkin).

Rougaille de Viande

Beef in Spicy Tomato Sauce

Ingredients (Serve 4):
- 1 kg cubed meat (2 cm cubes),
- 1 medium onion finely chopped,
- 425 g canned finely crushed tomatoes,
- 2 red chillies sliced -quantity to your preference,
- 1 sprig thyme,
- 3 tablespoons finely chopped parsley,
- 1 tablespoon crushed garlic,
- 1 tablespoon crushed ginger,
- Salt and pepper to taste,
- 1 cup hot water,
- 3 tablespoons vegetable oil.

Method:
1. Season beef cubes with salt and pepper to taste. Mix well.
2. In a deep saucepan over medium heat, heat 3 tablespoons of vegetable oil. Add the crushed garlic, ginger, finely chopped onion and thyme sprig. Stir fry until the finely chopped onions become transparent.
3. Add the finely crushed tomatoes, sliced red chillies and stir. Cover and simmer over medium high heat for 10-15 mins or until the tomatoes are cooked and the sauce well blended. Stir at intervals to prevent the sauce from burning. Add some hot water if necessary to maintain the sauce in a liquid state.
4. Add the beef cubes and stir well into the tomato sauce. Add 1 cup of hot water and mix well. Increase heat to high, cover saucepan until the sauce starts simmering again.
5. Reduce heat to medium, cover and simmer for 15-20 mins or until the sauce thickens and the meat cubes are cooked. Adjust sauce continually with hot water if necessary to maintain sauce in a liquid state. On the other hand, if the sauce is too liquid, uncover and simmer until sauce thickens to your preference. Make sure that the beef cubes are just cooked. Do not overcook.
6. Remove the thyme sprig. Finely chop the parsley (2 tablespoons) and add to the rougaille. Mix well. Cook for another minute. If necessary, season with salt and pepper to taste.
7. Sprinkle with 1 tablespoon of chopped parsley.
8. Serve hot and eat with bouillon brèdes or red (or black lentils) on rice.

Roti de Boeuf à la Moutarde

Roast Sirloin Beef in Mustard Sauce

Ingredients (Serve 6):
- 2 kg sirloin beef (roast),
- 900 ml of thickened cream,
- 125 g of wholegrain mustard,
- 3 tablespoons of hot English mustard,
- 5 garlic cloves.

Method:
1. Choose a beef cut such as sirloin suitable for roasting. Cut garlic cloves in halves lengthwise and insert into meat after making incisions with the end of a sharp knife.
2. Mix 600 ml of the thickened cream with 60 g of the wholegrain mustard and the hot English mustard. Place meat in a roasting tray and rub the mustard and thickened cream mixture into the meat. Cover with aluminium foil and marinate in fridge overnight, turning over once and basting with the marinade.
3. Heat oven to 250°C. Turn over the meat in the roasting tray and bake in oven in mid position for 30 mins. Remove foil, turn meat over, baste with mustard and thickened cream mixture. Mix the remaining thickened cream and wholegrain mustard, pour over the roast. Reduce heat to 200°C and bake roast uncovered until meat is cooked. Check at intervals. Turn the roast over to ensure even cooking. Roasting time depends upon the tenderness and cut of the meat. Test by inserting a skewer. If the skewer comes out clean, then the meat is cooked. If the meat bleeds, then it needs more cooking. Baste with the thickened cream and mustard mixture at regular intervals.
4. Remove from oven when cooked. Allow to cool and carve the roast into slices, according to your own preference. Reserve the sauce and thicken over low heat before serving with the sliced roast beef.
5. Enjoy. Perfect with steamed vegetables.

Sausages in Tomato Sauce
Rougaille de Saucisses

Ingredients (Serve 4):
- 1 kg Continental sausages,
- 1 kg red tomatoes (or use crushed tomatoes in cans),
- 1 medium onion chopped,
- 2-3 cloves of garlic crushed,
- 1 teaspoon of crushed ginger,
- 1 sprig thyme chopped,
- 1 sprig parsley chopped,
- Sliced green or red chillies *(as much as you can take)*,
- 3 tablespoons vegetable oil,
- Salt and pepper to taste.

Optional:
- 4 hard boiled eggs,
- 200 g frozen peas.

Tip: The frozen peas should be added to the sauce to cook slightly before adding the sausage pieces.

Method:
1. Blend tomatoes, garlic and crushed ginger in blender.
2. Prick sausages individually to prevent bursting (use tooth pick).
3. Heat saucepan under medium heat with vegetable oil to fry sausages to a uniform brown colour. Remove, pat dry, set aside and keep warm. Alternatively, cook in the microwave, initially for 2 mins. Repeat in 1 minute stages until slightly cooked. Remove and set aside on kitchen paper to allow oil to drain.
4. Reduce oil quantity in saucepan to 2 tablespoonfuls and gently fry onions to a golden brown colour.
5. Add blended mixture of tomatoes, garlic and ginger to onions in sauce pan and simmer with gentle stirring to a creamy consistency on low heat. Optional: *add frozen green peas.*
6. Cut sausages into serving portions. Along with chopped thyme, parsley and sliced chillies, add to the simmering sauce. Simmer for five mins or until sausages are well blended into the sauce.
7. Optional: *add halved boiled eggs. Stir in lightly.*
8. Serve hot on rice, with pulses or bouillon brèdes. Decorate with parsley sprigs.

Lima Beans & Tripes Curry
Cari Tripes Gros Pois

Ingredients (Serve 4):
- 375 g lima beans,
- 1 kg honeycomb tripes (beef tripes),
- 4 tablespoons curry powder,
- 4 tablespoons chopped coriander leaves,
- 7 cari poulet (or 3 kaffir lime) leaves,
- 4 cloves,
- 400 g canned chopped tomatoes,
- 1 medium onion chopped,
- 1 teaspoon crushed ginger,
- 1 teaspoon crushed garlic,
- Salt and pepper to taste.

Method:
1. Soak lima beans in cold water for 30 mins.
2. Cut tripes into bite size pieces.
3. Strain lima beans. Put lima beans and tripe pieces with 1 litre of clean water and cloves in casserole pan. Cover, bring to boil and simmer until both are thoroughly cooked and tender. A delicate balance between the tenderness of the tripe pieces and lima beans needs to be reached. Adjust cooking time to suit your preferences.
4. Remove pan from heat and put aside.
5. In another casserole pan, heat 2 tablespoons of oil. Add crushed garlic and ginger, chopped onions and cook until onions are soft and transparent. Add the chopped tomatoes, cari poulet (curry leaves) leaves and half the chopped coriander leaves. Stir well and simmer until ingredients are well blended and a cooked creamy consistency is obtained. Add curry powder to sauce and mix well. If sauce is too thick, add some hot water. Cover and simmer for 10-15 mins or until the sauce is well blended. Stir at intervals and add some more hot water if necessary, to prevent sauce from burning.
6. Add the lima beans, tripes and cooking water into the curry sauce. Cover and simmer for 30 mins. Stir regularly to mix well and scrape bottom of pan with a wooden spoon to prevent sauce from burning.
7. Cook until the desired consistency is reached. A little hot water can be added to adjust sauce to your preference. Add salt to taste.
8. Serve on hot basmati rice with tomato chutney.

Venison Curry with Lilva Beans
Cari Cerf Embrevades

Optional:
Use pork instead of venison.

Ingredients (Serve 4):
- 800 g venison,
- 400 g frozen, fresh or canned lilva beans,
- 400 g can of finely crushed tomatoes,
- 1 medium onion finely chopped,
- 1 tablespoon crushed garlic,
- 1 tablespoon crushed ginger,
- 1 tablespoon finely chopped thyme,
- 1 tablespoon finely chopped parsley,
- 3 tablespoons coarsely chopped coriander leaves,
- 5 cari poulet or 2 kaffir lime leaves,
- ½ cup dry white wine or dry sherry,
- 4 tablespoons curry powder hot or mild depending upon your preference,
- 4-5 tablespoons vegetable oil,
- Salt and pepper to taste.

Method:
1. Cut the venison meat into bite size pieces. Marinate the venison with the chopped onion, crushed garlic, crushed ginger, chopped thyme, finely chopped parsley, chopped coriander leaves, dry white wine or sherry. Cover and marinate overnight in the refrigerator. Stir once or twice if possible. If using pork, there is no need to marinate overnight. Just marinate the pork for 30 mins.
2. Heat oil in a deep and thick bottomed saucepan over medium high heat. Remove marinated venison or pork pieces from marinade. Keep the marinade for use later. When the oil is simmering, add the venison or pork pieces into saucepan and cook until meat is opaque, tender and lightly browned.
3. Add the marinade and finely crushed tomatoes. Mix well and simmer for 5 mins. Add the curry powder and mix well into the sauce and venison / pork pieces. Simmer without cover until sauce thickens and the crushed tomatoes are cooked. Add some hot water if necessary to maintain sauce consistency. Season with salt and pepper.

4. Add the lilva beans (if using canned lilva beans, drain first before adding the beans to the saucepan. Mix well without crushing. Cover and simmer until the beans are cooked. Stir at intervals to prevent the sauce from burning. Add a little hot water to maintain sauce consistency or to adjust sauce to your preference. Do not allow the curry sauce to dry up.
5. Taste sauce and if necessary season with salt and pepper to your preference. Transfer to a warmed serving dish and garnish with 1 tablespoon of coarsely chopped coriander leaves.
6. Eat with rice and tomato chutney (chatini pomme d'amour), grated carrot salad or salade cresson.
7. Enjoy during the deer hunting season.

Goyaves de Chine in wild deer country (Plaine Champagne)

Pork and Veal Terrine

Ingredients (Serve 5):
- 350 g lean pork mince,
- 350 g veal mince,
- 150 ml whisky or brandy,
- 150 g coarsely minced pork fat,
- 100 g shelled pistachios,
- 2 tablespoons finely chopped parsley,
- 2 tablespoons thyme leaves,
- 1 large garlic clove crushed,
- 1 medium onion finely chopped,
- 2 tablespoons duck fat,
- 1 egg slightly whisked,
- 5 rindless long bacon rashers,
- Salt and pepper to taste,
- Cornichons (French Gherkins) are the traditional accompaniment.

Method:
1. Gather the thyme leaves. Set aside.
2. Put the lean pork mince, veal mince, coarsely minced pork fat, thyme leaves, chopped parsley, pistachios, crushed garlic, whisky or brandy in a large stainless steel or glass container. Season with salt and pepper to your preference.
3. Mix all the ingredients well to obtain a uniform mix. Cover with cling wrap and marinate in the fridge for at least 4 hours or overnight. This will allow the seasoning, herbs and other ingredients to permeate into the meats.
4. Sauté the chopped onion in a small frying pan in the duck fat until translucent. Transfer to a large plate and allow to cool completely. Lightly whisk the egg.
5. Add the finely chopped onion and whisked egg to the meat mixture. Mix well. Marinate in the fridge for 1-2 hours, to allow the chopped onion and egg to permeate the meat mixture.
6. Preheat oven to 150°C. Line the base and sides of a 1.5 litre terrine mould with the bacon rashers. Allow the bacon rashers to overhang the sides of the terrine mould.
7. Spoon the meat mixture into the bacon lined terrine dish, pressing firmly. Fold back the bacon rashers and tuck into the opposite sides of the terrine mould.
8. Cover the mould with baking paper cut to size. Then cover with thick aluminium foil. If using thin foil, use two layers.
9. Place the covered terrine mould on to a baking tray lined with a folded kitchen drying towel. Fill the tray with hot water until half way up the terrine mould.
10. Place in mid position in the hot oven at 150°C and cook for 1 hour 30 mins to 2 hours or until a meat thermometer indicates that the cooked meat in the middle has reached 70°C. Alternatively, check with a bamboo or wood skewer to make sure that the meat mixture is cooked. It should come out clean if cooked.

11. Using kitchen gloves, remove terrine from baking tray in oven and leave to cool completely. Weigh down the top of the terrine mould with either a press plate if your terrine cookware has one, or by placing food cans on top of the aluminium foil. Place in fridge and chill for at least 4 hours.
12. Serve sliced from the mould with your chosen accompaniments. Or by placing the chilled mould in hot water for 30 mins, the contents are loosened enough to invert on to a flat plate
13. Enjoy with crispy baguette and Mauritians will need a chilli sauce to add more flavour to the terrine. Perfect as an entrée for a multi course dinner. Accompany with cornichons or French Gherkins. The cornichons will cut through the fat.

Bacon lined terrine before baking in oven

Poulet aux Petits Pois

Chicken with Green Peas

Ingredients (Serve 4):
- 1.2 kg chicken,
- 600 g frozen green peas,
- 150 g tomato paste,
- 1 tablespoon crushed garlic,
- 1 large onion finely chopped,
- 3 tablespoons vegetable oil,
- 2 tablespoons chopped parsley,
- ½ cup dry sherry,
- ½ cup dry red wine,
- 6 cloves,
- Salt and pepper to taste.

Method:
1. Cut the chicken into bite size pieces and mix with the garlic, onions, sherry, 1 tablespoon parsley, cloves, salt and pepper. Allow to marinate for 30 mins or desirably overnight in the fridge.
2. Heat oil in a deep saucepan to simmering point. Add the marinated chicken pieces and marinade into the pan. Stir thoroughly and cook until the chicken pieces are fried to a golden brown colour. Be careful not to overcook.
3. Stir in the tomato paste. Mix thoroughly and add ½ cup of hot water. Mix well, cover and simmer for 10 mins. Add ¼ cup of red wine, stir at intervals and simmer for 5 mins. If necessary, add a little hot water to avoid the sauce from drying up.
4. Add the frozen green peas and carefully mix with the chicken pieces and sauce. Avoid crushing the chicken or frozen green peas. Add ¼ cup of red wine. Simmer over low heat for 15 mins or until the frozen green peas are thoroughly cooked. Keep saucepan covered if sauce is to your preference. If too thick, add some hot water to lighten the sauce. If sauce is too liquid, simmer pan uncovered and allow excess water in sauce to evaporate. When sauce is to your preference and the chicken and peas are cooked, remove from heat and transfer to a warm serving dish. Garnish with 1 tablespoon of finely chopped parsley.
5. Serve on rice with a chatini pomme d'amour.

Rougaille de Corned Beef
Corned Beef in Spicy Tomato Sauce

Ingredients (Serve 2):
- 450 g lean canned corned beef,
- 1 medium onion finely chopped,
- 1 tablespoon finely chopped thyme leaves,
- 1 tablespoon finely chopped parsley leaves,
- 1 teaspoon crushed garlic,
- 1 teaspoon crushed ginger,
- 4 tablespoons vegetable oil,
- Cracked black pepper to taste,
- 400 g can finely crushed tomatoes.

Optional:
- 2 or more red chillies chopped.

Method:
1. Remove corned beef from can and cut into small cubes. Remove any visible extra fatty bits.
2. Heat 2 tablespoons of vegetable oil in a saucepan over medium heat. Fry the crushed garlic, crushed ginger, finely chopped onions and thyme until the onions become transparent.
3. Add the finely crushed tomatoes, cover and simmer for 15-20 mins or until the tomatoes are cooked and the sauce is well blended. Stir at intervals. If necessary, add a little hot water at a time to maintain sauce consistency and to prevent burning. Optional: *Add the chopped red chillies.*
4. Add the corned beef to the tomato sauce. Allow to soften and gently mix. Lower heat to medium low. Cover and simmer for another 10-15 mins. Sauce consistency can be adjusted to your own preference by either simmering without cover to thicken the sauce or adding a little hot water to create more sauce. Add a pinch of cracked black pepper and the finely chopped parsley. Stir and simmer for another 2-3 mins. Season to your preference with salt and pepper. Additional salt is rarely required.
5. Serve with rice and bouillon brêdes or black lentils. Perfect with fresh crusty bread.

Maddy's Fried Rice

Fried Rice with Chicken and Prawns

Ingredients (Serve 6):
- 150 g Chinese sausages,
- 300 g green prawns (whole),
- 200 g chicken fillet (skinned),
- 4-6 spring onions,
- 1 small pinch saffron yellow colouring, dissolved in 1 cup of warm water,
- 500 g basmati rice,
- 6 eggs,
- 1 cup dry white wine,
- 2 tablespoons fish sauce,
- 1-2 tablespoon(s) light soy sauce,
- 1-2 teaspoon(s) sesame oil,
- Salt and pepper to taste,
- Peanut oil for cooking.

Note: You can cook in two batches (use half quantities when stir frying the rice), then mix the two batches before serving.

Method:
1. Wash rice in running cold water several times. Cook rice in an equal + half volume of water so that the rice is cooked, but still separated and firm. When cooked, spread on a large plate, fluff up to separate the grains and allow to cool. Do this in advance.
2. Using a sharp knife, thinly slice the Chinese sausages at an angle. Set aside.
3. Shell and de-vein the prawns. Cut into halves or thirds, depending on size. Season with salt, pepper and fish sauce (1 teaspoon) to taste.
4. Cut the chicken fillet into bite size pieces. Season with salt, pepper and fish sauce (1 teaspoon) to taste. Set aside.
5. Clean spring onions and cut into thin slices.
6. Beat the eggs with 1 teaspoon of salt, dash of light soy sauce and 1 tablespoon of water.
7. Heat up a wok (or other similar wide frying pan) under high heat. Put in 2 tablespoons of oil and spread the oil to coat the wok all over.
8. Pour in the beaten eggs. Stir cook, break and scrape the omelette with a spatula until the scrambled egg mixture is broken into small pieces that are well cooked and light golden in colour.

9. Remove all scrambled egg pieces from the wok. Set aside. Clean wok with kitchen paper towel. Add two tablespoons of oil. Heat up to smoking point but not burning.
10. Fry the chicken pieces until thoroughly cooked and light golden in colour. Flavour the chicken by adding 1 teaspoon of sesame oil towards the end. Remove chicken pieces, set aside and allow excess oil to drain off.
11. Fry the sliced Chinese sausages until the slices start to become transparent. Remove from wok, set aside and allow excess oil to drain off. Add the prawns and stir fry until just cooked. Remove from wok, set aside and allow oil to drain off.
12. Top up oil in wok so that there are approximately 2 tablespoons. Stir in the rice in batches, making sure that rice is loose and not in lumps. Season with 1 tablespoon of fish sauce, half teaspoon of sesame oil. Mix well, add half cup of dry white wine and quickly stir fry for a few mins until well coated with the seasoning. Sprinkle sparingly with drops of the saffron coloured water to obtain a half yellow / half white rice mix. Stir fry for another minute. Sprinkle with 1 tablespoon of light soy sauce. Stir and mix well. Add remaining half cup of dry white wine and stir mix quickly while the wine evaporates.
13. Stir in the cooked Chinese sausages and chicken pieces, mix well. Stir cook for 2-3 mins. Add the scrambled eggs and prawns. Stir mix carefully so as not to damage the prawns for 2-3 mins. Stir in half the spring onions and mix well with the fried rice.
14. Remove from heat and stir mix the remaining spring onions.
15. Serve hot with garlic sauce, chilli sauce, or a tomato chutney with chillies.

Fried rice with ham and chicken

Moon Fan Mauricien

Chinese Bryani

Ingredients (Serve 6):
- 1.5 kg fresh chicken,
- 4 x 180ml cups of basmati rice,
- 150 g dried Chinese Shiitake mushrooms,
- 225 g canned bamboo shoots (or dried shrimps),
- 4 Chinese sausages,
- 1 medium onion,
- 5 spring onions,
- 500 ml beef stock,
- 3 tablespoons dark soy sauce,
- 3 tablespoons fish sauce,
- 1 teaspoon sesame oil,
- 5 tablespoons vegetable oil or as required,
- 1 tablespoon finely crushed garlic,
- 1 tablespoon finely crushed ginger,
- Water as required,
- Salt and pepper to taste.

Note:
If you do not have a rice cooker, you can also cook the rice in a large thick bottomed casserole saucepan over low to moderate heat. Cover whilst cooking to retain the moisture within the rice.

Method:
1. Soak dried Chinese Shiitake mushrooms in a bowlful of hot water for at least 2-3 hours to allow the dried mushrooms to plump up. Put a saucer upright on top to keep the dried mushrooms immersed. Similarly, if using dried shrimps soak in hot water for at least 3-4 hours or until hydrated and plump.
2. Remove skin and fatty bits from chicken. Debone and cut into bite size pieces. Season with 3 tablespoons of dark soy sauce, salt and pepper to taste. Mix well, cover and marinate for at least 30 mins. Stir gently at regular intervals.
3. Wash rice in cold water until it runs clear. Cook the 4 x 180 ml cups of rice, using 500 ml of beef stock and 550 ml of water, preferably in a rice cooker. Check at intervals and switch off rice cooker when rice is still very moist but not fully cooked. Keep covered. Water quantity could vary depending upon the basmati rice variety.
4. Finely chop onion, bamboo shoots (if used) and spring onions and set aside in separate containers.

5. Remove the soaked mushrooms from the bowl and gently squeeze out the water. Slice into 2 cm long by 1 cm wide strips. Set aside. If using dried shrimps, drain carefully to remove impurities and put aside.
6. Heat up wok or similar deep frying pan over medium to high heat. When wok is ready pour in 5 tablespoons of vegetable oil. Allow oil to sizzle. Fry the chicken pieces in 2-3 batches until golden brown. Move around carefully to ensure even frying and don't break up the chicken pieces. Remove and set aside on kitchen paper or grill to drain away the excess oil.
7. If there is not enough oil in the wok, add 2 tablespoons of vegetable oil or as required. Heat up over medium heat. Add the finely chopped onions, finely crushed garlic and ginger. Stir fry until the onion pieces become transparent. Add the sliced bamboo shoots, drained soaked shrimps (if used) and the soaked mushroom strips and stir fry mixture until cooked. Stir carefully using a flat wok spatula from the bottom at intervals to avoid burning the ingredients. Make sure that the mushroom strips are cooked and tender to the bite.
8. Add the fried chicken pieces to the other ingredients in the wok. Add the fish sauce. Stir and mix carefully without breaking or crushing the ingredients. Remove from heat and set aside. Divide the mixture into 3 equal portions.
9. Remove the partly cooked rice from the rice cooker and put in large container, leaving a small layer of rice at the bottom of rice cooker. Carefully place a layer of the chicken, bamboo shoots, cooked dried shrimps (if used), onion and mushroom mix into the rice cooker. Alternate layers of rice followed by the mix in three layers finishing with the rice spread evenly on top. Add 2 x 180 ml cups of water into the rice cooker. Sprinkle with 1 teaspoon of sesame oil. Close rice cooker and switch on. Allow to cook. Check rice when cooked to ensure that it is cooked to your preference. Water quantity can be adjusted to suit your taste.
10. Whilst the rice is cooking, finely slice the spring onions. Set aside. Finely angle-slice the Chinese sausages and place in a glass container. Cover with kitchen paper and cook the Chinese sausages in the microwave in 15 seconds instalments until just cooked and looking really appetising.
11. Serve the rice from the rice cooker by gently penetrating the layers and dishing out the various ingredients and rice proportionally. Decorate with the finely chopped spring onions and some slices of the Chinese sausages.
12. Ideally served with tomato chutney, including chopped chillies, onion slices and chopped coriander leaves.

Macaroni Cheese with Minced Beef

Ingredients (Serve 6):
- 1 kg minced beef,
- 500 g macaroni (dry pasta packet),
- 425 g can finely crushed tomatoes,
- 2 bacon rashers finely chopped,
- 50 g butter,
- 125 g freshly grated cheddar cheese,
- 2 eggs yolks,
- ½ cup milk,
- 1 medium onion finely chopped,
- 2 tablespoons finely chopped parsley,
- 1 tablespoon finely chopped thyme,
- 2 tablespoons vegetable oil,
- Salt and pepper to taste.

Optional:
- 125 g parmesan cheese.

Method:
1. Add the chopped bacon to the minced beef and mix well. Season with salt and pepper. In a deep saucepan, add 2 tablespoons of vegetable oil over medium high heat. Stir in the finely chopped onion, finely chopped thyme, crushed ginger and garlic. Stir fry until the onion pieces become transparent.
2. Add the minced beef and bacon. Cook until the meat becomes opaque and cooked. Taste and if necessary, season with salt and pepper again.
3. Add the finely crushed tomatoes to the minced beef and bacon. Stir in and cook over medium-high heat. Add a little hot water if necessary to obtain a bit more sauce.
4. Cover and simmer until the tomato pieces are cooked and the sauce is well blended. Simmer for approximately 20-25 mins or until the tomato pieces are well cooked. Stir at intervals to prevent burning. Add a little bit of hot water if necessary to keep the sauce semi liquid.
5. When the minced beef, bacon and finely crushed tomatoes are cooked, stir in 1 tablespoon of the chopped parsley. Remove saucepan from heat and set aside.
6. Bring 4 litres of water, plus 1 teaspoon of salt, to the boil in a covered deep pasta cooking pot. Add a further 2 teaspoons of salt. Quickly put in the macaroni when water is fully on boil and gently stir. Cover and cook for 10-12 mins or until the macaroni is "al dente" (cooked but firm to the touch). Strain and set aside. Empty pasta cooking pot.
7. Mix 2 egg yolks with ½ cup of milk in a bowl. Set aside.
8. Melt the butter in the pasta cooking pot or similar deep saucepan over medium low heat. Immediately, add the strained cooked macaroni and gently stir in the milk and egg yolk mixture. Mix gently and cook until the egg yolk/milk mixture is cooked. Stir in the freshly grated cheddar cheese and mix well.

9. Add the minced beef/bacon/tomato sauce mixture to the macaroni. Mix well taking care not to crush the macaroni. Transfer to a warmed serving dish. Garnish with 1 tablespoon of finely chopped parsley.
10. Alternatively, top the macaroni with breadcrumbs and *freshly grated parmesan cheese*. Put under grill and allow the crumbs and cheese to cook/melt to a light golden colour. Serve immediately.
11. Enjoy. Perfect with a chatini pomme d'amour (tomato with chillies chutney).

Madeleine tasting cousin Guito's cuisine

Mines Frire

Fried Noodles - Mauritian Chow Mein

Ingredients (Serve 4):
- 350 g dried Chinese noodles,
- 225 g skinless, boneless chicken breast,
- 2 Chinese sausages,
- 250 g shelled and de-veined green prawns,
- 2 eggs,
- 2 tablespoons mushroom soy sauce,
- 1 tablespoon fish sauce,
- 1 teaspoon garlic finely crushed,
- 2 tablespoons dry sherry,
- 1 ½ tablespoon sesame oil,
- 5 tablespoons vegetable oil,
- 2 garlic cloves finely chopped,
- 125 g bean sprouts,
- 4 spring onions,
- Salt and pepper to taste.

Method:
1. Cook the noodles in a saucepan of boiling water until tender but firm. Drain and rinse under cold water. Drain well again. Put aside.
2. Slice the chicken breast into small bite size pieces. Place in a bowl and add 1 tablespoon of the fish sauce, 1 tablespoon dry sherry and ½ tablespoon sesame oil. Add salt and pepper to taste. Mix well, cover and set aside to marinate.
3. Cut the prawns into bite size pieces. Add 1 tablespoon dry sherry. Add salt and pepper to taste. Mix well, cover and set aside to marinate.
4. Cut the Chinese sausages into thin slices at an angle. Place in a glass bowl, cover with kitchen paper and microwave for 20 seconds. Set aside.
5. Wash and clean the bean sprouts. Remove all the stringy bits, drain and put aside. Clean the spring onions and cut into thin slices.
6. Whisk the 2 eggs into an omelette batter. Add salt and pepper to taste.
7. Heat up a wok or large frying pan and add 1 tablespoon of vegetable oil. Spread the oil all over to coat the wok completely. Stir cook the egg omelette batter. Remove from frying pan. Allow to cool and cut into small pieces according to your preference. Remove all traces of cooked omelette from wok or frying pan to avoid burning of food later on.
8. Heat two tablespoons of vegetable oil in the wok over a high heat. When it starts smoking, add the chicken mixture. Stir fry for 2 mins or until thoroughly cooked. Remove fried chicken pieces from wok. Set aside and keep warm.

9. Add two tablespoons of vegetable oil to the wok. Heat to simmering point and stir in the garlic and prawns. Stir fry for one minute or until the prawns are slightly cooked. Remove prawns and set aside.
10. Place the sliced Chinese sausages in the pan and add the noodles gradually. Mix well and stir taking care to separate noodles rather than breaking them. Gradually mix in the fried chicken pieces. Sprinkle with 1 tablespoon of fish sauce, 2 tablespoons of mushroom soy sauce followed by 1 tablespoon of sesame oil. Gradually add the bean sprouts, sliced omelette and the prawns. Mix well without crushing the prawns or the noodles.
11. Stir fry until the noodles are heated through. Add the chopped spring onions and mix well. Serve at once and eat hot, with a chatini pomme d'amour (tomato with chilli chutney).

Fried noodles with chicken and Chinese sausages

Spaghetti Bolognese à la Créole

Ingredients (Serve 4):
- 450 g mince beef,
- 1 medium onion finely chopped,
- 1 teaspoon crushed garlic,
- 1 teaspoon crushed ginger,
- 500 g dried spaghetti pasta,
- 400 g can finely chopped tomatoes,
- 375 g plain tomato paste,
- ½ cup dry sherry or dry white wine,
- ½ cup freshly grated parmesan cheese,
- ½ cup of freshly grated tasty cheddar cheese,
- 3 tablespoons coarsely chopped basil leaves,
- 2 tablespoons vegetable oil,
- 1 tablespoon virgin olive oil,
- 1 tablespoon finely chopped thyme leaves,
- 10 cloves,
- ½ tablespoon dried mixed herbs,
- Salt and pepper to taste.

Optional:
- Chopped fresh red chillies as desired.

Method:
1. Season the mince beef with salt and pepper. Mix thoroughly. Cover and allow to rest at ambient room temperature for 20 mins.
2. If the canned crushed tomato is not finely crushed, use blender to further crush to a fine texture. Set aside
3. Heat oil in a deep heavy bottomed saucepan to simmering point over medium heat. Add the crushed garlic and ginger, finely chopped onion and chopped thyme leaves. Mix well and cook until the onion pieces become transparent.
4. Add the mince meat, mix well and allow to cook to a golden brown colour. Stir at intervals to ensure that meat does not burn or stick to the bottom of saucepan. Increase heat if necessary to cook the meat.
5. Add the tomato paste in small quantities and blend in well with the mince meat. Add the chopped tomatoes, 1½ tablespoons chopped basil leaves, mixed herbs, cloves and 1 cup of hot water. Mix and reduce heat to medium.
6. Cover and allow to simmer for 15-20 mins or until the sauce is well blended and cooked. Stir at regular intervals to ensure the blending of all ingredients and to make sure that the sauce does not burn at the bottom of saucepan.
7. Optional: *You can add the chopped red chillies at this point. This will also remove the sweet taste in canned tomatoes.* Mix well.

8. Check at regular intervals to ensure that the sauce does not dry up and burn. Add and mix in little quantities of hot water if the sauce dries up. If sauce becomes watery, uncover and simmer to allow water to evaporate to make sauce thicker. Adjust the sauce consistency to suit personal sauce preferences. Taste sauce at intervals and season with salt and pepper if desired. Stir at regular intervals to ensure the blending of all ingredients and to make sure that the sauce does not burn. The sauce must not be watery or it will not cling to the pasta. It should be consistent enough to stick to the pasta when mixed.
9. Optional: Add ½ cup of dry sherry or dry white wine and mix well. Allow to simmer for 2 more mins.
10. Transfer to a serving dish. Can be reheated in the microwave later as this needs to be served piping hot. Sprinkle with 1 ½ chopped basil leaves just before serving.
11. Cook the spaghetti pasta as per the instructions on the packet. Just prior to serving, reheat the spaghetti in the microwave and mix well with 1 tablespoon of extra virgin olive oil.
12. Serve the desired quantity of spaghetti on each plate, sprinkle with cheddar cheese according to taste, top with the desired amount of Bolognese meat sauce, sprinkle with the parmesan cheese.
13. Sit back and enjoy with a glass of full bodied red wine.

Madeleine with granddaughters Jennifer and Annabelle in the kitchen

Layered Cheese Lasagna

Ingredients (Serve 6):
- 1 kg lean mince beef,
- 2 x 400 g cans of crushed tomatoes,
- 1 cup (250 ml) tomato paste,
- 250 g shredded mozzarella cheese,
- 250 g grated parmesan cheese,
- 250 ml of dry sherry,
- ½ cup finely chopped onions,
- 1 teaspoon fennel seeds,
- 2 tablespoons coarsely chopped basil leaves,
- 4 tablespoons finely chopped parsley,
- 2 tablespoons honey or raw sugar,
- 600 g smooth ricotta cheese,
- ½ teaspoon grated nutmeg,
- 2 eggs,
- 1 tablespoon crushed garlic,
- Hot water as required
- Salt and pepper to taste,
- 500 g dried instant lasagna sheets.

Optional:
- 2 tablespoons crushed red chillies or to taste.

Method:
1. In a large heavy based saucepan heat 3 tablespoons of vegetable oil over medium to high setting.
2. Add the chopped onions and the crushed garlic. Allow the finely chopped onions to become transparent, add the mince beef. Stir until well mixed.
3. Allow the minced beef to brown and stir at intervals to prevent burning. If the minced beef releases a lot of fat or liquid, skim it off.
4. Add the crushed tomatoes, tomato paste and one cup of hot water to the cooked minced beef. Mix well. Allow to simmer for two mins.
5. Optional: *add finely crushed or chopped red chillies to taste.*
6. Meanwhile, place the lasagna sheets in hot water in a baking tray to soften.
7. Preheat oven at 180°C.
8. Add to the minced beef in the pan, the sugar or honey, chopped basil and half the parsley leaves, dry sherry, fennel seeds, salt and pepper to taste. Mix well. Cover and simmer for one hour over medium to low heat.

9. Stir at intervals to make sure that the minced beef or sauce does not stick to the pan or burn. Adjust the sauce with little quantities of hot water if necessary to maintain consistency if the mixture dries up. When well blended and cooked, remove from heat. Set aside.
10. Place the ricotta cheese in a large bowl, add 2 eggs, half teaspoon grated nutmeg and the remaining finely chopped parsley leaves. Mix well with a large spoon until uniformly blended. Set aside.
11. In a 25cm by 35cm baking pan or similar, spread no more than a third of the meat sauce on the bottom. Remove lasagna sheets from water one by one, allow the water to drip off and place one layer on top of the meat sauce. Spread a little less than half the ricotta cheese mixture over the lasagna layer. Spread a little less than half of the mozzarella cheese uniformly over the ricotta layer. Sprinkle with half the parmesan cheese.
12. Spread half of the remaining meat sauce over the cheese layer. Place another layer of lasagna sheets. Spread the remaining ricotta cheese mixture over the lasagna sheets. Spread the remaining mozzarella and parmesan cheeses as before, except save some (about a third) of the mozzarella and parmesan cheeses for use later.
13. Spread the remaining meat sauce over the cheese layer. Finish off by sprinkling the mozzarella cheese over the meat sauce, followed by the parmesan cheese.
14. Cover with aluminium foil and place in oven preheated at 180°C. Allow to bake for 25 mins. Remove foil and bake uncovered for 30 mins.
15. If the top layer of cheese has not attained a golden brown colour, remove from oven and place under grill. Watch closely and remove when golden brown.
16. Allow the lasagna to settle down for 10 to 15 mins. Cut into portions with a sharp knife in the tray. Carefully remove with a flat spatula.
17. Enjoy with a green salad.

Lasagna with Béchamel Sauce

Ingredients (Serve 6):
- 1 kg lean mince beef,
- 2 x 400 g cans of crushed tomatoes,
- 1 cup (250 ml) tomato paste,
- 250 g grated parmesan cheese,
- 250 ml of dry sherry,
- ½ cup finely chopped onions,
- 1 teaspoon fennel seeds,
- 2 tablespoons coarsely chopped basil leaves,
- 2 tablespoons finely chopped parsley,
- 2 tablespoons honey or raw sugar,
- 1 tablespoon crushed garlic,
- Hot water as required
- Salt and pepper to taste,
- 500 g dried instant lasagna sheets,
- 6 cups Béchamel sauce as per recipe in cauliflower in white sauce recipe. (page 103)

Optional:
- 2 tablespoons crushed red chillies or to taste.

Method:
1. In a large heavy based saucepan heat 3 tablespoons of vegetable oil over medium to high setting.
2. Add the chopped onions and the crushed garlic. Allow the finely chopped onions to become transparent, add the mince beef. Stir until well mixed.
3. Allow the minced beef to brown and stir at intervals to prevent from burning. If the minced beef releases a lot of fat or liquid, skim it off.
4. Place the lasagna sheets in hot water in a baking tray to soften.
5. Add the crushed tomatoes, tomato paste and one cup of hot water to the cooked minced beef. Mix well. Allow to simmer for two mins.
6. Add the sugar or honey, chopped basil and parsley leaves, dry sherry, fennel seeds, salt and pepper to taste. Optional: *add finely crushed or chopped red chillies to taste.* Mix the ingredients with the minced beef and tomato mixture. Cover and simmer for one hour over medium to low heat.
7. Stir at intervals to make sure that the minced beef or sauce does not stick to the pan or burn. Adjust the sauce with little quantities of hot water if necessary to maintain consistency if the mixture dries up. When well blended and cooked, remove from heat. Set aside.

8. Prepare the Béchamel sauce as described in the cauliflower in white sauce recipe.
9. In a 25cm by 35cm baking pan or similar, spread no more than a third of the meat sauce at the bottom. Remove lasagna sheets from water one by one, allow the water to drip off and place one layer on top of the meat sauce. Spread a thin layer of the Béchamel sauce over the lasagna sheets, followed by a third of the parmesan cheese.
10. Place another layer of lasagna sheets. Spread half of the remaining meat sauce over the lasagna sheets. Spread half of the remaining Béchamel sauce, followed by half the remaining parmesan cheese.
11. Place another layer of lasagna sheets. Spread the remaining meat sauce over the lasagna sheets. Spread the remaining Béchamel sauce, followed by the remaining parmesan cheese.
12. Cover with aluminium foil and place in oven preheated at 180 degrees Centigrade. Allow to bake for 25 mins. Remove foil and bake uncovered for 30 mins. If the top layer of cheese has not attained a golden brown colour, remove from oven and place under grill. Watch closely and remove when golden brown
13. Allow the lasagna to settle down for 5 to 10 mins. Cut into portions with a sharp knife in the tray. Carefully remove with a flat spatula.
14. Enjoy with a green salad.

Omelette aux Herbes

Ingredients (Serve 1):
- 2 eggs,
- 1 tablespoon butter,
- 1 tablespoon crème fraiche or sour cream,
- 1 tablespoon chopped herbs (such as thyme, parsley or marjoram),
- Salt and freshly ground black pepper.

Filling suggestions:
Chopped ham, shaved truffles, finely chopped crispy bacon or sauteed sliced mushrooms, sliced tomatoes, finely sliced onions or grated cheese.

Method:
1. Whisk the eggs, salt and pepper until well mixed.
2. Melt the butter in an omelette pan or small non-stick frying pan over medium high heat, until the butter is foamy and light nutty brown.
3. Pour in the beaten eggs. When the eggs start to set, lift up the sides with a palette knife and tilt the pan to allow the uncooked eggs to run underneath.
4. When the eggs are set enough so as not to run freely, but still soft and not completely cooked, spoon the crème fraiche on the middle of the omelette. Sprinkle with the freshly chopped herbs.
5. With a palette knife or two, ease off one third of the omelette and fold in over the middle. Tilt the pan and fold the other third over the folded portion.
6. Cook to your preference. Don't overcook.
7. Carefully slide out the omelette to a serving plate. Enjoy.

Truffles Omelette

Ingredients (Serve 2):
- 25 g truffles,
- 3 eggs at room temperature,
- 25 g butter,
- 2 tablespoons fresh cream,
- Salt and pepper to taste.

Top Tip:
Place the eggs and truffles in an airtight container for a few days before making the omelette. This allows the truffle to permeate the eggs.

Method:
1. Lightly whip the eggs and fresh cream with a wire whisk to obtain a uniform mixture. Season with salt and pepper to taste. Put aside.
2. Slice the truffles into thin shavings.
3. Melt the butter in a small saucepan over medium to high heat until the butter starts to foam. Add egg and fresh cream mixture to the pan. Using a small wooden spoon, bring the sides of the omelette into the centre and allow the uncooked omelette to run out. Use the pan handle to tilt the pan and assist the uncooked omelette in the centre to run out.
4. When the omelette is set to your preference with the centre part still runny, 4-5 mins, add the truffle shavings. Remove pan from heat and allow to stand for a minute or two. Then, carefully fold in the omelette into thirds.
5. Serve immediately with toasted sourdough bread. Enjoy.

Salt Fish in Spicy Tomato Sauce

Rougaille de Poisson Salé

Ingredients (Serve 3):
- 200 g salt fish (poisson salé),
- 1 medium onion finely chopped,
- 1 tablespoon finely chopped thyme leaves,
- 1 tablespoon finely chopped parsley leaves,
- 1 teaspoon crushed garlic,
- 1 teaspoon crushed ginger,
- 400 g can finely crushed tomatoes,
- 4 tablespoons vegetable oil,
- Cracked black pepper to taste.

Optional:
- 2 or more red chillies chopped.

Method:
1. Rinse salt fish whole in cold running water to wash the salt away. Soak in hot, but not boiling water, for 20 mins or until the fish skin is soft enough to be scraped off. Scrape the skin off the fish with a sharp knife. Rinse in cold running water. Boil fish whole over medium heat in a saucepan for 5 mins or until the fish is soft enough to be flaked into small pieces.
2. Drain, allow to cool down. De-bone and flake fish. Take care to remove all bones with the help of a small knife and fork.
3. In a frying pan, over high heat add 2 tablespoons of vegetable oil. Fry the flaked fish until golden brown. Stir at intervals to prevent burning. Do not overcook. Set aside.
4. In another saucepan, put 2 tablespoons of vegetable oil over medium heat. Fry the crushed garlic, crushed ginger, finely chopped onions and thyme until the onions are cooked and become transparent.
5. Add the finely crushed tomatoes, cover and allow to simmer for 15-20 mins or until the tomatoes are cooked and the sauce is well blended. Stir at intervals. If necessary, add a little hot water to maintain sauce consistency and to prevent burning. Optional: *Add the chopped red chillies and mix well into the sauce.*

6. Add the fried fish flakes to the tomato sauce and mix. Reduce heat to medium low. Cover and simmer for another 10-15 mins. Adjust the sauce consistency to your preference by either simmering without cover to thicken the sauce or adding a little hot water to create more sauce. Add a pinch of cracked black pepper and the finely chopped parsley. Stir and simmer for another 2-3 mins. Taste sauce and season to your preference with salt, if necessary, and pepper. Additional salt is rarely required.
7. Serve hot. Makes an excellent appetiser with rice and bouillon brèdes or black lentils.

Madeleine Philippe dining with friends in Paris

Oxtail Curry with Eggplant

Ingredients (Serve 4):
- 1 kg oxtail-separated at joints and meaty pieces,
- 1 kg Lebanese eggplants,
- 400 g canned finely chopped tomatoes,
- 4 tablespoons curry powder of your choice,
- 1 medium onion finely chopped,
- 1 teaspoon finely crushed garlic,
- 1 teaspoon finely crushed ginger,
- 1 tablespoon finely chopped thyme,
- 1 heaped tablespoon chopped coriander leaves, including root stems,
- 6 curry leaves - alternatively use kaffir lime leaves,
- 1 heaped tablespoon coarsely chopped coriander leaves for sprinkling on finished curry,
- Salt and pepper to taste,
- 2 tablespoons vegetable oil.

Method:
1. Cut oxtail at joints or ask your butcher to saw-cut the oxtail. Carefully remove all excess fat, without damaging the oxtail pieces. Put oxtail pieces in pressure cooker. Just cover with cold water. Add 1 teaspoon of salt and a pinch of ground black pepper.
2. Cover and pressure cook over medium high heat for 20 mins or until just cooked and tender, but firm. If necessary, cook again for a few mins at a time to ensure that meat is cooked and tender. Do not overcook. Remove pressure cooker from heat and set aside. Do not pour out the cooking water.
3. Wash the eggplant and cut into halves lengthwise. Cut the eggplant halves into 2 cm slices.
4. In a deep saucepan, add 2 tablespoons of vegetable oil, 1 teaspoon each of finely chopped garlic and ginger, curry leaves, 1 tablespoon chopped coriander root stems and leaves, finely chopped thyme leaves and onion.
5. Stir fry over medium high heat until onion pieces become transparent. Add the finely crushed tomatoes. Stir well and add salt to taste. Mix well, cover and simmer over medium high heat, until tomatoes are cooked and well blended with the spices and herbs. Stir sauce at intervals to prevent from burning.
6. If sauce becomes too thick, add some of the oxtail cooking water. Add 4 tablespoons of curry powder. Mix well and simmer for a further 2-3 mins.

7. Add oxtail pieces. Mix with the curry sauce until all the oxtail pieces are covered in sauce. If sauce is or becomes too thick, add little quantities of the oxtail cooking water. Stir well, cover saucepan and simmer over medium low heat for 20-30 mins or until the oxtail pieces are cooked to your preference. Gently stir at intervals to prevent curry sauce and oxtail pieces from burning.
8. Add the eggplant pieces to the oxtail in curry sauce mixture. Gently stir and cover. Cook for a further 15-20 mins to blend the curry sauce, oxtail and eggplant pieces. Stir at intervals to make sure that the sauce does not burn. The eggplant pieces will collapse and blend in with the sauce.
9. Add salt and pepper to taste. Mix well.
10. Gently transfer the oxtail pieces to a serving dish. Pour over the curry sauce. Decorate with the coarsely chopped coriander leaves.
11. Serve hot on rice with a tomato with chilli chutney or cucumber salad.
12. Enjoy.

Jack fruit curry on rice (page 168)

Rougaille Ourite Sec
Dried Octopus Rougaille

Ingredients (Serve 2):
- 350 g dried octopus,
- 1 large onion finely chopped,
- 1 tablespoon crushed garlic,
- 1 tablespoon crushed ginger,
- 400 g canned finely crushed tomatoes,
- 2 tablespoons chopped coriander leaves,
- 2 tablespoons vegetable oil,
- Salt and pepper to taste.

Optional:
- Chopped red chillies.

Method:
1. Cut the dried octopus in lengths to fit into a deep saucepan. Soak the octopus in water overnight and leave at room temperature. Cover the container to avoid the dried octopus aroma from permeating through the house.
2. Drain the octopus. Boil in water for about 30-45 mins or until the texture is very soft and suitable for eating. Test with a small knife or small skewer. Remove from the boiling water. With a very sharp knife cut into half cm pieces. Set aside.
3. Alternatively heat up a non stick wok and stir fry the boiled octopus without oil to impart a slightly grilled flavor and texture. Do this very quickly and remove the octopus pieces to stop burning this precious ingredient. Transfer to a bowl and set aside. If some of the octopus pieces are too tough, use a meat pounder to tenderize.
4. Heat up two tablespoons of vegetable oil in a casserole pan over medium to high heat. Stir fry the freshly crushed garlic, ginger and finely chopped onion. When the onion pieces become transparent, add the finely crushed tomatoes and stir in 1 cup of hot water. Cover and simmer until the tomato sauce is blended with the other ingredients. Stir at intervals to prevent the sauce from sticking to the pan. Add small quantities of hot water if necessary to keep the sauce liquid. Optional: *add the finely chopped red chillies.*
5. Add the slightly grilled octopus pieces to the tomato sauce. Add the finely chopped coriander leaves. Gently stir and simmer over medium to low heat. Cook until the octopus pieces are softened to your preference.
6. If the octopus pieces do not soften enough, add small quantities of hot water to further cook in the sauce.
7. Adjust the sauce consistency to your preference by either adding small quantities of hot water or simmer uncovered to thicken the sauce. Add salt and pepper to taste. Transfer to serving dish and decorate with chopped coriander leaves.
8. Enjoy with main courses with rice. Dried octopus has this unique flavour and taste.

Grilling dried octopus and tomatoes to make chatini ourite sec

Jackfruit Curry
Cari Jacques

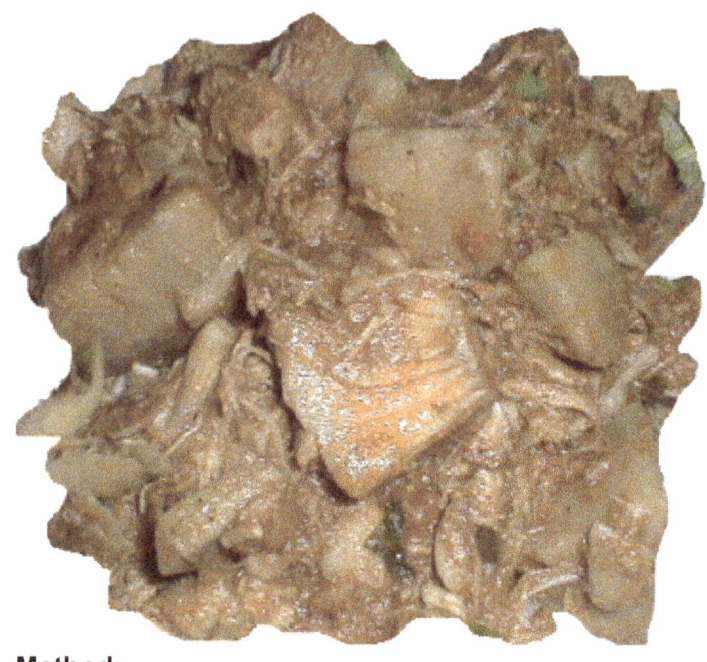

Ingredients (Serve 4):
- 500 g pork,
- 1 kg green jackfruit unpeeled (or 425 g canned jackfruit,
- 1 medium onion finely chopped,
- 1 teaspoon crushed garlic,
- 1 teaspoon crushed ginger,
- 1 tablespoon chopped thyme leaves,
- 2 tablespoons chopped coriander leaves,
- 3-5 cari poulet leaves (alternatively use kaffir lime or bay leaves),
- 3 tablespoons vegetable oil,
- 250 g canned finely crushed tomatoes,
- 4 tablespoons curry powder,
- Salt to taste.

Method:
1. Cut pork into bite size pieces. Season with salt and pepper. Set aside.
2. Oil both sides of the blade of a large, sharp kitchen knife.
3. Cut the green jackfruit into quarters. Peel the jack fruit pieces and cut flesh into bite size pieces. Drop into a bowl of cold water to prevent the jackfruit pieces from browning. Alternatively, use canned jackfruit.
4. Heat 3 tablespoons of oil to simmering point. Add the pork pieces. Stir and cook until tender. Stir at intervals.
5. Add the crushed garlic and ginger, chopped thyme leaves, chopped onions and 250 g canned finely crushed tomatoes.
6. Mix well and simmer until the tomatoes are cooked and the sauce is well blended. Do not overcook and add a little hot water if necessary to prevent sauce from drying up. Stir at intervals to prevent the sauce from burning.
7. Mix well and add the curry powder, 1 tablespoon chopped coriander leaves, cari poulet leaves and 1 cup hot water. Simmer until the sauce is well blended.
8. Add the jackfruit pieces. Mix well, cover and simmer until jackfruit pieces are cooked and tender. If there is not enough sauce or jackfruit is not cooked, add little quantities of hot water. Stir and simmer until both jackfruit and pork are cooked and tender. Taste sauce and season with salt to taste. Enjoy.

Spare Ribs in Black Bean Sauce

Ingredients (Serve 4):
- 5 tablespoons vegetable oil,
- 750 g pork spare ribs, cut into 5 cm lengths,
- 3 tablespoons black bean paste. Alternatively: use 6-7 tablespoons of black bean sauce,
- 2 spring onions, finely chopped,
- 2 thin slices root ginger, peeled and finely chopped,
- 1 garlic clove, crushed,
- 2 dried chillies, finely chopped,
- 1 tablespoon Chinese wine or dry sherry,
- 2 tablespoons soy sauce,
- 1½ teaspoons sugar,
- 2 teaspoons cornflour,
- 1 tablespoon water,
- 2 coriander sprigs,
- Chopped spring onions.

Method:
1. Heat the oil in a wok until smoking. Add the spare ribs. Stir fry for about 2 mins or until slightly golden, then transfer the ribs to a heatproof bowl.
2. Pour off most of the oil, leaving about 1 tablespoon, and reheat. Add the black bean paste, half the spring onions, the ginger, garlic and chillies. Stir fry for about 30 seconds, then add the wine, soy sauce and sugar. Mix well, then stir into the bowl with the spare ribs. Place the bowl in a steamer and steam for 1 hour or until meat is tender.
3. Pour off the liquid from the bowl into a pan and bring to the boil. Blend the cornflour with the water, and stir into the pan to make a smooth sauce.
4. Transfer the spare ribs to a warmed serving dish. Pour the hot sauce over the ribs, decorate with the coriander sprigs and remaining chopped spring onions. Serve immediately.
5. Eat with rice and stir fried Chinese green vegetables (eg Bok Choy or alternatively Cos Lettuce).

Pork Spare Ribs with Oyster Sauce

Ingredients (Serve 4):
- 1 kg pork spare ribs 4 cm wide strips,
- 2 teaspoons cornflour,
- ½ cup cornflour for dredging,
- 4 teaspoons peanut oil,
- 1 cup peanut oil for deep frying,
- 4 tablespoons oyster sauce (not oyster flavoured sauce),
- ½ teaspoon black soy sauce,
- ½ teaspoon sugar,
- 4 spring onions, cut into 5 cm pieces,
- 2 garlic cloves finely crushed,
- 3 tablespoons finely shredded ginger,
- 4 teaspoons dry sherry,
- 1 teaspoon soy sauce,
- ½ teaspoon ground black pepper,
- 2 teaspoons sesame oil,
- ½ cup chicken stock.

Method:
1. Separate the spare ribs into individual pieces 4cm long. Leaving the meat on, trim any excess meat to make extra meat pieces.
2. Blend 2 teaspoons of cornflour, 2 teaspoons dry sherry, 1 teaspoon soy sauce, ½ teaspoon ground black pepper and 1 teaspoon sesame oil. Coat the spare ribs and meat pieces to ensure that they are well marinated. Cover and set aside for 2 hours in a cool spot.
3. Mix well to ensure that all the spare rib and meat pieces are well marinated. Set aside, cover and marinate for 2 hours in a cool spot.
4. In another container, combine the chicken stock, oyster sauce, black soy sauce, sugar, 2 teaspoons dry sherry, 1 teaspoon sesame oil and ground black pepper. Mix well and set aside.
5. Cut the spring onions into 5 cm pieces.
6. Lightly dredge the individual pieces of pork spare ribs and meat pieces in ½ cup of cornflour.
7. Meanwhile, heat up a wok or similar cooking pan over high heat until the wok is very hot. Add 1 cup peanut oil and swirl around to coat the whole wok surface.
8. When the oil starts to sizzle, add the pork spare ribs and meat pieces in small batches and deep fry until light golden, turning often to ensure uniform cooking. Remove and drain over kitchen paper towels or drip tray.
9. Empty the wok of all oil. Wipe clean with kitchen paper towels and put wok back on high heat. Allow to heat up until it starts smoking. Add 4 tablespoons of peanut oil. Add the spring onion pieces and stir fry for 10 seconds. Add the finely crushed garlic and shredded ginger. Stir fry for another 10 seconds. Add the fried spare rib and meat pieces. Stir in the reserved chicken stock and other ingredients from 4.

10. Stir fry until the spare ribs and meat pieces are cooked through and the sauce well combined. This should not take long (only ½ to 1 minute) and do not overcook the spare ribs and meat pieces. If sauce is too liquid, thicken the sauce by adding 1 teaspoon of cornflour dissolved into ¼ cup of cold water. Allow more cooking time to blend in the added water/cornflour. If too thick, thin the sauce by adding a little hot water.
11. Transfer the spare ribs and meat pieces to a serving plate. The spare ribs and meat pieces will taste even better if allowed to rest under cover overnight, to allow the sauce to permeate the meat. Heat up in microwave before serving.
12. Serve with plain white rice or fried rice and some stir fried greens. Enjoy.

Pork and eggplant curry (page 194)

Breaded Pork Chops

Ingredients (Serve 4):
- 4 thin pork chops,
- 1½ cups seasoned bread crumbs,
- 3 tablespoons milk,
- 3 eggs lightly beaten,
- ½ cup grated Parmesan cheese,
- 3 tablespoons dried parsley,
- 3 tablespoons vegetable oil,
- Salt and pepper to taste.

Method:
1. Season the pork chops with salt and pepper on both sides and allow to rest.
2. Preheat oven to 170°C.
3. Beat the eggs in a small bowl with the milk.
4. In another bowl, mix the grated Parmesan cheese, dried parsley and seasoned bread crumbs together.
5. In a thick bottomed skillet, place 3 tablespoons vegetable oil over medium high heat.
6. When oil starts to sizzle, dip each pork chop into the egg mixture, then into the bread crumbs mixture. Shake off any excess bread crumbs.
7. Place pork chop in skillet and fry both sides to a light golden brown colour (about five mins). Repeat with the remaining pork chops.
8. Place on a grill/tray combination and allow excess oil to drain. Place grill/tray in oven and cook for 30 mins or until the pork is cooked to your preference. Check at intervals to ensure the chops do not burn.
9. Remove from oven when cooked and enjoy, with cauliflower in white sauce.

Lamb Roast with Herbs in Butter and Red Wine

Ingredients (Serve 6):
- 2 kg leg of lamb,
- 100 g soft butter,
- 2 tablespoons finely crushed garlic,
- 3 tablespoons chopped parsley,
- 3 tablespoons chopped mint leaves,
- 2 tablespoons chopped rosemary,
- 1 tablespoon chopped thyme leaves,
- 2 tablespoons plain white flour,
- 100 ml red wine,
- 300 ml vegetable stock,
- Salt and pepper to taste.

Method:
1. Add the butter to the herbs and garlic. Mix well. Season with salt and pepper to taste.
2. With a small sharp knife, puncture the leg of lamb in 6 places right to the joint. Be careful not to cut open the leg of lamb.
3. Heat the oven to 200°C.
4. Place sheets of aluminium foil in an oven tray with enough wrap around to totally enclose. Place the leg of lamb on the foil in the middle of an oven tray. Rub and spread the butter and herbs mixture over the top of the leg of lamb. Wrap the aluminium foil over the lamb.
5. Place the oven tray in the oven (mid rack position) and allow to cook for 2 hours. After 2 hours, open up the aluminium foil and continue to cook for 30 mins or until the lamb is lightly roasted to a golden brown colour or to your preference. Do not overcook.
6. Remove the roasted leg of lamb carefully and place in a serving dish. Keep warm.
7. Pour the juices from the oven into a container. Separate the floating lamb fat using a large spoon or by decanting.
8. Pour the clarified juice into a small casserole pan. Place over medium heat and when the juice starts to simmer, sprinkle and blend in the white flour through a small sieve into the simmering juice. Continuously stir with a wooden spoon to blend the flour into the juice.
9. Allow the juice and flour mixture to brown. Add the wine and vegetable stock gradually into the mixture to form a thin or thick gravy, to your preference. Should the gravy be too liquid, mix 1 teaspoon of cornflour in half a glass of water and stir into the mixture. Simmer for a little while or until the gravy thickens.
10. Cut the lamb roast into serving slices and top with the rich gravy.

Fettucine Clancy

Ingredients (Serve 2):
- 500 g dried egg fettucine pasta,
- 6 ripe tomatoes (medium size),
- 2 green chillies chopped,
- 1 teaspoon chopped coriander leaves,
- 1 medium onion finely sliced,
- ½ teaspoon vegetable oil,
- Salt to taste.

Method:
1. Remove stem eyes from tomatoes. Finely chop with sharp knife. Add the chillies to the chopped tomatoes.
2. Add finely sliced onion and finely chopped coriander leaves. Mix the ingredients and sprinkle ½ teaspoon vegetable oil on top.
3. Bring a large pot of water to the boil. Add 1 teaspoon of salt. Wait until the water is bubbling before adding the fettucine. Make sure that there is enough room for the pasta to boil freely. Cook until al dente
4. Drain the pasta when cooked. Put the pasta back in the pot, add a splash of virgin olive oil and mix gently. Serve the fettucine on individual plates.
5. Thoroughly mix the ingredients from step 2 adding salt to taste. Serve on top of the fettucine.
6. Gently stir in with a fork and enjoy this fusion of Italian and Mauritian cuisines.

Ham Hock Terrine

Ingredients (Serve 2):
- 2 ham hocks,
- 2 carrots chopped,
- 3 celery chopped,
- 5 cloves garlic, peeled and halved,
- 2 teaspoons black peppercorns,
- 5 star anise,
- 2 bay leaves,
- ½ teaspoon coriander seeds,
- ½ bunch chopped coriander leaves,
- ½ bunch chopped parsley,
- Salt and pepper to taste.

Method:
1. Place ham hocks in a large pot, cover with cold water and bring to the boil, immediately drain and rinse. Place the hocks back into the empty pot with the chopped carrots and celery, garlic, 1 teaspoon black pepper corns, star anises, and bay leaves. Cover with cold water and bring to the boil, reduce the heat to a simmer cover and cook for around 1½ hours or until flesh is tender and comes away from the bone easily.
2. Remove from heat and set aside to cool for 2 hours to allow the gelatin from the hock to dissolve in to the liquid. Remove the hocks and strain the liquid into a clean pot. Return the strained liquid to the heat and simmer until reduce by half
3. Flake the hocks into a large bowl and add coriander seeds, 1 teaspoon lightly crushed black peppercorns, chopped coriander and chopped parsley. Mix through the ham. Season with salt and pepper to taste.
4. Add the reduced liquid a little at a time till there is enough liquid that when you squeeze a hand full of mix, it sticks together.
5. Line a terrine mould with cling film and pack in your ham mix, cover the top with cling film and then weight down over night in the fridge.
6. Serve sliced from the mould with your chosen accompaniments. You can also invert the terrine from the mould onto a flat plate.
7. Enjoy with crispy baguette and Mauritians will need a pickle or chilli sauce to add more flavour to the terrine. Perfect as an entrée for a multi course dinner.

Madeleine Philippe doing what she enjoys best

Vegetables and Pulses

The best description of Mauritian cuisine under British Rule in 1830 is narrated in an official report written by Charles Telfair, dated Jan 15, 1830, stating that "a mixture of animal and vegetable foods seems to form a diet most conducive to health and strength. When animal food cannot be furnished in large quantity, the best substitute is a mixture of farinaceous and herbaceous products, with the addition of proper condiments, to stimulate the stomach and to secure general healthy action."

Mauritian cuisine has been recognised as being within the top four dietary patterns based on its contents in healthful foods and nutrients. A systematic assessment was conducted by the Global Burden of Diseases Nutrition and Chronic Diseases Expert Group (NutriCODE) "Dietary quality among men and women in 187 countries in 1990 and 2010: a systematic assessment. Lancet Glob Health 2015; 3:e132-142", has confirmed that Mauritian Cuisine is among the best in the world. This high rating is driven by the high consumption of ten healthy items consumed within traditional Mauritian cuisine. Those ten healthy items include the consumption of fruits, vegetables, beans (pulses) and legumes, nuts and seeds, whole grains, milk, total polyunsaturated fatty acids, fish, plant omega-3's and dietary fibre.

Brèdes songe that contains amino acids, omega-3, potassium and antioxydants

Vegetables are a very important source of many nutrients, including omega-3's *potassium*, fibre, folate *(*folic acid*)* and vitamins A, E and C. Pulses typically contain about twice the amount of protein found in whole grain cereals like wheat, oats, barley and rice, as well as a significant source of vitamins, amino acids and minerals, such as iron, zinc, folate, and magnesium. Mauritian cuisine has a very high vegetable and whole grain content, cooked with a wide selection of herbs, spices and meats. The most popular pulses consumed in Mauritius are red and black lentils, dhall and kidney beans (haricots rouges).

Black Lentils

Fricassée Lentilles Noires

Ingredients (Serve 4):
1. 250 g black lentils,
2. 5 curry leaves,
3. 1 sprig thyme,
4. 2 large red tomatoes finely chopped,
5. 2 large onions finely chopped,
6. 1 tablespoon crushed garlic,
7. 1 teaspoon garlic,
8. 1 tablespoon crushed ginger,
9. 2 tablespoons chopped parsley,
10. 2 tablespoons vegetable oil,
11. Salt and pepper to taste.

Method:
1. Check lentils for impurities. Wash in cold running water. Soak for 30 mins. Place in pressure cooker with enough water to cover. Add curry leaves and thyme sprig. Cook over medium high heat under pressure for 10-15 mins, until tender or creamy according to taste.
2. Remove curry leaves and thyme sprig.
3. In a deep saucepan, large enough to contain the cooked lentils, add 2 tablespoons vegetable oil. Over medium heat, fry the chopped onions, garlic and ginger. Add the chopped tomatoes and parsley. Pour the cooked lentils into the saucepan with the other ingredients. Mix well. Allow to simmer for 5-10 mins. Add salt and pepper to taste.
4. Serve on rice with a steak, rougaille, chicken fricassée or vindaloo.
5. Excellent with rougaille poisson salé as shown.

Lentilles Rouges
Red Lentils

Ingredients (Serve 2):
- 1 ½ cups split red lentils,
- 1 small onion finely chopped,
- 1 tablespoon crushed garlic,
- 1 tablespoon crushed ginger,
- 2 tablespoons vegetable oil,
- 1 tablespoon chopped thyme leaves,
- 1 tablespoon chopped fresh parsley,
- Water,
- Salt to taste.

Method:
1. Soak the red lentils in cold water for 30 mins. Drain and rinse in cold water 2 to 3 times. Drain all water and remove any impurities. Set aside.
2. Add 2 tablespoons of vegetable oil to saucepan over medium heat. Stir fry the finely chopped onion, crushed ginger, crushed garlic and thyme leaves until the onion is cooked and becomes transparent. Add the red lentils and mix well together. Add salt to taste. Add 4-5 cups of cold water and mix.
3. Simmer uncovered for 30-45 mins or until the red lentils are cooked and become creamy. Stir in some hot water a little at a time if the mixture dries up, until the red lentils are cooked to your preference. Stir continually to ensure even cooking and to prevent burning.
4. Mix 1 tablespoon of chopped fresh parsley into the cooked lentils.
5. Serve over rice with a steak, fried fish or rougaille (salt fish or sausage).

Haricots Blancs with Smoked Pork

Borlotti Beans with Smoked Pork

Ingredients (Serve 4):
- 375 g Borlotti beans,
- 500 g smoked pork,
- 1 medium onion finely chopped,
- 1 tablespoon finely chopped thyme leaves,
- 2 tablespoons chopped parsley,
- 1 teaspoon crushed garlic,
- 1 teaspoon crushed ginger,
- 2 tablespoons oil,
- 6-8 cloves,
- Salt to taste,
- Water as required.

Method:
1. Soak the Borlotti beans in cold water for 1 hour.
2. Cut smoked pork into 2 cm cubes
3. Drain the beans in a colander. This will allow all impurities to drain away. Put the beans and cloves in a pressure cooker. Fill with clean cold water until a 2 cm water cover is obtained.
4. Bring to pressure over medium heat and cook for 15 mins. Remove from heat and allow to cool. Remove the cloves.
5. Carefully remove the cooked beans with a slotted spoon and put into casserole saucepan with the smoked pork and other ingredients. Add some of the water in which the beans were cooked to allow the mixture to simmer gently.
6. Cover and cook over medium heat. Stir gently at intervals to prevent the ingredients from sticking. Some people like the beans half cooked, others want it creamy. Cook according to your preference.
7. If necessary, add some more of the cooking water to adjust the sauce to your taste. Alternatively, allow the sauce to thicken by removing cover from saucepan. Season with salt to taste.
8. Carefully transfer to warm serving bowl. Sprinkle with chopped parsley and enjoy.

Cari Dholl

Yellow Split Peas Curry

Ingredients (Serve 4):
- 250 g dholl (dhal) peas,
- 1 tablespoon turmeric powder,
- 1 teaspoon crushed cumin seeds,
- 1 medium onion finely sliced,
- 2 tablespoons coarsely chopped coriander leaves,
- 4-5 curry leaves finger crushed,
- 1 tablespoon crushed garlic,
- 1 tablespoon crushed ginger,
- 1 teaspoon chopped thyme leaves,
- Water to boil yellow split peas,
- Salt to taste.

Optional:
- Bony piece of salt fish (poisson salé).

Method:
1. Soak the dholl for 30 mins in cold water. Drain and transfer to a deep saucepan. Add just enough cold water to cover. Add 1 teaspoon salt, 1 teaspoon crushed cumin seeds and 1 tablespoon turmeric powder to the water. Cook for 20-25 mins uncovered over medium high heat or until the peas are tender. When it starts to boil, reduce heat to low. Be careful as the water may overflow when boiling. Remove from heat when dholl is cooked and tender. Set aside.
2. Heat 3 tablespoons of vegetable oil in a deep saucepan. Add sliced onions, chopped thyme leaves, crushed garlic and crushed ginger. Stir fry until the onion becomes transparent. Optional: *If you have a bony piece of salt fish (poisson salé), add it and stir fry until the oil absorbs its flavour.*
3. Add the finger-crushed curry leaves and stir. Add the cooked dholl including the cooking water, into the saucepan with the other ingredients. Add 1 tablespoon chopped coriander leaves. Mix well together and allow to simmer over medium low heat uncovered for 15-20 mins or until the dholl is creamy and tender, or to your preference. Stir at intervals.
4. Season with salt to taste. Remove the salt fish bone(s) if added. Transfer to a serving bowl and sprinkle with 1 tablespoon of coarsely chopped coriander leaves.
5. Serve over rice with fried salt fish.
6. Just perfect. One of the joys of Mauritian Cuisine.

Red Kidney Beans with Minced Beef

Ingredients (Serve 4):
- 375 g red kidney beans,
- 500 g lean mince beef,
- 1 medium onion finely chopped,
- 1 tablespoon finely chopped thyme,
- 2 tablespoons chopped parsley,
- 1 teaspoon crushed garlic,
- 1 teaspoon crushed ginger,
- 2-3 heaped tablespoons organic tomato paste,
- 500 ml chicken stock,
- 3 tablespoons oil,
- 6-8 cloves,
- Salt and pepper to taste.

Method:
1. Soak the red kidney beans in cold water for 1 hour. Season the minced beef with salt and pepper to taste. Allow to rest.
2. Drain the red kidney beans of all water in a colander. Put the soaked beans and cloves in a pressure cooker. Pour in clean cold water to cover the beans to a depth of 2-3 cm. Stir in one tablespoon of salt or to taste. Place lid on pressure cooker. Cook over medium heat for 15 mins under pressure. Remove the cloves.
3. Place three tablespoons of oil in a deep casserole saucepan over medium heat. When hot, add the minced beef, finely chopped onion, crushed garlic and ginger, thyme and half the parsley. Stir fry gently until the minced beef is cooked.
4. Add the tomato paste and incorporate with the minced beef. Simmer for 3-5 mins or until well integrated. If needs be, add some chicken or beef stock to prevent the minced beef from burning.
5. Carefully remove the cooked beans with a slotted spoon and put into casserole saucepan with the minced beef and other ingredients. Add some more chicken stock. Gently mix and avoid crushing the red beans, cover the saucepan and simmer. Stir at intervals to prevent the meat and beans from burning.
6. Adjust the sauce by adding some more chicken stock. Similarly, if there is too much sauce, uncover and allow the water to evaporate. Cook under medium heat, stir at regular intervals to avoid the ingredients from burning and simmer until cooked to your preference. Place in serving dish with chopped parsley.

Snake Beans & Pork Stir Fry

Ingredients (Serve 4):
- 800 g snake beans,
- 500 g smoked bacon or pork,
- 1 tablespoon white vinegar,
- 1 tablespoon light soy sauce,
- 3 tablespoons fish sauce,
- 2-3 tablespoons oyster sauce,
- 1 teaspoon cornflour,
- 3 tablespoons vegetable oil,
- 1 tablespoon crushed garlic,
- 1 tablespoon finely crushed ginger,
- 2 spring onions finely chopped,
- Salt and pepper to taste,
- Sliced red chillies to taste.

Method:
1. Cut the smoked bacon/pork into bite size pieces. Season with 1 tablespoon light soy sauce, 2 tablespoons fish sauce, salt and pepper. Mix well and allow marinate for 30 mins.
2. Wash the snake beans. Cut off the end bits. Cut into bite lengths (5 cms) with a sharp knife. Set aside.
3. Mix the vinegar, 1 tablespoon fish sauce and 2 tablespoons oyster sauce together in a separate container. Set aside.
4. Pour enough water into a large saucepan to blanch the snake beans, with 2 tablespoons salt. Allow water to boil. Add cut snake beans.
5. Blanch the snake beans for one minute. Remove from the boiling water and immerse into running cold water to stop the cooking. The snake beans will turn into a vibrant green colour. Drain and set aside.
6. Put 3 tablespoons vegetable oil in wok or saucepan on medium high heat. When the oil starts to sizzle, stir fry the sliced red chillies, crushed garlic and ginger, followed by the smoked bacon/pork pieces. Stir at intervals, allow the smoked bacon/pork pieces to cook thoroughly and turn into a light golden brown colour.
7. Add the snake beans and gently mix. Add the vinegar, fish and oyster sauce mix. Mix gently to blend in with the meat and snake beans.
8. Cover and cook over medium heat until the sauce starts forming and the snake beans are fully cooked and tender. Uncover and simmer until the sauce thickens to desired consistency. If sauce is too thin, thicken by adding one teaspoon of cornflour dissolved in a little bit of water. Mix well.
9. Transfer onto a warm serving plate and garnish with chopped spring onions.

Fricassée of Cabbage and Carrots with Sausages

Ingredients (Serve 4):
- 1 medium cabbage,
- 4 medium carrots,
- 500 g spicy sausages,
- 1 medium onion finely sliced,
- 2 tablespoons finely crushed garlic,
- 1 tablespoon finely chopped ginger,
- 3 tablespoons of vegetable oil,
- 4 tablespoons finely chopped parsley,
- 4 sprigs thyme,
- 1 cup chicken stock,
- Salt and pepper to taste.

Optional:
- Sliced red chillies according to taste.

Enjoy with rice, tomato chutney or vegetable achar.

Method:
1. Remove the outer leaves of the cabbage that are not suitable for cooking. Wash the cabbage and wipe dry with a kitchen paper towel. With a sharp knife, cut the cabbage into halves. Carefully cut out the triangular hard core stems.
2. Cut the cabbage halves into quarters. With a sharp knife, cut into 2 cm thick slices. Set aside.
3. Peel the carrots, cut the end bits and slice into ½ cm thick pieces. Set aside.
4. In a heavy bottomed saucepan large enough to contain all the ingredients, add 4 tablespoons vegetable oil. Allow oil to start sizzling over medium high heat. Carefully add the individual sausages and fry on all sides until light golden brown. Remove sausages from pan and place on kitchen paper towels to allow the surplus oil to drain away. Cut the sausages into thirds.
5. Heat the oil in the saucepan over medium-high heat and stir fry the sliced onions, crushed garlic and chopped ginger.
6. When the onion becomes transparent, add half the cabbage and carrot slices. Add the sausages, remaining cabbage and carrot slices. Gently mix the ingredients together and add half the finely chopped parsley and thyme sprigs. Make sure that the sausages are well distributed within the mix. Add 1 cup chicken stock. Gently mix.
7. Optional: *stir in the sliced red chillies.*
8. Reduce heat to low, cover the saucepan and simmer.
9. Check at intervals and using a wooden spoon, bring up the bottom ingredients and mix gently to make sure that the bottom ingredients do not burn. Repeat at regular intervals.
10. Taste the cabbage and carrots slices to make sure they are cooked to your preference. Season with salt and pepper to taste. Garnish with finely chopped parsley.

Fricassée of Brèdes Songe

Ingredients (Serve 4):
- 500 g taro leaves & stems,
- 1 tablespoon crushed garlic,
- 1 tablespoon crushed ginger,
- 1 medium onion finely chopped,
- 2 large ripe tomatoes coarsely chopped,
- 2 tablespoons tamarind paste without seeds,
- ½ cup hot water,
- 1 teaspoon salt,
- 110 g canned sardines,
- 2 tablespoons vegetable oil.

Optional:
- 2 fresh or dried red chillies sliced lengthwise.

Serve with rice and a vegetable pickle.

Method:
1. Dissolve the tamarind paste in ½ cup of hot water. Put aside.
2. Wash the taro leaves and stems in cold running water. Using plastic gloves, cut the taro leaves in 2-3 cm pieces. Cut the stems into 2 cm pieces and carefully remove the stringy bits.
3. Add vegetable oil to a deep saucepan over medium heat. When hot, stir fry the crushed garlic, crushed ginger and finely chopped onion. Cook over medium heat until the onion pieces become transparent.
4. Gradually add the cut taro leaves and stem pieces. Add the chopped tomatoes. Stir in and reduce the heat to medium low. Add 1 teaspoon of salt (or to taste) and mix well. Keep stirring until the collapsed taro leaves and stems blend in with the chopped tomato pieces.
5. If necessary, add some hot water to stop the taro leaves from burning.
6. Cover saucepan and cook for 30 mins or until the taro leaves are cooked to a creamy consistency and change to a dark colour. Refer to photo. Stir at regular intervals and scrape the bottom of the pan with a wooden spoon to re-incorporate the sticky bits into the mix if necessary. Watch carefully to make sure the cooked taro leaves and other ingredients do not stick and burn. Add some hot water if necessary. Add tamarind paste dissolved in water from step 1 to taro leaves. Mix well and cook over medium heat for another 10 mins.
7. If the cooked taro leaves and other ingredients become too watery, you can allow the stew to simmer uncovered over low heat to reduce the water content to your preference. Optional: *Stir in the sliced red chillies and allow to cook for another 5 mins.*
8. Just before serving, add the drained canned sardines into the stewed taro. Mix well without crushing the sardines. Enjoy with rice.

Stir Fried Beef with Broccoli

Ingredients (Serve 4):
- 500 g beef thinly sliced (refer to photo),
- 750 g broccoli florets,
- 2 tablespoons fish sauce,
- 1 tablespoon dry sherry or white wine,
- 1 tablespoon cornflour,
- ½ cup cold water,
- 1 tablespoon light soy sauce,
- 2 tablespoons vegetable oil,
- Salt and pepper to taste.

Method:
1. Season beef with salt and pepper. Add the fish sauce and dry sherry or white wine. Mix well together. Cover and marinate for 15-30 mins.
2. Heat vegetable oil in a wok or similar saucepan. Stir fry the beef slices with the marinade, until the beef is cooked and light golden in colour. Add the broccoli florets, mix gently, cover and allow to simmer for 10-15 mins or until the broccoli is cooked.
3. Stir at intervals to ensure even cooking. Do not overcook the broccoli. Add a little bit of hot water if the sauce is not liquid enough. Uncover if sauce is too liquid and allow liquid to evaporate.
4. Taste and season with salt and pepper to your preference.
5. Mix the cornflour in ½ cup of cold water. Add 1 tablespoon of light soy sauce. Stir and add to the beef and broccoli. Mix well. Cook until the sauce thickens.
6. Transfer to a warm serving dish. Serve immediately and eat with rice.

Kat Kat Manioc

Ingredients (Serve 4):
- 1 kg manioc (cassava),
- 500 g corned silverside (viande salée), alternatively use bacon pieces,
- 1 medium chopped onion,
- 1 teaspoon crushed garlic,
- 1 teaspoon crushed ginger,
- 2 medium tomatoes chopped,
- ½ tablespoon chopped thyme,
- ½ tablespoon chopped parsley,
- Brèdes martin leaves (quantity as desired),
- 4 cups water,
- 2 tablespoons vegetable oil,
- Salt and pepper to taste.

Method:
1. Peel manioc and cut in half lengthwise. Remove strings in the middle and cut into bite sizes (2 cm cubes).
2. Cut corned silverside into 2 cm cubes. Wash under running cold water several times to remove surplus brine. Drain and pat dry with kitchen paper towel. Set aside.
3. Heat oil in pressure cooker. Allow to reach frying temperature and add corned silverside pieces. Stir fry until light golden brown. Add chopped onion, thyme, parsley, garlic, ginger and stir fry until onion pieces become transparent.
4. Add chopped tomatoes and cook until well blended with the other ingredients. Stir occasionally to avoid burning the corned silverside.
5. Add the manioc pieces. Stir in with the other ingredients except for the brèdes martin leaves, and add 4 cups of water (quantity may need to be adjusted later depending upon the dryness of the manioc pieces). Stir once more to blend everything together. Close pressure cooker and allow to pressure cook for ten mins.
6. Reduce pressure. Remove lid. Carefully add a little hot water at this point to reach desired consistency. Check if manioc is tender. If not, cover again and cook for a little longer. When manioc is tender, stir in brèdes martin leaves. Simmer on low heat, without lid, for another five mins. Stir occasionally to ensure that manioc pieces do not stick to bottom of pan.
7. Enjoy on its own, with a little hot piment ecrasé (hot chilli paste).

Pipengaille Fricassée with Dried Prawns

Ingredients (Serve 4):
- 1 kg pipengaille *luffa acutangula*,
- 100 g dried prawns (Asian shop),
- 1 medium onion finely chopped,
- 3 tablespoons finely chopped parsley,
- 3 tablespoons finely chopped thyme,
- 2 tablespoons crushed garlic,
- 2 tablespoons crushed ginger,
- 2 medium ripe tomatoes quartered,
- 4 tablespoons vegetable oil,
- 1 cup chicken stock,
- Salt and pepper to taste.

Tip: *Use the pipengaille skin to make a chutney.*

Method:
1. Wash the dried prawns and soak in lukewarm water overnight. Avoid dried prawns with artificial colouring.
2. Using a sharp knife, cut the pipengaille into 15 cm lengths and remove the green skin. Be careful not to overcut. Only slice off the green parts. With a sharp knife cut the white pieces of pipengaille into ½ cm thick slices. Set aside.
3. In a heavy bottomed saucepan, stir fry in 4 tablespoons of vegetable oil, the chopped onions, finely crushed garlic and ginger. Mix gently and cook until the onions become transparent. Stir at intervals to avoid burning the ingredients.
4. Add the drained prawns and stir fry gently to semi cook the prawns. Add the quartered tomatoes, cover the saucepan and allow the tomato pieces to cook. Stir at intervals to blend in the tomato pieces with the prawns.
5. Add the pipengaille slices, the chopped parsley and thyme, mix well. Add the chicken stock to enrich the flavour of the dish. Stir carefully without crushing. Cover and cook over medium low heat. Check and carefully stir at intervals to avoid burning the ingredients.
6. You can control the amount of sauce by either uncovering the saucepan to reduce the sauce or add a little bit of hot water to obtain more sauce. If the prawns are not fully cooked, add a little hot water if necessary to prolong the cooking. Be careful not to add too much.
7. Season with salt to taste and serve hot on rice.

Pipengaille Fricassée with Pork Spare Ribs

Ingredients (Serve 4):
- 1 kg pipengaille *luffa acutangula*,
- 1 kg pork spare ribs optional,
- 1 medium onion finely chopped,
- 3 tablespoons finely chopped parsley,
- 3 tablespoons finely chopped thyme,
- 2 tablespoons crushed garlic,
- 2 tablespoons crushed ginger,
- 2 medium ripe tomatoes quartered,
- 4 tablespoons vegetable oil,
- Salt and pepper to taste.

Method:
1. Cut the pork spare ribs into bite size pieces and season with salt and pepper. For more flavour add 3 tablespoons of fish sauce. Optional: *People who do not eat pork or want to cook the pipengaille by itself, please omit this step.*
2. Using a sharp knife, cut the pipengaille into 15 cm lengths. With a very sharp knife peel the green skin from the pipengaille and set aside. (*You can make a chatini with the hard green peels*). Be careful not to overcut. With a sharp knife cut the white pieces of the pipengaille into ½ cm slices. Set aside.
3. In a heavy bottomed saucepan, add 4 tablespoons of vegetable oil. Heat to simmering point.
4. Add the finely crushed garlic and ginger, chopped onions, thyme and parsley. Mix gently and cook until the onions become transparent.
5. Stir at intervals to avoid burning the ingredients. Add the quartered tomatoes, cover the saucepan and allow the tomato pieces to cook. Carefully crush the tomato pieces to add some extra sauce to the dish.
6. Add the marinated pork pieces and mix well with the other ingredients. Cook the pork until it reaches a light golden colour, stirring at intervals to prevent the ingredients from burning. Do not cover the saucepan to allow any excess moisture from the pork pieces to evaporate. (Omit this step if you are not adding any pork to this dish).
7. Add the pipengaille slices, mix with the other ingredients and continue cooking over a low to medium heat.
8. Stir at intervals to ensure the pipengaille cooks and softens to your preference being careful not to crush the ingredients. Add a little hot water if necessary to maintain the sauce. Taste and add salt as necessary.
9. When cooked and the sauce is to your desired consistency, remove from heat. Cover and put aside. Sprinkle with some finely chopped parsley to finish off.
10. Enjoy with rice and a good chatini or pickle.

Vegetable stalls in Port Louis market

Stir Fried Cos Lettuce

Ingredients (Serve 2):
- 1 medium cos lettuce,
- 1 tablespoon crushed ginger,
- 2 tablespoons vegetable oil,
- ½ cup chicken stock.

Method:
1. Separate the cos lettuce leaves. Cut off the woody stems and damaged sections. Wash individually to remove any grit and soil. Bundle the leaves together and cut across the width into 1-2 cm strips. Cut the tender parts into 2 cm strips and the not so tender parts into 1 cm strips. This will enable even cooking of all pieces when stir fried.
2. In a wok over high heat, add 2 tablespoons of vegetable oil. When the oil is hot, add 1 tablespoon of crushed ginger. Stir fry and when the ginger starts to fizzle, add the cos lettuce. Take care to drain the lettuce strips so that you do not pour water into the hot oil.
3. Stir the lettuce continually to ensure even cooking bringing the bottom pieces to the top and vice versa. Add ½ cup of chicken stock. Mix well together. When the cos lettuce pieces just start to collapse and are just cooked, remove from the wok and serve immediately.
4. Enjoy.

Vegetable Fried Rice

Ingredients (Serve 4):
- 2 ½ cups of basmati rice,
- 2 cups vegetable stock,
- 6 large dried shitake mushrooms,
- 1 medium carrot,
- 1 small fennel,
- ¼ of small cabbage,
- 125 g frozen baby peas,
- 300 g corn kernels,
- 3-4 tablespoons of light soy sauce,
- 1-2 teaspoon(s) sesame oil,
- 1 tablespoon freshly crushed garlic,
- 1 tablespoon of finely chopped ginger,
- 4 spring onions finely chopped,
- 3 ½ cups of water,
- Vegetable oil for cooking.

Optional:
- 1 large mild red chilli,
- 1 large mild green chilli.

Method:
(Note: Cook in two batches, then mix together before serving. It makes it easier to handle.)
1. Soak the dried shitake mushrooms in a bowl of warm water overnight, using an inverted teacup saucer to keep the dried mushrooms immersed.
2. Wash the rice in running water, at least three times until the water runs clear. Cook the rice in 3 ½ cups of water, until the water is fully absorbed. Make sure the rice is cooked and not hard. Add a little hot water and cook for a few mins more if necessary. Allow to cool, place in an open dish/plate and fluff gently until the cooked grains of rice are separated. Leave rice to dry in an open platter.
3. Wash the shitake mushrooms and gently hand press to expel the absorbed water. Cut into thin slices, taking care to remove any hard stems that have not softened. Set aside.
4. Using a vegetable peeler, peel off the carrot skin. Using a vegetable peeler, peel off the carrot skin and then shave off thin strips from the carrot. Shave off thin strips from the carrot, Shave off as much of the carrot as you can. Position all the shaved strips lengthwise and cut into 4-5 cm lengths. Set aside.
5. Wash the fennel. Cut off the stems and the hard bottom. Cut fennel in halves and finely slice into thin strips. Chop the slices again into 4-5 cm lengths.
6. Wash the cabbage. Remove the hard part at the bottom. Slice the cabbage into thin slices. Then, cut the slices again into 4-5 cm lengths. Remove any hard bits. Set aside.
7. Optional: *Wash the chillies. Thinly slice at an angle to obtain delicately angled pieces. Set aside.*
8. Heat wok or other similar pan over medium high heat, until the wok starts smoking. Add 2 tablespoons of the vegetable oil and swirl using a wok spatula.

9. Add the fennel and mushroom pieces and stir fry until the mushroom pieces are just cooked. Add some vegetable stock if the mushroom and fennel pieces start drying up. Add the carrot shavings and stir fry until just cooked. Remove from the wok and set aside.
10. Add two tablespoons of vegetable oil to the wok over medium to high heat. Add the fluffed rice (if wok is small, cook in half batches). Stir fry the rice and add some of the vegetable stock to stop the rice from sticking to the wok, followed with 2 tablespoons of light soy sauce. You can adjust the addition of the soy sauce to suit your preference. Stir fry and mix the rice into the soy sauce and vegetable stock. Add the mushroom, fennel and carrot slices to the rice. Combine gently without crushing.
11. Cook until the rice absorbs the soy sauce and vegetable stock. Only add small amounts of vegetable stock to flavor the rice and to stop it from sticking to the wok.
12. Add the sliced cabbage and gently stir at intervals to ensure uniform cooking. Add some vegetable stock if necessary.
13. Add the corn kernels and gently mix. Add 1-2 teaspoons of sesame oil and gently stir. Add the chilli slices and gently mix. Add some more vegetable stock if necessary.
14. Add the frozen baby peas and gently stir without crushing. The peas will soften very quickly. Add half of the finely sliced spring onions and gently stir. Remove wok from heat.
15. Transfer into a warm serving dish. Garnish with the remaining finely sliced spring onions. Serve immediately.

Madeleine Philippe with guests Cynthia and Marie-Rose

Eggplant with Pork Fricassée

Ingredients (Serve 4):
- 1 kg pork spare ribs
  Option: substitute the pork with other meats,
- 2 tablespoons crushed garlic,
- 2 large onions finely chopped,
- 125 ml vegetable oil,
- 1 ½ kg eggplant,
- 250 ml chicken stock,
- 400 g finely chopped canned tomatoes,
- ½ teaspoon fresh cinnamon powder,
- ½ teaspoon allspice powder,
- ½ teaspoon fresh ground cloves,
- 1 tablespoon red wine vinegar,
- 4 tablespoons chopped parsley,
- 100 ml dry sherry,
- Cornflour as required,
- Salt and pepper to taste.

Method (Slow Cooker):
1. Cut the pork (or other meat) into bite size pieces and mix with the garlic, onions, sherry, 1 tablespoon parsley, cloves, salt and pepper. Allow to marinate for 30 mins or desirably overnight in the fridge.
2. Clean the eggplant and cut into bite size pieces. Season with salt and pepper to taste.
3. Heat the oil in a deep saucepan to simmering point. Add pork pieces and marinade to the pan. Stir thoroughly and cook until the pork is fried to a golden brown colour. Be careful not to overcook.
4. Stir in the eggplant pieces with the pork. Mix gently and stir at intervals to prevent the ingredients from burning. Cook the mixture until the eggplant starts to turn a light golden colour. Remove from stove.
5. Transfer the pork and eggplant into a slow cooker. Add the remaining ingredients and slow cook for five to six hours or until the sauce thickens to your preference. Stir gently once or twice to ensure even cooking.
6. If the sauce is too liquid, you can thicken the sauce by adding 1 teaspoon of cornflour dissolved in two tablespoons of water. Mix the cornflour into the mixture without crushing the eggplant. Wait for sauce to thicken and transfer to a warm serving dish.

Cauliflower Sauce Blanche

Ingredients (Serve 2):
- 1 medium cauliflower,
- 3 egg yolks,
- 2 tablespoons flour,
- 2 cups milk,
- 2 tablespoons butter,
- 3 tablespoons chopped parsley,
- ½ teaspoon salt,
- Salt and pepper to taste.

Optional:
- Replace cauliflower with chokoes.

Sauce Blanche is also known as Béchamel Sauce.

Method:
1. Remove outer leaves from cauliflower. Wash in cold running water. With a sharp knife, cut out the florets at the base of the stems. Place in a steamer. Steam until tender.
2. Alternatively, boil in enough water with half teaspoon salt, to cover cauliflower florets until tender, but not soft.
3. Remove cauliflower florets from steamer/pan. Drain if necessary and allow to cool. Place in a deep and wide serving dish.
4. Melt butter in a saucepan and gradually sprinkle and stir in the flour. Mix well with a wooden spatula and cook for 1 to 2 mins.
5. Add milk gradually to the flour and butter mix. Mix well. Bring back to boil stirring constantly. Simmer for 2-3 mins. Keep stirring to blend the flour and butter.
6. Beat egg yolks in a bowl. Beat in a few tablespoons of hot sauce. Blend well together. Use a blender or a wire whisk to obtain a homogenous mix. Return to remaining sauce. Whisk together again and simmer until the sauce thickens to your preference. If you get lumpy bits, use a whisk or a stick blender to blend. Season with salt and pepper to taste.
7. Pour over cauliflower florets. Sprinkle with chopped parsley. Ideally, served with roast chicken and freshly baked bread.

Buttered Cabbage

Ingredients (Serve 2):
- 1 white cabbage (500 g),
- 60 g butter,
- 1 large onion finely chopped,
- 60 ml of cider vinegar,
- 10 ml of honey,
- 120 ml of red wine,
- 120 ml of chicken stock,
- Salt to taste.

Optional:
- 100 g bacon pieces.

Method:
1. Remove the outer leaves of the cabbage. Cut into quarters and remove the central stalk. Cut each quarter into fine strips as shown above. Option: cut into larger pieces just like Grandma used to do.
2. Heat a large and deep saucepan.
3. Add the butter until melted, (optional: *add bacon pieces at this point and fry to a golden brown colour before adding the rest of the ingredients*), then the finely chopped onion, cider vinegar, red wine, honey and chicken stock. Allow the mixture to boil. Reduce the heat to medium high.
4. Add the cabbage strips or pieces, mix well with the ingredients in the pan.
5. Cover and cook until the cabbage is tender but firm. Gently stir at intervals to prevent the cabbage from burning.
6. Taste the cabbage and add salt to taste if necessary.
7. When cooked, transfer to a warm serving plate.
8. Normally eaten with rice and a chatini pomme d'amour or an omelette.

Fricassée le Chou

Stewed Cabbage

Ingredients (Serve 4):
- 1 white cabbage (medium size),
- 275 g corned silverside (viande salée),
- 4 medium ripe red tomatoes,
- 1 onion finely sliced (medium size),
- 1 tablespoon crushed ginger,
- 1 tablespoon crushed garlic,
- 10 cloves,
- cracked black pepper,
- 5 tablespoons vegetable oil,
- Salt and pepper to taste.

Method:
1. Remove the outer leaves of the cabbage. Cut into quarters and remove the central stalk. Cut each quarter into bite size pieces (as shown in photo). Wash in cold water and drain.
2. Cut up the corned silverside into bite size cubes. Wash in running cold water and dry thoroughly with a kitchen paper towel. Sprinkle the corned silverside cubes with cracked black pepper. Set aside.
3. Finely chop the tomatoes without crushing.
4. In a deep saucepan, add 5 tablespoons of vegetable oil. Heat under medium-high. Add the finely sliced onions, crushed ginger and garlic. Cook until the onion slices become transparent. Add the chopped tomatoes, stir and cook until the sauce is well blended 5-10 mins. Add a little hot water if necessary to prevent the sauce from burning.
5. Add the corned silverside pieces and stir in with the tomato sauce. Allow to simmer until the corned silverside pieces are cooked and become opaque. Add a little bit of hot water if necessary to prevent the corned silverside from burning.
6. Stir in the chopped cabbage leaves and the cloves. Mix well together. Cover the saucepan and simmer over low heat until the cabbage is cooked to your preference. Stir at intervals to ensure even cooking and prevent burning. Add a little hot water if necessary.
7. Taste the cooked cabbage pieces and if necessary, season with salt and pepper to your preference. Mix well after adding the salt.
8. Serve over rice with a chatini pomme d'amour (tomato chutney).

Vegetable Bryani

Ingredients (Serve 4):
- 2 cups basmati rice,
- 6-7 saffron strands in 2 tablespoons warm milk,
- 2 medium ripe tomatoes,
- 4-5 green chillies,
- 1 medium carrot,
- 1 teaspoon red chilli powder,
- 10-15 green beans,
- 1 tablespoon coriander powder,
- ½ teaspoon garam masala powder,
- 2 tablespoons vegetable oil,
- vegetable oil to deep fry,
- ½ teaspoon caraway seeds,
- ½ tablespoon ginger paste,
- ½ tablespoon garlic paste,
- 1 teaspoon turmeric powder,
- 1 black cardamom,
- 2-3 green cardamoms,
- ¼ medium cauliflower,
- 4 medium onions,
- ¾ cup yoghurt,
- 2-3 cloves,
- 2 ½ cm stick cinnamon,
- 1 kaffir lime leaf,
- ½ cup frozen green peas,
- 2 tablespoons chopped coriander leaves,
- 2 tablespoons chopped mint leaves,
- 2 tablespoons ghee,
- Salt to taste.

Method:
1. Finely chop 1 onion and finely slice the others.
2. Soak the basmati rice for 15 mins, wash in running water until the water runs clear. Drain and cook the rice in 2 ½ cups of boiling salted water with the slightly crushed green and black cardamoms, cloves, cinnamon and kaffir lime leaf.
3. Finely chop the tomatoes into eight pieces each. Chop the green chillies into small pieces, peel and cut the carrot into ½ cm cubes. String the green beans and cut into 1 cm lengths. Cut the cauliflower into small florets.
4. Mix together the carrot cubes, cauliflower florets, green bean pieces and frozen peas. Blanch in boiling water for 1-2 mins until the vegetables turn into bright colours. Immediately drain and plunge into very cold water. Drain and set aside.
5. Heat enough oil in a thick bottomed saucepan over medium to high heat. Deep fry the onion slices until golden brown. Drain on kitchen paper towel and set aside.
6. Heat 2 tablespoons oil over medium-high heat in a thick bottomed saucepan. Add the caraway seeds. When they begin to change colour, add the finely chopped onions and sauté until golden brown. Add the chopped chillies, crushed ginger and garlic.
7. Add the coriander powder, turmeric powder, red chilli powder, garam masala and yoghurt. Mix well together. Add the chopped tomatoes and cook on medium heat until the oil separates. Add the blanched vegetables, mix well and add salt to taste. Set aside.

8. In a rice cooker or in a deep baking tray, place alternate layers of cooked rice and vegetables, starting with and finishing with rice. Garnish the layers with the fried onion slices, chopped coriander and mint leaves.
9. Add one cup of water, drizzle the top layer with the melted ghee and saffron strands soaked in milk.
10. Cook to your liking in the rice cooker.
11. Alternatively, cover the oven tray with aluminium foil and place the oven tray in a 180°C oven in mid position, cook for 15-20 mins. Check at intervals and serve when ready. Serve with a grated carrot or cucumber salad with onions and chopped green chillies.

Etouffée de brèdes malbar (Amaranth) with pork (page 218)

Gratin de Giraumon
Pumpkin Gratin

Ingredients (Serve 4):
- 1 kg diced pumpkin,
- 1 tablespoon butter,
- 100 ml milk,
- 2 egg yolks,
- 1 cup grated Cheddar cheese,
- Grated Parmesan cheese for topping,
- Bread crumbs,
- Salt and pepper to taste.

Method:
1. Peel pumpkin, remove seeds and stringy bits. Dice into 2-3 cm cubes and wash in running cold water. Boil diced pumpkin until tender and ready to be mashed. Drain cooked pumpkin pieces. Mash to a smooth purée while still hot. Add 1 tablespoon butter and 1 cup grated Cheddar cheese. Mix well together. Season with salt and pepper to taste. Add 2 egg yolks. Mix well together and gradually add 100 ml milk. Blend manually until well blended.
2. Pour the purée into a non-stick or pre-buttered baking dish. Top with breadcrumbs and grated Parmesan cheese. Bake in a pre-heated oven in mid position at 180°C. Cook until the topping turns a light golden colour.
3. Serve as an accompaniment for roasts and steaks, with fresh crusty French baguette bread.

Gratin de Manioc
Cassava Gratin
(Serge Paruit's Recipe)

Ingredients (Serve 4):
- 1 kg manioc (cassava) peeled,
- 1 medium onion finely sliced,
- 1 teaspoon garlic finely crushed,
- ½ cup milk,
- 1cup grated cheddar cheese,
- 1 teaspoon thyme leaves,
- 2 egg yolks,
- Parsley sprigs,
- Breadcrumbs,
- 3 tablespoons vegetable oil,
- Salt to taste.

Method:
1. Boil the peeled manioc (cassava) in salt water over medium high heat until softened but not mushy. Remove from water and allow to cool. Keep the water for later use. Mash up the manioc (cassava) to a creamy consistency. Remove the stringy bits. Add salt to taste and mix well. Set aside.
2. Fry the onion slices and crushed garlic in the vegetable oil until light golden. Remove from the oil and drain.
3. Beat up the egg yolks. Set aside.
4. Heat up the oven to 180°C.
5. Add the fried onion slices to the mashed manioc (cassava). Mix well. Add the grated cheese, thyme leaves and egg yolks. Mix well. Gradually blend in the milk until the mixture is creamy but not watery.
6. Grease an oven proof gratin dish. Spoon the mixture into the dish. Place in oven in mid position. Cook until the top starts to turn light golden brown. Sprinkle the top with the bread crumbs. Reduce heat to 150°C. Continue to bake until crumbs are cooked to a light golden colour.
7. Remove from oven. Garnish with parsley sprigs.

Haricots Verts à l'Ail

Green Beans with Garlic

Ingredients (Serve 4):
- 750 g tender and slender green beans,
- 2 tablespoons extra virgin olive oil,
- 6 cloves garlic, finely minced,
- 2 tablespoons dried white bread crumbs,
- 2 tablespoons chopped parsley,
- Salt and ground black pepper to taste,
- 25 g butter.

Method:
1. Remove the stalks and stringy bits from the green beans. Cut into serve lengths 4 cm.
2. Drop the green beans into a large pot of boiling salted water and cook uncovered over high heat for about 3-4 mins or until cooked but slightly crisp.
3. Drain the beans into a colander and immediately immerse into very cold water to stop the cooking and retain the bright green colour. Drain again and set aside.
4. Heat the olive oil in a large non stick sauté pan over low heat. Add the garlic, breadcrumbs, parsley, salt and pepper. Stir cook for 1 minute. Add the butter and when melted, add the drained green beans and stir cook for 1 minute. Just long enough for the green beans to absorb the flavours and reheat without frying.
5. Remove from pan and place in a warm serving dish.
6. Serve immediately. Ideal to eat with meat dishes.

Potato Chips
Pommes Frites

Ingredients:
- Medium potatoes (use Bintje, Yukon Gold or Russett Burbank variety),
- Peanut oil for deep frying,
- Salt and freshly ground black pepper.

Method (French Style):
1. Peel the potatoes. Cut them in slices 1 cm thick and cut again into 1 cm square chips.
2. Put the chips in cold water for a few mins. This will wash out much of the starch and make the chips less sticky after the first frying, and crispier after the second. Remove from the cold water and drain.
3. Dry the chips in kitchen towel paper.
4. Heat the oil in a hot frying pan or deep fryer to a temperature of 160°C. Put in a handful of chips: not too many at once because the oil will cool down too much. Fry for 4-8 mins depending on the variety of potatoes to blanch the chips. Stir regularly to prevent sticking.
5. Remove and drain chips. Spread the blanched chips out on an oven grill lined with kitchen paper towel. Allow to cool and 'sweat' for at least ½ hour. Repeat with the remaining chips.
6. Finally reheat the oil in the deep fryer to 190°C and fry the blanched chips in batches for 2 mins or until crispy and golden brown. This way the fries will be crispy on the outside and soft on the inside.
7. Remove and drain the crispy and golden fries over kitchen paper towel. Season with salt and pepper to taste.

Potato Salad

Salade de Pomme de Terre

Ingredients (Serve 4):
- 1 kg potatoes,
- 1 medium onion sliced or chopped,
- 5 spring onions finely sliced,
- ½ - 1 cup Mauritian mayonnaise,
- ½ - 1 cup plain yoghurt,
- 4 hard boiled eggs quartered,
- 2 rashers bacon trimmed of fat,
- Salt and pepper to taste.

Method:
1. Place bacon rashers between kitchen paper towel and microwave for 30-60 seconds on high. Cut into thin strips with a sharp knife. Set aside.
2. Peel potatoes and cut into 2 cm cubes. Boil in water with 1 teaspoon of salt until just tender and cooked. Drain and allow to cool. Do not overcook.
3. Quarter the hard boiled eggs. Set aside.
4. Combine the mayonnaise and yoghurt. Add to the potato cubes and gently combine without crushing the potato pieces, with the onion slices and finely sliced spring onions. Season with salt and pepper to taste.
5. Transfer to a serving dish and top with the bacon strips and quartered hard boiled eggs.
6. Serve at room temperature. Enjoy.

Salade Chou Chou

Choko Salad

Ingredients (Serve 4):
- 1 kg chokos/chayote squash/christophene,
- 1 tablespoon white vinegar,
- 3 tablespoons extra virgin olive oil,
- 1 tablespoon freshly crushed garlic,
- 1 medium onion finely sliced,
- 1 tablespoon chopped fresh green chillies,
- Salt and freshly ground black pepper.

Method:
1. Heat water in a saucepan. Add salt and stir to dissolve completely. Add the chokos and boil for about 20 mins or until tender. Remove from boiling water and set aside to cool.
2. Peel and halve the chokos. Discard the seed membrane and cut into slices according to your preference.
3. Mix the oil, vinegar, freshly crushed garlic, salt and pepper to taste, freshly chopped green chillies (if desired) and sliced onions together.
4. Pour over the sliced chokos. Carefully mix without breaking the chokos.
5. This salad makes a good addition to any meal as a side dish.
6. Sit back and enjoy.

Salade Palmiste
Palm Heart Salad

Ingredients (Serve 6):
- 3 hearts of palm,
- Juice from 2 lemons (medium),
- 2 tablespoons white vinegar,
- 4 tablespoons vegetable oil,
- Salt and pepper to taste.

Note: It is not recommended that sliced onions be added to the salad to preserve the delicate flavour of the palm heart.

Method:
1. Remove the tender inner part of the palm heart. The less tender outer parts can be used to make achards.
2. Slice the tender heart of palm crosswise into thin slices. Immediately immerse into a mixture of half water and half milk to prevent the palm heart slices from browning.
3. In a large serving bowl, mix well together the lemon juice, vinegar and vegetable oil.
4. To serve, remove the quantity of sliced palm heart required. Pat dry with kitchen paper towel and incorporate with the lemon juice, vinegar and vegetable oil mixture. Add salt and pepper to taste.
5. Eat immediately when the palm heart slices are still crisp.
6. Serve with "Sauce Rouge Camarons" (King prawns in rich tomato sauce-page 243) and crisp bread, as an entrée.

Heart of Palm with Parmesan Salad

Alternative using Canned Hearts of Palm

Ingredients (Serve 4):
- 400 g can hearts of palm, drained & rinsed
- 2 medium tomatoes, seeded & chopped,
- 3 garlic cloves, finely chopped,
- 2 tablespoons extra virgin olive oil,
- Salt and pepper (use fresh cracked pepper),
- 2 ounces parmesan cheese, freshly shaved,
- 2 tablespoons fresh basil, chopped.

Method:
1. Cut the hearts of palm into 1-2 cm thick pieces Combine all ingredients, except the parmesan, salt and pepper in a large bowl.
2. Season with salt and pepper to taste.
3. Toss and leave at room temperature for 30 mins to allow the flavours to blend. Serve with shavings of parmesan cheese on top of a lettuce salad.

Sauce Blanche Chou Chou

Chokos in White Sauce

Ingredients (Serve 4):
- 4 medium green (or white) chokos,
- 3 egg yolks,
- 2 tablespoons flour,
- 2 cups milk,
- 2 tablespoons butter,
- 3 tablespoons chopped parsley,
- ½ teaspoon salt,
- Salt and pepper to taste.

Optional:
- Replace chokos with cauliflower.

Method:
1. Peel and cut chokos into 3 cm pieces.
2. Boil in water with half teaspoon salt, enough water to cover choko pieces, until tender but not soft.
3. Remove from pan, strain and place in deep serving dish. Allow to cool.
4. Melt butter in a saucepan and add flour. Mix well and cook for 1 minute. Remove from heat and mix well together.
5. Add milk gradually to the flour and butter mix. Blend gradually. Bring back to boil stirring constantly.
6. Simmer for 2-3 mins. Keep stirring to blend the milk, flour and butter well. Reduce heat or temporarily remove from stove.
7. Beat egg yolks in a bowl. Add a few tablespoons of the hot sauce. Blend well together using a blender or a wire whisk to obtain a homogenous mix.
8. Add the egg yolk mix to the milk, flour and butter sauce. Mix well and return to stove over low heat. Simmer until the sauce thickens to your preference. If you get lumpy bits, use a stick blender or similar to blend the sauce to a homogenous mix. Season with salt and pepper to taste.
9. Pour over choko pieces. Sprinkle with chopped parsley.
10. Serve with roast chicken and freshly baked bread.

Stewed Okra
Lalos with Red Chillies

Ingredients (Serve 4):
- 500 g okras (lalos) (choose tender ones),
- 1 medium onion finely sliced,
- 1 tablespoon crushed garlic,
- 1 tablespoon crushed ginger,
- 3 red chillies,
- 2-3 tablespoons vegetable oil,
- 1 tablespoon finely chopped parsley,
- Salt and pepper to taste.

Optional:
- 1 bacon rasher.

Method:
1. Wash okras and cut off stems. Remove stems from the red chillies and slice into halves lengthwise. Optional: Cut off the fat from a bacon rasher and finely slice the lean part into thin strips.
2. In a heavy based saucepan, heat 2-3 tablespoons of vegetable oil over medium heat.
3. Optional: *Stir fry the thin bacon strips.*
4. Add the crushed garlic, crushed ginger, sliced onion and the sliced red chillies. Stir fry until the sliced onion is cooked and becomes transparent.
5. Add the okras and gently mix with the other ingredients. Reduce heat to medium-low. Allow to stew and gently stir at intervals until the okras are cooked and tender. Be careful not to squash the okras. Season with salt and pepper to taste.
6. Serve hot and garnish with the chopped parsley.
7. Eat with rice, black lentils or meat.

Stir Fried Bok Choy

Stir Fried Chinese Greens

Ingredients (Serve 4):
- 450 g bok choy (or any other green Chinese vegetables - Cos Lettuce can also be used),
- 1 teaspoon salt,
- 4 tablespoons vegetable oil,
- 2 teaspoons finely chopped garlic,
- ½ teaspoon sugar dissolved in 1 tablespoon water.

Method:
1. Cut the bok choy into 2-3 cm long pieces. You may reduce the size of the tougher sections to ensure uniform cooking. Cover with water, add the salt and leave to soak for 10 mins. Remove from the water and allow to drain thoroughly.
2. Heat the oil in a wok until smoking. Add the garlic, stir fry for a few seconds to flavour the oil. Add the greens, sugar and water. Stir fry for 1-2 mins or until the colour changes to transparent green. Transfer to a hot serving dish and serve immediately.
3. Ideal to eat with fried rice.

Bitter Melon with Prawns Stir Fry

Ingredients (Serve 4):
- 650 g fresh bitter melons,
- 2 medium red tomatoes,
- 1 medium onion thinly sliced,
- 1 tablespoon crushed garlic,
- 1 tablespoon finely chopped ginger,
- 250 g green prawns,
- Chopped red chillies to taste,
- 2 tablespoons vegetable oil,
- 1 cup chicken stock,
- 2 medium size eggs,
- 3 tablespoons finely chopped spring onions,
- Salt and pepper to taste.

Method:
1. Cut bitter melons in half lengthwise. Using a spoon, scrape out the centre whitish parts. Soak in lightly salted water for 30 mins.
2. Remove from salt water and wash in running cold water. Pat dry and using a very sharp knife, cut into bite size pieces or to your preference. Set aside.
3. Cut the tomatoes into quarters then into eighths. Set aside.
4. Heat oil in thick based saucepan over medium heat. Stir in the onions, crushed garlic and finely chopped ginger. Stir fry until the onions become transparent.
5. Add the tomato pieces and stir fry. Crush the tomato pieces with a wooden spoon until half blended into the onions. Add the bitter melon pieces and mix well with the ingredients in the saucepan. Add the chicken stock and the finely chopped red chillies. Mix the ingredients together. Cover and simmer over medium heat.
6. When the bitter melon pieces are half cooked, add the prawns. Mix well together, cover and simmer gently. Stir at intervals and mix the ingredients to ensure even cooking.
7. Carefully stir the ingredients from the bottom of the pan to ensure that you don't burn the bitter melon and prawns.
8. Check at intervals to see if the bitter melon pieces and prawns are cooked. Check the sauce and add salt and pepper to taste. If the sauce is too watery, uncover and allow the sauce to thicken. On the other hand if sauce is too dry, add a little bit of hot water or chicken stock to adjust sauce consistency to your taste.
9. Before serving, whip the two eggs in a bowl and pour in a thin stream over the bitter melon pieces and the prawns. Allow to cook a bit on the surface, then gently stir mix the whipped eggs, bitter melon pieces and prawns. Allow the eggs to cook.
10. Transfer to the serving dish and sprinkle with the finely chopped spring onions. Serve with rice.

Vegetables and herbs in Rose Hill market

Jardinière de Boeuf

Beef with Vegetables

Ingredients (Serve 4):
- Half cauliflower (250 g),
- 2-3 carrots (200 g),
- 200 g stringless green beans (haricots verts),
- 2 medium potatoes,
- 500 g beef,
- 1 medium onion,
- 2 medium red tomatoes,
- 1 tablespoon crushed garlic,
- 1 tablespoon crushed ginger,
- 3 tablespoons vegetable oil,
- 10 cloves,
- 1 cup chicken stock,
- Salt and pepper to taste.

Method:
1. Cut the beef into bite size cubes. Season with salt and pepper to taste. Set aside.
2. Cut the cauliflower into florets. Finely slice the onion. Scrape off the carrot skins, wash and cut into ½ cm thick slices. Peel and cube the potatoes, keep immersed in cold water until ready to use to prevent oxidation.
3. Remove the stalky end bits from the green beans, slice into thin strips lengthwise. Cut the tomatoes into quarters, de-seed, cut the quarters into further halves.
4. Over high heat in a large saucepan, add 3 tablespoons of vegetable oil. When oil is hot, add the beef cubes and stir fry to seal in the juices until the beef is cooked to an opaque colour (3-4 mins). If the beef releases water, cook for longer until the liquid evaporates and the beef is cooked. Stir constantly to ensure even cooking.
5. Add the sliced onions, crushed garlic and ginger. Mix well with the beef cubes and cook until the onion slices become transparent. Reduce heat to medium-low. Stir at intervals to ensure even cooking. Add the carrot slices and cook for a few mins. Add the sliced green beans and mix with the carrot slices and the beef cubes. Take care not to crush the vegetables. Simmer for 1-2 mins.
6. Add the potato cubes and mix well with the other ingredients. Add the cloves and cook for 1-2 mins. Add the cauliflower florets and stir in gently. Mix well together taking care not to crush the vegetables. Add the tomato pieces, the chicken stock and ½ cup of hot water. Gently mix well together. Taste the sauce and season with salt, if necessary. Cover and simmer for 30-45 mins or until the vegetables are cooked and tender.
7. Serve over rice with a tomato chatini.

Cassoulet Mauricien
Mauritian Cassoulet

Ingredients (Serve 4):
- 500 g Cannellini beans,
- 1 medium onion, finely chopped,
- 500 g Continental sausages,
- 200 g smoked bacon, medium sliced and cut into 3 cm pieces,
- 500 g beef,
- 225 g canned finely crushed tomatoes,
- 1 tablespoon chopped parsley,
- 1 tablespoon chopped thyme,
- 8 cloves,
- 1 teaspoon garlic crushed,
- 1 teaspoon ginger crushed,
- Salt to taste,
- Oil as indicated,
- 1 litre water.

Optional:
- 4 medium red chillies.

Method:
1. Wash Cannellini beans in running cold water. Soak in cold water for 1 hour. Drain, place in pressure cooker with 1 litre of water. Add the cloves and salt to taste. Bring to boil and cook under pressure for 15-20 mins. Release pressure and check if beans are cooked but still firm. If not, cook under pressure for a few mins more. Remove from heat. Set aside.
2. Place sausages in a microwave proof dish in one layer. Prick each sausage with a toothpick all over (to prevent bursting). Cover with kitchen paper towel and cook under high for 6 mins. Remove and allow to cool. Cut into 2-3 cm long pieces or according to your own preference.
3. Cut beef into bite size pieces. Season with salt and crushed black pepper to taste.
4. Heat a large casserole pan over medium high heat and add 4 tablespoons oil. Add the sliced onion, crushed garlic, crushed ginger and thyme. Stir fry until the onions slices become transparent. Add the finely crushed tomatoes, simmer until the sauce is well blended. Stir at intervals to prevent the sauce from burning.
5. Add beef pieces to tomato sauce and mix well. Continue to cook for about 10 mins or until the meat becomes opaque. Optional: *add the sliced red chillies.* Add the cut sausages, bacon pieces and mix well together without crushing the sausages. Cook over low heat for a further 5 mins or until bacon pieces are cooked.

6. Drain the Cannellini beans from the cooking water. Retain the water for adding to the dish later. Add the cooked Cannellini beans to the beef, sausage, bacon and tomato mixture in the pan and carefully mix together. Do not mash up the beans. Cook for a further 10 mins.
7. Add the retained boiled water to the pan and carefully mix. Cook for a further 20 mins or until the sauce reaches the desired consistency, according to your own preference. It has to be semi liquid as the beans will continue to absorb the water. If there is not enough sauce you can stir in some hot water.
8. Add salt to taste.
9. Serve hot and eat with bread or rice.

Home made sausages by Clancy Philippe

Spiced Boiled Chickpeas
Gram Bouilli

Ingredients (Serve 6):
- 1 kg dried chickpeas,
- 2 tablespoons cumin seeds,
- 2 teaspoons mustard seeds,
- 2 teaspoons paprika,
- 2 teaspoons turmeric powder,
- 2 teaspoons garam masala,
- juice from 1 lemon,
- 4 sliced green or red chillies quantity to taste,
- 1 tablespoon crushed ginger,
- 1 tablespoon crushed garlic,
- 3 tablespoons vegetable oil,
- 1 tomato finely chopped,
- 4 tablespoons chopped coriander leaves,
- Salt to taste.

Method:
1. Choose chickpeas that are large in size and pale in colour. Soak overnight in cold water. In the morning, carefully drain and wash chickpeas in running cold water. Drain and set aside.
2. Bring a large saucepan full of water to the boil, stir in 2 teaspoons salt and add the drained chickpeas. Check the chickpeas at intervals and skim off any scum forming on top. When cooked to just soft, (that is soft to the bite), drain the boiled chickpeas and immediately wash in cold running water. Set aside.
3. Over medium to high heat, heat up the oil in a large saucepan (Chinese wok is perfect) and sizzle the cumin and mustard seeds. When the cumin and mustard seeds start to splutter, add the crushed ginger, crushed garlic and sliced green chillies (alternatively use red chillies). Stir fry for 2-3 mins.
4. Add the drained boiled chickpeas and carefully stir. Mix gently and carefully so as not to crush the chickpeas. When the chickpeas are coated with the spices, add the chopped tomato and 2 teaspoons of salt. Mix well without crushing. Add the remaining spices, juice from one lemon and stir mix into the chickpeas.
5. Cook until the chickpeas have been well seasoned with the spicy ingredients and not too moist. Season to taste with salt, if necessary.
6. Transfer to a serving dish and garnish with the chopped coriander leaves.

Chicken Stir Fry with Vegetables

Ingredients (Serve 4):
- 350 g chicken fillets,
- 200 g carrots,
- 150 g bean sprouts,
- 100 g snow peas,
- 5 spring onions,
- 2 sticks celery,
- 200 g cauliflower,
- 100 g broccoli florets,
- 1 large onion sliced,
- 1 tablespoon cornflour,
- 1 tablespoon light soy sauce,
- 3 tablespoons vegetable oil,
- 1 ½ teaspoons sesame oil,
- 50 ml water,
- 2 tablespoons dry sherry,
- 3 tablespoons fish sauce,
- Salt and pepper to taste.

Method:
1. Cut the chicken into thin strips. Season with 3 tablespoons fish sauce, ½ teaspoon sesame oil, salt and pepper to taste. Set aside.
2. Wash the vegetables in cold water. Remove the stringy ends from the bean sprouts, wash and put aside. Cut the spring onions into 2 cm lengths.
3. Finely slice the onion halves. Cut the broccoli and cauliflower florets into bite sizes. Chop the celery into 2 cm pieces. Julienne the carrots. Remove the strings from the snow peas.
4. In a wok or similar saucepan, heat 3 tablespoons of vegetable oil over high heat. Stir fry the chicken strips with the marinade until the chicken is cooked to a light golden brown or to your preference. Remove the fried chicken strips from the oil, drain on kitchen paper towel. Set aside.
5. In the remaining oil (if necessary add some more oil), stir in and cook in the following order, the carrots, cauliflower, broccoli, celery, onions and snow peas. Stir fry until the vegetables are just cooked and still crisp. Put the fried chicken strips back into the saucepan. Mix together without crushing the ingredients.
6. Season with 1 teaspoon sesame oil. Cover and cook for 2-3 mins over medium heat. Do not overcook.
7. In a cup, prepare a mixture of 50 ml water, 1 tablespoon cornflour, 1 tablespoon light soy sauce and 2 tablespoons dry sherry. Stir the cornflour mixture into the saucepan. Gently mix together and cook for a few mins to allow the sauce to thicken and blend in. Taste and season with salt if necessary. Remove from heat and gently stir in the bean sprouts. Cover for 1 minute. Serve immediately on rice.

Etouffée de Brèdes Malbar
Amaranth Greens

Ingredients (Serve 4):
- 2 medium bunches of brèdes malbar (amaranth),
- 2 medium ripe red tomatoes,
- ½ cup vegetable or chicken stock,
- 1 onion finely sliced (medium size),
- 1 tablespoon crushed ginger,
- 1 tablespoon crushed garlic,
- 2 tablespoons vegetable oil,
- Salt and pepper to taste.

Optional:
- 2 slices bacon.

Method:
1. Break off the shoots and tender parts of the brèdes malbar. Do not use the hard stems. Wash in cold running water. Drain and set aside.
2. Optional: Cut the bacon slices into thin strips.
3. Finely chop the tomatoes without crushing.
4. In a deep saucepan, add 2 tablespoons of vegetable oil. Heat over medium-high. Add the finely sliced onions, crushed ginger and garlic. Cook until the onion slices become transparent.
5. Add the chopped tomatoes, stir and cook until the sauce is well blended 5-10 mins. Add a little hot water if necessary to prevent the sauce from burning.
6. Optional: *Add the bacon pieces and stir in with the tomato sauce. Simmer until the bacon pieces are slightly cooked.* Add a little bit of the vegetable or chicken stock if necessary to prevent the ingredients in the pan from burning.
7. Stir in the brèdes. Mix well. Cover the saucepan and simmer over low heat until the brèdes are cooked to your preference. Stir at intervals to ensure even cooking and prevent burning. Add a little vegetable or chicken stock if necessary. Do not overcook.
8. Taste the brèdes malbar and if necessary, season with salt to your preference.
9. Serve over rice with a vegetable achar.

Etouffée de Brèdes Mouroum
Moringa Greens

Ingredients (Serve 4):
- 2 medium bunches of brèdes mouroum (moringa),
- 2 slices poisson salé blanc (white salt fish)
- 2 medium ripe red tomatoes,
- ½ cup vegetable or chicken stock,
- 1 onion finely sliced (medium size),
- 1 tablespoon crushed ginger,
- 1 tablespoon crushed garlic,
- 2 tablespoons vegetable oil,
- Salt and pepper to taste.

Method:
1. Wash the brèdes mouroum. Shake dry. Break off the leaves from the brèdes and place in a container. Keep moist.
2. Soak the poisson salé blanc in cold water for 30 mins. Wash and cut into small pieces 4-5 cm long. Boil in a small container for 5 mins or until half cooked. Remove and drain. Set aside.
3. Finely chop the tomatoes without crushing. Set aside.
4. In a deep saucepan, add 2 tablespoons of vegetable oil. Over medium heat, stir fry the poisson salé pieces until cooked. Add the finely sliced onions, crushed ginger and garlic.
5. Cook until the onion slices become transparent. Add the chopped tomatoes, stir and cook until the sauce is well blended 5-10 mins. Add a little stock if necessary to keep the sauce moist.
6. Stir in the brèdes. Mix well. Cover the saucepan and simmer over low heat until the brèdes are cooked to your preference. Stir at intervals to ensure even cooking and prevent burning. You may add a little vegetable or chicken stock if necessary. Do not overcook. Taste the brèdes and season with salt to your preference.
7. Serve over rice with a vegetable achar.

Cassoulet de Carcassonne

Ingredients (Serve 6):
- 500g white kidney beans,
- 1 pork trotter, cut into two lengthwise,
- 1 ham bone,
- 250g pig skin with fat,
- 500g sausages (Toulouse style),
- 150g salt pork,
- 3 duck breast confits,
- 100g duck fat,
- 500g lean pork,
- 5 medium onions,
- 3 medium carrots,
- 1 leek,
- 1 celery stick with leaves,
- 5 medium garlic cloves,
- 5 cloves,
- 10 black peppercorns,
- 1 bunch parsley,
- 2 sprigs thyme,
- 2 bay leaves,
- Salt and pepper to taste.

Method:
1. Soak the white kidney beans overnight in 3 litres of cold water.
2. Prepare a bouillon in a large pot with 4 litres of cold water, with the pork trotter halves, ham bone, the pork skin with fat rolled and tied up, 3 onions (one onion spiked with the cloves), 10 black peppercorns and one bouquet garni consisting of parsley, bay leaf, thyme sprigs, celery leaf and half of the green part of the leek-tied together. Bring to boil and simmer for 2 hours over low heat.
3. Peel the carrots and finely cut into small cubes. Finely chop half the celery stick and the remaining green leek. Finely chop the garlic cloves. Set aside.
4. Cut the lean pork into 2 cm cubes. Season the pork cubes with salt and pepper. Set aside for 15 mins. Cut the salt pork into thin strips. Brown the pork cubes and salt pork in half the duck fat. Add the finely cut carrots, chopped celery, green leek and finely chopped garlic cloves. Mix well with the browned pork and stew over low heat. Add some of the stock from 2. Cook until the pork is tender. Stir at intervals to prevent the pork from burning. Add some more stock if necessary. Remove the cooked pork from the saucepan.
5. Deglaze the saucepan with some of the stock from 2. Pour the rich sauce from the saucepan back into the stock.
6. In the remaining duck fat, brown the sausages. Put the browned sausages aside and deglaze the frying pan. Return the sauce into the stock.
7. In another frying pan without any fat, gently heat up the duck breast confits. Turn and allow the duck breast confits to sweat off some fat. Set the duck breast confits aside and deglaze the frying pan with some more stock. Pour the deglazed sauce back into the stock.

8. Filter the stock into another stock pot and retrieve the rolled up pork skin and trotters.
9. Drain the white kidney beans and blanch in boiling water until a scum starts forming. Remove scum and transfer the white kidney beans into the filtered stock. Bring to the boil and simmer over low heat for 2 hours until beans are tender but still whole.
10. Meanwhile, debone the pork trotters and cut pork meat into small bite size pieces. Unroll the cooked pork skin and cut into small bite size strips. Season with salt and pepper to taste and set aside.
11. Heat up the oven to 150°C. When white kidney beans are cooked but still whole, remove from stock with a strainer sieve and set aside. Keep stock. Lightly season the cooked white kidney beans with salt and pepper to taste. Do not crush the beans.
12. Allow the filtered stock to simmer and reduce by half into a concentrate over low heat.
13. In a casserole (or similar oven safe earthenware or stoneware bowl), line up the bowl with the cooked pork skin, place a layer of the white kidney beans, add a layer of the cooked meats (except the sausages and duck breast confits), add another layer of the white kidney beans with the sausages and duck breast confits in between. Add the remaining white kidney beans. Add the stock concentrate until the beans, sausage and duck breast confits are just covered.
14. Place cassole into oven in mid position and allow to cook for 1 hour or longer until the cassoulet starts simmering. Push down any meat that shows through and add a little stock to keep the white kidney beans and meats immersed.
15. When the cassoulet starts simmering, increase oven temperature to 175°C and continue cooking. A crust will start forming. Carefully push down the crust just before it starts to burn. Continue cooking until the topmost layer of beans, sausages and duck breast confits are well cooked and to your taste.
16. Enjoy with crusty baguette and a lettuce salad. Bon Appetit.

Clancy Philippe with Cassoulet Chef Jean Claude Rodriguez and Paul Rizzardi in Carcassonne

Clancy Philippe at Maison du Cassoulet in Carcassonne

Seafoods

Mauritians are blessed with a cornucopia of seafoods. The Indian Ocean is teeming with sea life that have for centuries provided the local population and tourists with tasty 'fruits de mer' (local appellation for seafood). The sea is rich in vitamins, minerals and protein, and sea creatures collect all these valuable nutrients when they eat. When we eat seafood, we benefit from these same nutrients. The delicate flavor of seafood, plus their low calorie, high energy content, make their consumption a very healthy choice.

The protein in seafood is also easier to digest because it has less connective tissue than red meats and poultry. This is one reason why fish muscle is so fragile, and why it flakes when cooked and can be eaten without further cutting or slicing. For certain groups of people such as the elderly who may have difficulty chewing or digesting their food, seafood can be a good choice to help them obtain their daily protein needs. It is also to be remembered that the first settlers in Isle de France (Mauritius) depended upon seafood for a substantial proportion of their food supplies.

Weather and seasons play a big part in the availability of seafood. The varieties of fish most consumed in Mauritius are tuna, dorade (bream), sacré chien rouge (ruby snapper), marlin, licorne (unicorn), cateau (parrot fish), cordonnier (shoemaker), batardé, capitaine (spangled snapper (poisson la perle), sacré chien (red snapper), and vieille rouge (grouper). These are consumed cooked, grilled, in curries or bouillon. The marlin and other big game fish are also smoked and sold as a delicacy that is in great demand worldwide. The most popular shellfish are lobster, tec tec (pipis), oysters, crabs and bigornos (winkles). It is even said that a bouillon of crabs or tec tec and bigornos has aphrodisiac properties. The Chinese harvest the sea cucumber (banbaras) for its health imparting benefits. The octopus caught in the tropical waters around the island, are used to make beautiful curries, stews and salads. In its sun dried form, the octopus provides one of the most sought after delicacies consumed by Mauritians worldwide. Rodriguan salted fish is very popular and when cooked in a rougaille, constitutes a dish that is unique in flavor and taste. Not to be forgotten either are freshwater fish and prawns. The most popular of the latter are the Rosenbergi prawns, locally named camarons that is very much in demand in Mauritian cuisine.

Rosenbergii giant river prawns (Camarons)

It is also a well known fact that seafood caught in the warm tropical waters of the Indian Ocean is tastier than seafood caught in the cold waters of oceans such as along the southern coastline of Australia. Seafood is an integral part of Mauritian cuisine, to be enjoyed by Mauritians and lovers of Mauritian cuisine worldwide. In Australia for example, the Mauritian community loves to cook the same seafood using products harvested in Australia and South East Asian waters.

It is not very well known that almost half of the seafood we eat comes from farms. And seafood farming (aquaculture) is the fastest growing food production system in the world. At first glance, farmed fish may seem like a good idea to help protect wild seafood populations from overfishing while meeting the nutritional needs of an ever-expanding global population. I have also seen farmed fish enclosures along the east coast of Mauritius. In reality, the industry is plagued with many of the same problems surrounding land-based concentrated animal feeding operations (CAFOs), including pollution, disease and inferior nutritional quality. It is also reported that in some countries, farm produced fish and prawns are regularly treated with growth hormones and antibiotics to maintain production quotas and prevent the occurrence of diseases. When buying seafood, please ensure that you are buying products from reputable sources.

Cooking seafood with various herbs and spices can also be beneficial to health, supplementing seafood with garlic can significantly lower cholesterol and triglyceride levels. Herbs are normally anti-oxidants as well. The addition of herbs helps to preserve the essential fatty acid value of seafood and reduce the formation of potentially harmful chemicals such as heterocyclic amines (derivates of amino acids in proteins) if seafood is over-cooked. Nutritionists increasingly advocate for the inclusion of seafood as a healthy dietary component for people at risk or suffering from coronary heart disease. Seafood is important in disease prevention but should not be considered in isolation. It has a premium place in a healthy diet for most people.

The constituent cultures making up Mauritian cuisine have led to the enhancement of seafood preparation into a galaxy of food presentation, taste, texture, colour and flavour. French seafood preparation is exemplified in classy dishes such as "bisque de homard" (lobster soup), "poisson aux fines herbes" (fish with herbs) and "gratin de morue" (salt cod with mashed potatoes). Creole cuisine has created one of the most popular Mauritian signature dish in "poisson sale rougaille" (saltfish in spicy tomato sauce) that is loved and adored by all Mauritians. Indian cuisine uses seafood to deliver the most umami rich, aromatic and luscious curries such as fish and octopus curries, second to none in taste. Chinese cuisine makes the preparation of seafood an artform. Their sweet and sour fish, chilli prawns, "bouillon crabes" (crab soup), crispy salt and pepper calamari bites, chilli crabs and seafood noodles are unique in taste, texture, colour and presentation.

Bouillabaisse

Ingredients (Serve 6):
- 500 g king prawns deveined and shelled (keep shells and heads for stock),
- 500 g white fleshed fish, skinned, boned and cut into bite size pieces (keep head and bones for stock),
- 12 mussels scrubbed and beards removed,
- 250 g crabs,
- 1 cup dry white wine,
- 2 cups water,
- ½ red onion chopped,
- 2 teaspoons finely chopped garlic,
- 1 bay (or cari poulet) leaf,
- ¼ cup olive oil,
- 2 red onions finely chopped,
- 1 small leek, finely sliced,
- 1 cup fish stock,
- 1 tablespoon crushed garlic,
- 450 g can chopped tomatoes,
- 3 tablespoons tomato paste,
- ¼ teaspoon saffron powder,
- 2 bay leaves,
- 1 tablespoon chopped basil leaves,
- 1 teaspoon fennel seeds,
- 4 cm piece orange rind,
- Salt and pepper to taste,
- ½ cup finely chopped parsley leaves.

Method:
1. Soak mussels in cold water for one hour. Clean crabs, break or cut into serve sizes and retain shells.
2. Prepare stock by boiling crab shells, fish head and bones, prawn shells and heads in 1 cup of fish stock, together with white wine, water, red onion, garlic and one bay or carri poulet leaf. Bring to boil, reduce heat and simmer for 20 mins. Strain and reserve liquid.
3. Heat oil in large casserole pan. Add finely chopped red onions, chopped leek and crushed garlic. Cover and cook on low heat for 20 mins, stirring occasionally until onion is softened but not browned. Add chopped tomatoes, tomato paste, saffron powder, bay leaves, basil, fennel seeds, and orange rind. Stir well and cook uncovered for 10 mins, stirring frequently.
4. Add strained fish stock and bring to boil. Boil for 10 mins, stirring often. Reduce heat and add fish pieces, crab pieces and mussels. Cover and simmer for 4-5 mins. Add prawns and simmer covered for 3-4 mins. Do not overcook the prawns. Season with salt and pepper to taste.
5. Remove orange rind and bay or cari poulet leaves. Transfer to warm serving bowls. Sprinkle with parsley.
6. Serve on freshly cooked hot basmati rice or with fresh crispy bread. Accompany with tomato chutney.

Octopus Salad
Salade Ourite

Ingredients (Serve 4):
- 1 kg octopus,
- Juice of half a lemon,
- 4 tablespoons oil,
- Chopped parsley,
- 2 small onions finely sliced,
- 2 finely chopped green chillies,
- 200 g white flour,
- Salt and pepper to taste.

Method:
1. Clean the octopus and carefully remove and discard the ink sac. Rub with white flour to thoroughly clean the octopus and wash in running water.
2. Heat a deep thick bottom saucepan. When the saucepan becomes very hot, using a pair of tongs lower the octopus into the saucepan. Allow the octopus to contract, lift it out of the pan and lower again. Do this three to four times. The contraction of the octopus will tenderise the octopus. Add the ground black pepper and ground cloves.
3. Leave the octopus in the pan and move around occasionally to prevent burning. Cook for 15 to 20 mins and simmer until the octopus is thoroughly cooked to a pink colour and tender, with the juice almost all evaporated. Retain the remaining juice for later use. Do not overcook as this will toughen the octopus. Remove octopus from pan.
4. Drain well and set aside to cool down. Using a very sharp knife, cut into small bite size slices.
5. Mix together lemon juice, oil and some salt and pepper.
6. Add parsley, onions, chillies and octopus pieces to mixture. Mix thoroughly.
7. Serve cold with bread.

Fish with Béchamel Sauce
Béchamel de Poisson

Ingredients (Serve 2):
For cooking fish prior to serving with Béchamel sauce:
- 650 g white flesh fish (whole),
- ½ cup white wine,
- Bouquet garni (thyme, parsley & coriander leaves),
- 5 cups water,
- 1 medium onion minced,
- 2 slices lemon,
- Salt and pepper to taste.

Béchamel Sauce:
- 4 tablespoons butter,
- 6 tablespoons plain white flour,
- 2 cups milk,
- 2 bay leaves,
- Freshly grated nutmeg,
- Salt and pepper to taste,
- 2 parsley sprigs for decoration.

For the Béchamel sauce, you may adjust ingredients to suit the quantity of sauce required.

Clean and scale fish while keeping the whole fish in one piece.

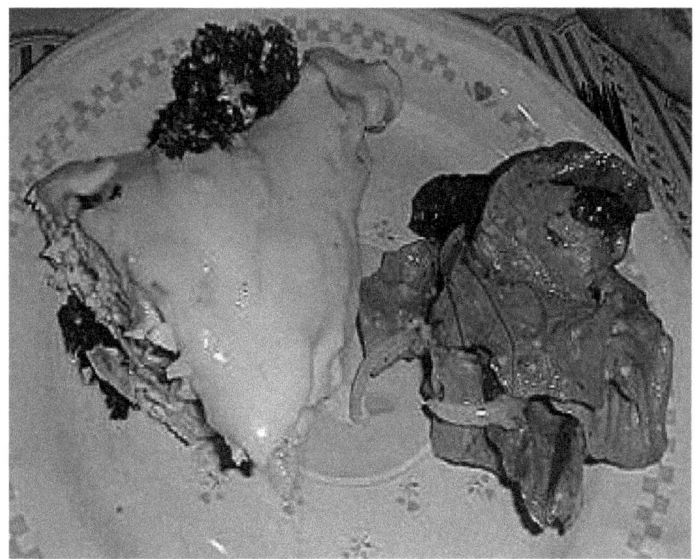

Method:
1. Place the fish in a large and deep saucepan with all the ingredients listed for cooking the fish. Bring to the boil over medium low heat. Make sure there is enough water to keep the fish immersed at all times.
2. Allow the fish to simmer until it is cooked to your preference. Make sure that the fish is not overcooked. Check at regular intervals until fish is just cooked without breaking into pieces.
3. Carefully remove the fish in one piece and transfer to a serving dish.
4. Melt the butter for the Béchamel in a heavy saucepan over medium heat. Add the flour and cook until just golden, stirring constantly to ensure a smooth blend.
5. Pour in half the milk, stirring vigorously until smooth, then stir in the remaining milk. Use a blender if necessary. Add the bay leaves.
6. Season with salt, pepper and nutmeg to taste. Reduce heat to medium low, cover and simmer gently for about 5-10 mins, stirring occasionally. Make sure that the sauce consistency is neither too thick nor too liquid.
7. Pour on top of the cooked fish in the serving plate and serve immediately. Decorate with the parsley sprigs. Serve with salad and fresh crispy bread.

Fish Bryani

Ingredients (Serve 5-6):
(Alternatively use prawns)
- 700 g white flesh fish cutlets (or prawns),
- 1 cup plain yoghurt,
- ½ teaspoon turmeric powder,
- Oil to fry fish (1 cup),
- 3 medium onions thinly sliced,
- 1 tablespoon crushed garlic,
- 1 tablespoon crushed ginger,
- 1 medium ripe tomato finely chopped,
- 1 tablespoon garam masala powder,
- ½ cup chopped coriander leaves and roots,
- 2 heaped tablespoons chopped mint leaves,
- 3 tablespoons ghee,
- 1 tablespoon salt,
- 1 tablespoon chopped coriander leaves for decoration,
- ¼ teaspoon saffron colouring.

Rice:
- 3 cups basmati rice,
- 1 medium onion thinly sliced,
- 2 tablespoons ghee,
- 4 cardamon pods,
- 4 cinnamon sticks,
- 4 cloves,
- 4 black peppercorns,
- 6 cups hot water,
- 2 teaspoons salt.

You can substitute the fish with prawns. However, do not fry the prawns beforehand. Just place the marinated prawns into the spice mix and cook until the prawns are thoroughly cooked, but not overcooked.

Method:
Marinated Fish:
1. Carefully cut fish into 2cm cubes using a very sharp knife, eliminating any fish bones. Put into a large bowl and sprinkle with the turmeric powder and 1 tablespoon salt.
2. Gently mix together and avoid breaking up or crushing the fish cubes. Cover and allow to marinate for 2 hours or overnight in refrigerator.

Rice Preparation:
1. Wash rice in cold water until it runs clear. Drain all water from rice. Set aside.
2. Heat ghee in a casserole pan large enough to cook and contain the cooked rice, over medium low heat. Add the cardamom pods, cinnamon sticks, cloves and black peppercorn. Stir fry for 1 minute. Add the finely sliced onion and stir fry until the onion slices become transparent.
3. Add the drained rice to the pan with other spices. Mix well together and make sure that the rice does not stick to the bottom of pan. Add 6 cups of hot water to rice, add 2 teaspoons of salt, mix well, cover and cook over low to medium heat.

4. Watch rice carefully and make sure that it is not under or overcooked. When ready, remove from heat and set aside for five mins. Fluff the rice carefully and gently to loosen the cooked rice grains. Do not scrape nor bring up (if any) burnt layer of rice from the bottom of pan.

Fish and Bryani Sauce:
1. In a deep frying pan, pour 1 cup of vegetable oil. Heat oil over low to medium heat. When oil starts to sizzle, carefully place the fish cubes in batches without touching each other in the pan. Fry fish cubes in batches until a golden colour, carefully remove from pan and drain over kitchen paper towel. Set aside.
2. Remove oil from frying pan, except for three tablespoons. Add sliced onions and fry over low heat until slightly golden brown.
3. Increase heat to medium and add the finely chopped tomato, optional chilli paste, crushed ginger and garlic. Stir fry for 5 mins until the tomato pieces are cooked.
4. Add the garam masala powder, yoghurt, salt to taste (1 tablespoon), chopped coriander and mint leaves. Stir fry for 5 mins over medium heat. Make sure that mixture does not stick to the bottom of pan by gently stirring the ingredients.
5. Add fried fish cubes (or prawns) and gently mix with the bryani sauce in pan. Continue cooking until mixture starts to boil. Remove from heat and set aside.

Presentation:
1. In a deep baking tray large enough to contain the rice and fish (or prawn) bryani, place a thin layer of rice alternating with the bryani mix and a thicker layer of rice. Carefully place the ingredients making sure that the fish (or prawn) and bryani sauce are evenly distributed. The dish looks better if the final layer shows an even combination of rice and fish (or prawn) with bryani sauce.
2. Melt 3 tablespoons ghee and sprinkle over mixture in pan. Dissolve ¼ teaspoon saffron colouring in 100 ml of hot water, sprinkle over rice. Cover with aluminium foil and place in oven at 150°C to keep warm. Allow rice to heat through for 20 mins.
3. Just before serving, remove foil and decorate with chopped coriander leaves.
4. Serve with a grated cucumber and carrot salad.

Chilli Crabs

Ingredients (Serve 2):
- 3 (1 kg) large fresh crabs,
- 6 fresh red chillies finely chopped,
- 20 mm piece of ginger finely chopped,
- 4 cloves garlic finely crushed,
- Peanut oil for deep frying,
- 1 tablespoon sugar,
- 300 ml chicken stock,
- 2 tablespoons vinegar,
- 2 tablespoons light soy sauce,
- 1 tablespoon sesame oil,
- 1 tablespoon corn flour, mixed with 3 tablespoons water,
- 2-4 tablespoons red chilli paste, vary quantity according to preference,
- ½ cup finely crushed canned tomatoes,
- 2 heaped tablespoons finely chopped spring onions,
- 1 egg, lightly beaten,
- Salt and pepper to taste.

Method:
1. Scrub the crabs and rinse well under cold water. Remove the claws and smash lightly. Chop the crabs into halves, discarding the grey and pulpy parts. Wash the crab pieces in cold running water. Set aside in colander and allow to drain.
2. In a deep thick bottom saucepan suitable for deep frying, heat the oil and deep fry the crabs for 1-2 mins, stirring frequently until just bright red. Remove saucepan from heat. Remove the fried crab pieces from the oil. Drain and set aside.
3. Remove the frying oil from the pan except for 60 ml (¼ cup oil). Heat under medium to high heat. Add the finely chopped red chillies, ginger and garlic. Stir fry for 2 mins or until you can smell the chillies. Add the finely crushed tomatoes, chilli paste, sugar, sesame oil and soy sauce. Simmer over low heat for 2-3 mins or until the finely crushed tomatoes are cooked and the sauce is thoroughly blended. Add salt and pepper to taste. The sauce should still be semi liquid to coat the crab pieces. Add some hot water if necessary.
4. Add crab pieces to the sauce. Stir gently until uniformly coated. Pour in the chicken stock and cook over high heat for 3 mins. Stir at intervals.
5. Dissolve the cornflour in 3 tablespoons of cold water and stir into the mixture. Add the lightly beaten egg and stir in gently. Check the sauce for taste and season with salt and pepper again if necessary.
6. Transfer to warmed serving dish. Sprinkle with chopped spring onions.
7. Serve hot with bread or as an appetiser.

Chilli Prawns

Ingredients (Serve 2-3):
- 450 g uncooked prawns, peeled and deveined,
- 2 egg whites,
- 75 g plus 1 tablespoon cornflour,
- 2 teaspoons salt,
- 1 tablespoon dry sherry,
- 300 ml vegetable oil,
- 2 teaspoons tomato paste,
- Pinch of ground white pepper,
- 1 teaspoon sugar,
- 2 spring onions, finely chopped,
- 1 teaspoon freshly crushed ginger,
- Red chillies (finely chopped) as many as you can handle,
- 1 medium onion sliced,
- 1 tablespoon chicken stock,
- 1 teaspoon sesame oil.

Method:
1. Mix together the egg whites, cornflour, 1 teaspoon of salt and the dry sherry. Coat the prawns uniformly.
2. Heat the oil to sizzling point in a wok. Add the prawns and stir fry for two mins or until lightly cooked. Do not overcook. Remove prawns from pan, drain oil and place on absorbent kitchen paper towels.
3. Pour most of the oil, leaving about 1 tablespoon to coat the bottom of the wok. Reheat the wok. Quickly stir fry the sliced onions. Add the tomato paste, white pepper, remaining salt and sugar. Return the prawns to the wok along with the finely chopped spring onions, crushed ginger and chopped red chillies. Stir fry for 1 minute.
4. Blend 1 tablespoon cornflour with the chicken stock and stir into the wok to thicken the sauce.
5. Pour onto a plate and sprinkle with the sesame oil. Serve with rice and stir fried bok choy.
6. Enjoy and see yourself in l'hotel Chinois Maurice.

Octopus Stew
Daube Ourite

Ingredients (Serve 3-4):
- 1.5 kg octopus,
- 2 medium onions finely chopped,
- 1 tablespoon finely chopped thyme,
- 3 tablespoons chopped parsley,
- 1 tablespoon crushed garlic,
- 1 tablespoon crushed ginger,
- 2 tablespoons vegetable oil,
- ½ cup dry sherry or dry white wine,
- 450 g can of finely chopped tomatoes,
- 6 cloves,
- 200 g white flour,
- Salt and pepper to taste.

Method:
1. Clean the octopus and carefully remove the ink sac. Rub with white flour to thoroughly clean the octopus and wash in running water.
2. Heat a deep thick bottom saucepan. When the saucepan becomes very hot, using a pair of tongs lower the octopus into the saucepan. Allow the octopus to contract, lift it out of the pan and lower again. Do this three to four times. The contraction of the octopus will tenderise the octopus.
3. Leave the octopus in the pan and move around occasionally to prevent burning. Cook for 15 to 20 mins and simmer until the octopus is thoroughly cooked to a pink colour and tender, with the juice almost all evaporated. Retain the remaining juice for later use. Do not overcook as this will toughen the octopus. Remove octopus from pan.
4. Drain well and set aside to cool down. Using a very sharp knife, cut into small bite size pieces.
5. Heat vegetable oil in deep saucepan.
6. Add the finely chopped onions, cloves, crushed ginger and garlic until the onions are cooked and become transparent.
7. Add finely chopped tomatoes and allow to simmer for 15 mins or until sauce is cooked and well blended. Add ½ cup of reserved octopus juice or hot water. Add two tablespoons of chopped parsley and the finely chopped thyme. Mix well. Add salt and pepper to taste. Allow to simmer for 5 more mins.
8. Add ½ cup dry sherry or dry white wine. Add the octopus pieces and mix well.
9. Simmer for 15 mins or until octopus pieces are tender and cooked to your taste.
10. You may add hot water in small quantities to adjust the sauce to your own preference.
11. Taste the sauce and add salt if necessary to taste.
12. Transfer to a serving dish and sprinkle with 1 tablespoon of chopped parsley.
13. Serve on a bed of rice with a green salad or tomato chutney.

Fish Bouillon with Okras

Bouillon Poisson avec Lalos (Okras)

Ingredients (Serve 4):
- 1 kg whole fish (cleaned and scaled),
- 10 small and tender okras with stems cut off,
- 2 medium onions finely chopped,
- 1 can (450 g) finely chopped tomatoes,
- Vegetable oil to fry fish slices,
- 1 tablespoon crushed ginger,
- 1 tablespoon crushed garlic,
- 1 tablespoon chopped thyme,
- 2 tablespoon chopped coriander leaves,
- 3 lemon slices,
- 3 curry leaves,
- Salt and pepper to taste,
- Hot water as required,
- Salt to taste.

Method:
1. Clean the fish and using a very sharp knife, cut into serve slices. Season with salt and pepper to taste.
2. Deep fry fish slices and fish head(s) in batches until golden brown. Set fish aside on kitchen paper towel to drain any excess oil.
3. Remove all oil from pan, except for 3 tablespoons.
4. Heat oil to simmering point. Add chopped onions, thyme, 1 tablespoon coriander leaves, curry leaves, crushed ginger and garlic. Mix well and cook until onions become transparent.
5. Add finely crushed tomatoes. Mix well and simmer for 15 mins or until sauce is cooked and well blended. Add salt and pepper to taste.
6. You may add some hot water to adjust the sauce consistency and to prevent it from drying up.
7. Add fish head(s) and mix well with the sauce. Cover and simmer for 10 mins. Add hot water in sufficient quantity to obtain a bouillon to your liking. Add the lemon slices, cover and simmer for 20 mins. Season with salt and pepper to taste.
8. Add the okras (lalos) into the bouillon and allow to simmer until the okras are cooked.
9. Add the fried fish slices and carefully stir into the bouillon without breaking the okras and fish slices. Simmer for another 5 mins.
10. Carefully remove the fish pieces and place into a deep serving dish. Pour the bouillon into the dish and sprinkle with the finely chopped coriander leaves.
11. Serve on a bed of rice and coriander tomato chutney.

Fish Curry
Cari Poisson

Ingredients (Serve 3-4):
- 1.2 kg whole white flesh fish cleaned and scaled,
- 2-4 tablespoons cornflour,
- 4 tablespoons curry powder, mild or hot to your preference,
- 1 medium onion finely chopped,
- 450 g can of finely crushed tomatoes,
- 1 tablespoon thyme finely chopped,
- 2 tablespoons chopped coriander leaves,
- 1 teaspoon crushed garlic,
- 1 teaspoon crushed ginger,
- 5-6 curry leaves,
- 3 cups water,
- 3 tablespoons vegetable oil,
- Oil to deep fry fish,
- Salt and pepper to taste.

Method:
1. Cut fish into slices (serve sizes). You may separate the fish head into halves lengthwise. Wash in cold running water, pat dry with kitchen towel paper. Season with salt and pepper to taste. Sprinkle fish slices with the cornflour to ensure a light even coating. Set the fish head pieces aside. Alternatively, toss the fish pieces in a large plastic bag with the corn flour. The cornflour will give the fish a crisp golden texture when fried.
2. Deep fry the fish slices to a crisp golden finish. Drain on kitchen paper towel. Do not fry the fish head pieces.
3. Add 3 tablespoons of the vegetable oil to a deep thick bottomed saucepan over medium-high heat. Stir in the crushed garlic, crushed ginger, finely chopped onion and thyme. Stir fry until the onions become transparent. Add the curry leaves (alternatively use kaffir lime leaves), stir in and cook for 2 mins.
4. Add the finely crushed tomatoes and simmer until the tomatoes are cooked and the sauce is well blended. Add hot water to prevent burning if necessary. Stir at intervals. When the sauce is nearly cooked, stir in 1 tablespoon of the finely chopped coriander leaves.

5. Add 4 tablespoons of curry powder into the tomato sauce. Stir in and simmer for a further 2-3 mins. Progressively add 1 cup of hot water and simmer to obtain a creamy curry sauce. Add the raw fish head pieces and gently stir into the curry sauce. Progressively, add 2 cups of hot water into the sauce and mix carefully. Cover and simmer for 20-25 mins or until the fish head pieces are cooked. Stir at intervals and turn over the fish head pieces once. You may adjust the sauce consistency to your preference by either adding more hot water (little at a time) to have more sauce or simmer without cover to thicken the sauce.
6. Taste sauce and season with salt and pepper to your preference. Carefully remove the fish head pieces and place in a warmed serving dish. Carefully add the fried fish slices to the sauce. Stir gently and simmer for a further 10-15 mins. Make sure that the fish slices are fully immersed into the sauce.
7. Remove from heat and allow the fish slices to rest in the sauce for at least 30 mins. Warm over low heat just before serving. Carefully transfer the fish slices and sauce into the serving dish with the fish head pieces. Sprinkle with the remaining chopped coriander leaves.
8. Enjoy and serve over rice. Just beautiful.

Licorne fish fried with onions by Lindsay Noe

Garlic Prawns
Crevettes à l'aïoli

Ingredients (Serve 3):
- 750 g prawns uncooked,
- 3 tablespoons crushed garlic,
- ½ cup aïoli,
- 3-4 tablespoons light olive oil,
- 1 sprig thyme finely chopped,
- 1 tablespoon lemon juice,
- Salt and pepper to taste.

Aïoli (will make 1cup)
- 2 egg yolks,
- 1/2 teaspoon Dijon mustard,
- 1 cup light olive oil,
- 1 tablespoon lemon juice,
- 1 tablespoon crushed garlic,
- Ground pepper to taste.

Method:
1. Prepare the aïoli first. All ingredients must be at room temperature. Whisk egg yolks, crushed garlic, mustard and pepper until it becomes sticky. Gradually add ½ cup oil, in a thin stream, stirring constantly. Use a blender to whisk the ingredients together. Add 1 tablespoon lemon juice. Continue blending. Gradually dribble in more oil, whisking constantly until fully blended. Set aside.
2. Shell the prawns leaving the head and tail. Remove the dorsal vein using a sharp knife. Heat the light olive oil in a heavy based frying pan over medium heat. Add the crushed garlic and cook until it sizzles. Add the prawns, stirring constantly until cooked and red in colour. Do not overcook. Remove pan from heat and carefully stir in ½ cup of the aïoli, thyme and lemon juice. Add salt and pepper to taste.
3. Serve individual portions with hot crusty bread, with the remaining aïoli for dipping in the bread.

Salt Cod with Mashed Potatoes
Gratin de Morue

Ingredients (Serve 4):
- 500 g salt cod (skinned and boned),
- 125 g cheddar cheese,
- 1.5 kg potatoes,
- 1 medium onion, finely chopped,
- 2 tablespoons parsley, finely chopped,
- 3 tablespoons butter,
- 2 eggs,
- 2 cups cold milk,
- Pinch of ground black pepper,
- 1 tablespoon olive oil,
- 1 teaspoon crushed garlic,
- Parmesan cheese grated for topping,
- Bread crumbs for topping,
- Salt to taste (sparingly as salt cod is salty).

Method:
1. Place salt cod in cold water and soak for 30 mins. Pour out water, wash and soak again. Repeat two or three times until the salt is washed out. Drain and cut into large portions. Set aside.
2. Peel potatoes. Boil in water until very soft and ready to mash. Remove from pan and drain. Add 2 tablespoons of butter and mash to a puree. Add 2 eggs and 1½ cups milk. Mash and blend well together until soft and fluffy. Add a pinch of ground black pepper and half the grated cheddar cheese. Mix well.
3. Boil the salt cod in a large saucepan until very tender, but not soft. Use a skewer to test. Remove from the pan and drain.
4. Flake the salt cod with a fork into very small pieces. Remove fish bones if any.
5. Gently heat 1 tablespoon of butter and 1 tablespoon olive oil in a large saucepan.. Fry the onions until transparent with 1 teaspoon crushed garlic. Add flaked salt cod and reduce heat to low. After a few mins, add the remaining cheddar cheese and finely chopped parsley. Mix well and cook for another 2 mins until the flaked salt cod salt is well blended with the cheese. Heat oven to 250°C.
6. Add the mashed potatoes to the pan and mix well. Add ½ cup milk.
7. Stir the mixture until very creamy. Taste for salt. Add more if desired.
8. Butter an oven proof gratin dish. Transfer mashed potato and salt cod mixture into the gratin dish. Spread uniformly and top with bread crumbs and parmesan cheese.
9. Place gratin dish in oven (mid position). When the gratin starts to cook, reduce heat to 200°C. Cook until topping turns golden brown. Serve with hot French bread and a green salad.

Fish Vindaloo
Fish Vindaille

Ingredients (Serve 4):
- 1 kg fish fillet (fresh),
- 6 cloves garlic,
- 2 tablespoons freshly ground mustard seeds,
- 1 tablespoon turmeric powder,
- 3 medium onions coarsely sliced,
- Green chillies (sliced lengthwise)-quantity to taste,
- Cornflour for dusting fish,
- Salt and pepper to taste,
- 2 tablespoons white vinegar,
- ½ cup vegetable oil.

Method:
1. Cut fish fillets into serve sizes according to your own preferences. Season with salt and pepper to taste. Lightly dust with cornflour. Using vegetable oil, deep fry fish in batches until golden brown. Drain and set aside.
2. Slice each garlic clove lengthwise into 3-4 slices. Slice the chillies lengthwise into halves.
3. Heat to simmering point 3 tablespoons of the oil used to fry the fish. Add the sliced onions, garlic slices and chillies. Cook until the onion slices become transparent. Add two tablespoons of the freshly ground mustard seeds, white vinegar and the turmeric powder. Mix well. Add the fried fish pieces and carefully blend with the spices. Reduce the heat to medium low and cook for a further ~~one~~ minute.
4. Remove fish and other ingredients carefully from the pan and place on a serving dish. (Keep the fish in the vindaloo sauce overnight in the fridge in a covered container. Will taste much better).
5. Serve with rice and black lentils or bouillon bredes. Can also be eaten with fresh bread.
6. Fish vindaloo can be stored in the fridge for 3 to 4 days and may be eaten cold.

Octopus Vindaloo
Vindaye Ourite

Ingredients (Serve 4):
- 1 kg octopus,
- 2 medium onions finely sliced,
- 5 garlic cloves quartered lengthwise,
- 1 teaspoon ground cloves,
- 1 teaspoon ground pepper,
- 5 red or green chillies sliced lengthwise,
- 2 tablespoons crushed black mustard seeds,
- 4 level tablespoons turmeric powder,
- 100 ml white vinegar,
- 200 g white flour,
- 3 tablespoons vegetable oil,
- Salt to taste.

Method:
1. Clean the octopus and carefully remove the ink sac. Rub with white flour to thoroughly clean the octopus and wash in running water.
2. Place a deep thick bottom saucepan over high heat. When very hot, use a pair of tongs to lower the octopus into the saucepan. Allow the octopus to contract, lift it out of the pan and lower again. Do this three to four times. The contractions will tenderise the octopus.
3. Add the ground black pepper and ground cloves. Leave the octopus in the pan and move around occasionally to prevent burning. Simmer for 15 to 20 mins or until thoroughly cooked to a pink colour and tender, with the juice almost all evaporated. Retain the remaining juice for later use. Do not overcook. Overcooking will toughen the octopus.
4. Remove the cooked octopus and set aside to cool down. Cut into bite sizes or according to your preference.
5. Heat up 3 tablespoons of vegetable oil in a deep thick bottom saucepan over medium to high heat. Add the onions, garlic cloves and chillies. Stir fry for 1 minute or until the onion slices are just cooked. Do not overcook. Add the crushed black mustard seeds. Add the turmeric powder and mix together. Reduce heat to medium low.
6. Add the octopus pieces and mix until well coated with the turmeric. Cook for 2-3 mins or until the turmeric powder is cooked. Stir occasionally. Add the white vinegar and stir into the mixture. Remove saucepan from heat. Allow the vindaloo to sit for 1-2 hours at room temperature before serving, gently stir mix occasionally.
7. Better still, leave vindaloo in fridge overnight to allow the octopus to marinate. Gently mix well together and warm up in microwave before serving.
8. Serve on rice with black lentils or bouillon brêdes. Also, very tasty when eaten in fresh crusty bread.

Fish with Herbs in Tomato Sauce

Poisson aux Fines Herbes

Ingredients (Serve 3):
- 1 kg whole white flesh fish (cleaned and scaled),
- ¼ cup finely chopped parsley leaves,
- ¼ cup finely chopped coriander leaves,
- 400 g canned finely crushed tomatoes,
- 1 medium onion finely chopped,
- 1 tablespoon freshly crushed garlic,
- 1 tablespoon freshly crushed ginger,
- 1 tablespoon finely chopped thyme leaves,
- ½ cup dry sherry,
- Juice from 1 lemon,
- 4 tablespoons plain tomato paste,
- 2 tablespoons vegetable oil.

Method:
1. Heat oven to 250°C.
2. Cut fish into serving slices such that you can reassemble the whole fish again. Season with salt and pepper to taste.
3. Reassemble whole fish on an oven safe serving dish. Place dish mid position in oven and bake until slightly cooked. Approximately 10-15 mins. Just long enough to evaporate all water from fish. Remove from oven and set aside.
4. Heat oil in frying pan to simmering point.
5. Stir in finely chopped onion, ginger, garlic and thyme. Cook until onion becomes transparent.
6. Add finely crushed tomatoes and tomato paste. Mix well together. Add salt and pepper to taste. Cook until the sauce is well blended and the finely crushed tomatoes are cooked. Gradually the dry sherry little by little.
7. Add half the chopped parsley, half the chopped coriander leaves and lemon juice. Mix well together and continue to cook until the sauce thickens to your preferred consistency. There should be enough sauce to oven bake the fish
8. Lower oven heat to 200°C.
9. Sprinkle the remaining chopped parsley and coriander on the fish. Pour the tomato sauce in a uniform manner so as to distribute evenly.
10. Put the fish back into the oven and cook for 10 mins. Reduce heat to 150°C. Continue to cook until sauce thickens further to your preferred sauce consistency. Be careful not to overcook.
11. Serve immediately and eat with fresh bread and a salad.

Poisson Salé
Salt Fish

Ingredients (Serve 3):
- 250 g poisson salé (alternatively use salt cod) cut into 4 cm pieces,
- 1 onion cut in halves then sliced,
- 2 spring onions finely chopped,
- 3 "piment carri" green chillies sliced,
- 1 tablespoon chopped coriander leaves,
- 4 tablespoons vegetable oil,
- 1 tablespoon chopped coriander leaves to garnish.

Method:
1. Soak and wash alternately the poisson salé (or salt cod) pieces in cold water. Do this at least three times over a half hour period (adjust time depending upon dryness of salt fish). Drain and set aside.
2. Place poisson salé (or salt cod) pieces in a saucepan with enough cold water to cover. Bring to the boil and allow to simmer for about 10 mins until tender, but not too soft. Remove from pan and using a small fork, hand-break into small pieces removing any bones and skin. Set aside.
3. Heat oil in frying pan and fry poisson salé (or salt cod) small pieces until nearly golden brown. Stir in the rest of the ingredients and continue to stir fry until onions become transparent and poisson salé (or salt cod) pieces turn rich golden brown. Do not overcook. Garnish with chopped coriander leaves.
4. Serve hot as an accompaniment for rice with lentilles rouges (noires) or bouillon bredes.

Fish in Sweet and Sour Sauce

Ingredients (Serve 4-5):
- 1.5 kg whole white flesh fish, cleaned and scaled,
- 2 carrots peeled and sliced diagonally,
- 2 tablespoons vegetable oil,
- 1 tablespoon crushed garlic,
- 1 tablespoon crushed ginger,
- 1 medium onion, cut into wedges,
- 3 spring onions cut into 4 cm pieces (keep some for decorating the dish),
- 4 fresh mushrooms, sliced,
- 125 g bamboo shoots, shredded,
- 1 green capsicum,
- 1 beaten egg,
- Cornflour to dredge fish,
- Peanut oil for deep frying fish,
- Sweet and sour sauce, as per recipe,
- Ginger strips.

Sweet and Sour Sauce Ingredients (2 cups):
- ½ cup sugar,
- ½ cup vinegar,
- 4-5 tablespoons light soy sauce,
- 1 tablespoon dark soy sauce,
- 2 tablespoons sherry,
- 1½ tablespoons cornflour blended with ½ cup cold water.

Method for Sweet and Sour Sauce:
1. Combine sugar, vinegar, light soy sauce, dark soy sauce and sherry. Bring to boil over low heat and stir in the blended cornflour to thicken. Remove from heat. This sauce can be used for all sweet and sour sauce dishes. Set aside.

Method for Fish:
1. Score fish lightly on both sides.
2. Parboil carrots in water for 4-5 mins. Cool immediately under cold running water. Drain and put aside. Slice mushrooms. Cut capsicum into strips.
3. Heat 2 tablespoons of peanut oil in wok over medium-high heat. Add garlic and ginger strips, stir fry for 1 minute. Add onion wedges, mushroom strips, parboiled carrots and shredded bamboo shoots. Stir fry for 2-3 mins or until just cooked. Quickly add the spring onions pieces and stir cook for 30 seconds. Remove from heat. Set aside.
4. Heat oil for deep frying fish on high heat. Brush fish inside and out with beaten eggs. Dredge with cornflour. Deep fry for about 6 mins or until golden brown and tender. Remove fish with a skimmer and drain on kitchen paper towels.
5. Warm the sweet and sour sauce.
6. Heat up stir fried ingredients on medium high heat from step 3. Add the sweet and sour sauce and mix thoroughly. Cook for 1 minute or until the sweet and sour sauce is hot.
7. Place fish on a warm serving dish and cover with sweet and sour mixture. Pour sweet and sour sauce with other ingredients on fish. Decorate with the cut spring onions.

King Prawns in Red Sauce
Crevettes Sauce Rouge

Ingredients (Serve 3):
- 12 king prawns (uncooked),
- 1 large onion (finely chopped),
- 500 g can finely crushed red tomatoes,
- vegetable oil,
- 3 garlic cloves crushed,
- 1 teaspoon crushed ginger,
- 2 tablespoons tomato paste,
- 1 sprig of thyme,
- 1 tablespoon of chopped parsley,
- 2 hard boiled eggs sliced,
- 1 tablespoon lemon juice,
- 50 ml dry sherry,
- Salt and pepper to taste.

Method:
1. Shell prawns keeping the tail pieces. Keep the shells. Remove the dorsal vein off the prawns by slightly slicing open the prawns' dorsal part lengthwise. Wash and put aside.
2. Place shells in blender to form a fine paste. Add the paste to 500 ml of water in a saucepan and boil until reduced by half. Stir at intervals. Blend shell paste again and pass through a very fine sieve. Keep the strained liquid.
3. Fry chopped onions in a small quantity of oil until slightly cooked. Add the garlic, ginger and tomato paste. Stir and simmer for 30 seconds or until the chopped onions become transparent. Add the finely crushed tomatoes and the thyme. Mix well together and simmer until the sauce is well blended and the tomatoes cooked. Gradually, add the strained prawn shell sauce and simmer again.
4. Allow the sauce to thicken to your preference. Stir at intervals to avoid burning. Add the lemon juice and dry sherry. Mix well together. Season with salt and pepper to taste. Add the chopped parsley and the prawns. Simmer and cook prawns for 5 mins or until only just cooked. Do not overcook.
5. Serve on a warmed plate and decorate with sliced boiled eggs. Serve with a salad and fresh crispy bread.

Saumon Maddy

Saveur des îles

Plat crée par Henri Maurel, en souvenir de Madeleine Philippe
(Inserted in French to keep the recipe as per original).

Ingredients (par personne):
- 1 pavé de saumon 150 grs,
- 1 échalote hachée finement,
- 3 gousses d'ail hachée finement,
- 1 branche de persil hachée finement,
- 1 branche de coriandre fraîche pour la decoration,
- grains de poivre vert,
- d'huile d'olive,
- 10 grs de beurre,
- 25 cc de vin blanc sec,
- Sel , poivre,
- safran (curcuma) 2 pincées,
- cannelle en poudre,
- zeste de combava râpé (1 petite cuillère à café),
- 1 branche de thym frais,
- 1 carotte,
- 1 petite courgette,
- 2 champignons de Paris ou equivalent,
- 2 tomates-cerises,
- 50 grs de haricots verts ou trois têtes d'asperges vertes,
- 50 grs (une joue) de mangue ½ mûre,
- 100 grs de pomme de terre en quartier (ou en lamelles).

Méthode:
1. <u>Préparation de la mangue:</u>
   Émincer finement en dés de 2 mm de côté (environ), saler délicatement, ajouter le zeste de combava râpé, 1 cuillère à café d'huile d'olive, mélanger, réserver hors chaleur.
2. <u>Cuisson des pommes de terre:</u>
   Les peler et les faire rôtir et dorer à la poêle dans 10 grs de beurre et 1 cuillère à soupe d'huile d'olive, saler et saupoudrer de persil hâché. Réserver au four température 60 ° C.
3. <u>Préparation des légumes:</u>
   Épluchez la partie vert foncé de l'asperge ne conserver que la partie tendre. Glisser l'éplucheur de la pointe vers l'extrémité de la queue. Préparer les haricots verts, en coupant les extrémités et enlever le fil éventuel.
   Dans de l'eau en ébullition, faire cuire les haricots verts ou têtes d'asperges vertes pendant quelques mins, vérifier qu'ils demeurent "croquants". Égoutter et réserver.
   Peler la carotte, puis en découper de très files lamelles dans le sens de la longueur avec un éplucheur de légume ou une mandoline. Faites de même avec les courgettes.
   Laver et enlever le pied des champignons.
   Laver et égoutter les tomates.

4. Cuisson des légumes: feu très doux
   Dans une sauteuse, 1 cuillère à soupe d'huile d'olive, faire fondre la moitié de l'échalote. Ajouter la moitié de l'ail, le thym.
   Faire cuire les haricots verts ou asperges, les lamelles de carotte et de courgette, les 2 tomates-cerises, ajouter sel, poivre et saupoudrer délicatement de cannelle. Tourner délicatement. Les légumes doivent rester croquants.
   Réserver au four température 60° C avec les pommes de terre.
5. Préparation du saumon: feu doux
   Saupoudrer au préalable, chaque face du saumon avec du safran et de la cannelle en poudre et une pincée de sel.
   Dans une poêle anti-adhésive, faire cuire et dorer le saumon sur les deux faces. Placer les grains de poivre vert autour du saumon.
   Dresser le saumon seul dans une assiette et réserver au four température 60 ° C.
6. Remettre la poêle sur le feu ajouter et faire fondre le reste d'échalote et d'ail, puis verser le vin blanc. Avec une spatule en bois, bien décoller le résidu de cuisson et les grains de poivre vert, laisser réduire - ajouter du sel si besoin.
7. Dressage: Positionner le saumon, les légumes, les pommes de terres, la mangue selon votre inspiration, verser la sauce du saumon sur celui-ci, décorer de la branche de coriandre.

Nota: à la place des pommes de terre, se servir de riz ou spaghetti ou autres...

Henri Loulou Maurel de Nice, France

Prawns in Spicy Sauce

Ingredients (Serve 4):
For the prawns:
- 1 kg medium raw prawns- peeled and deveined,
- Juice of ½ lemon,
- 1 teaspoon chilli powder,
- 1 teaspoon turmeric powder,
- 6 crushed garlic cloves,
- 2 medium onions finely chopped,
- 450 g canned crushed tomatoes,
- 1 tablespoon chopped coriander leaves,
- 2 tablespoons vegetable oil,
- Salt to taste.

For the Spicy Sauce:
- 1 teaspoon cumin seeds,
- 1 tablespoon coriander seeds,
- ½ teaspoon black peppercorns,
- 4 cloves,
- 2 cm cinnamon stick,
- Seeds from 4 green cardamom pods,
- 1 kafir lime leaf,
- 6 whole dried red chillies,
- 2.5 cm peeled piece of ginger,
- 6 peeled garlic cloves,
- 1 teaspoon turmeric,
- 2 tablespoons white vinegar.

Method:
1. Wash and dry the prawns on kitchen paper towel. Place in bowl and marinate with the lemon juice, salt, chilli powder and turmeric. Mix well and cover.
2. Blend all the ingredients for the spicy sauce until very smooth. If necessary, add some more vinegar to form the paste. Remove and set aside.
3. Add vegetable oil to a large pan over medium to high heat. When oil starts sizzling, add the garlic and finely chopped onions. Stir fry for a few mins until the onion becomes transparent. Add the spice paste and stir fry for a few mins or until cooked and blended with the onion pieces.
4. Add the finely crushed tomatoes and mix well. Cook and stir at intervals to avoid burning the sauce.
5. Allow the sauce to thicken to your preference. You can adjust by adding little quantities of hot water or by allowing the water in the sauce to evaporate. If the sauce stays watery, you can bind the sauce by dissolving 1 teaspoon of cornflour in cold water, then stir into the sauce.
6. When sauce is ready, add the marinated prawns. Gently stir in the prawns and simmer until just cooked. Adjust the salt seasoning, place in hot serving dish and sprinkle with chopped coriander leaves.
7. Enjoy. Eat with bouillon brèdes or red lentils on rice.

Garlic Cream Prawns

Ingredients (Serve 2 or 4):
- 500 g shelled prawns uncooked,
- 3 tablespoons crushed garlic,
- 3 tablespoons butter,
- 2 cups of cooked rice,
- 250 mm thickened cream,
- 2 tablespoons basil leaves,
- Salt and pepper to taste.

Method:
1. Cook the rice so that it is fluffy and separated.
2. Devein the prawns, wash and set aside on kitchen paper towel to drain.
3. Add the butter to a large non stick saucepan over medium low heat. Add the prawns and stir fry until just cooked. Do not to overcook. Stir in the crushed garlic and gently mix. When the garlic is just starting to brown, pour in the cream and mix. Stir at intervals to prevent the sauce from burning and sticking to the pan. Simmer until the cream thickens to a semi liquid consistency. Be careful not to overcook.
4. Meanwhile, divide the rice into 2 or 4 portions, depending upon whether you serve this as an entrée or main course. Place in suitably sized bowls. Gently compact the rice so that when the cup or bowl is turned upside down on a plate, the rice sticks together. Place the rice on the plate as shown and remove cup or bowl leaving a small rice mound.
5. Remove the prawns from the creamy garlic sauce and carefully place individually on the plates besides the rice mound. Arrange delicately and gently spoon the creamy garlic sauce onto the prawns and partly over the top of the rice.
6. Decorate with the chopped or whole basil leaves to your preference.
7. Enjoy with a dry or sweet white wine.

Octopus Curry
Cari Ourite

Ingredients (Serve 3):
- 1 kg octopus,
- 450 g can of finely chopped tomatoes,
- 3 tablespoons curry powder hot or mild,
- 1 medium onion finely chopped,
- 1 tablespoon crushed garlic,
- 1 tablespoon crushed ginger,
- 1 tablespoon chopped thyme leaves,
- 2 tablespoons roughly chopped curry leaves,
- Small bunch of coriander leaves chopped,
- ½ teaspoon ground black pepper,
- 200 g white flour,
- ½ teaspoon ground cloves,
- 3 tablespoons vegetable oil,
- Finely sliced red or green chillies to taste,
- Salt to taste.

Method:
1. Clean the octopus and carefully remove the ink sac. Rub with white flour to thoroughly clean the octopus and wash in running water.
2. Heat up a deep thick bottom saucepan until very hot. Using a pair of tongs lower the octopus into the saucepan. Allow the octopus to contract, lift it out of the pan and lower again. Do this three to four times. The contraction of the octopus will tenderise the octopus.
3. Add the ground black pepper and ground cloves. Leave the octopus in the pan and move around occasionally to prevent burning. Cook for 15 to 20 mins and simmer until the octopus is thoroughly cooked and tender, with the juice almost all evaporated. Retain the remaining juice for later use. Do not overcook.
4. Remove the cooked octopus and set aside. Using a very sharp knife, cut into bite size pieces. Set aside.
5. Add 3 tablespoons of vegetable oil to a deep thick bottom saucepan over high heat. Add the chopped onion, crushed garlic, crushed ginger and thyme leaves. Cook until the onion pieces are transparent. Stir occasionally to ensure even cooking. Add the crushed tomatoes and stir. Reduce heat to medium high. Simmer for 20-25 mins or until tomato sauce is cooked. Stir occasionally to prevent the sauce from burning. If necessary, add some hot water to stop sauce from thickening. If you like a lot of curry sauce, add some more hot water
6. Add 3 tablespoons of curry powder. Mix well. Cook for 5-10 mins or until the curry powder is well blended into the sauce. Stir at intervals to prevent sauce from burning.
7. Add the chopped curry leaves and half the chopped coriander leaves. Stir well. Cook until the curry sauce separates from the saucepan when stirred. Add salt to taste.

8. Add the octopus pieces and the reserved octopus juice. Mix well ensuring the pieces are well coated with the sauce. Add ¼ to ½ cup of hot water. Mix thoroughly. Simmer on low heat, stirring occasionally for 20-30 mins or until the octopus pieces are just cooked. Do not overcook. You can adjust the sauce to your preference by either adding some hot water or simmering the sauce over low heat to thicken.
9. Transfer to a warm serving dish. Sprinkle with the remaining coarsely chopped coriander leaves. Eat with rice accompanied with a tomato chutney or watercress salad.

Tenderising octopus in hot pan, the Madeleine way

Tropical Carbonara with Prawns

Ingredients (Serve 3):
- 250 g shelled and deveined green prawns,
- 500 g dried egg fettucine pasta,
- 4 eggs,
- 80 g freshly grated parmesan cheese,
- 300 ml fresh cream,
- 1 tablespoon butter,
- 1 tablespoon vegetable oil,
- 2 tablespoons dry sherry,
- 2 tablespoon of virgin olive oil,
- Salt and black pepper to taste.

You can substitute the prawns with other sea foods cut into bite size portions. As usual, do not overcook as this would toughen sea foods such as calamari, pipis or octopus.

Method:
1. Season the prawns with the dry sherry, salt and pepper to taste. Allow to marinate for 10-15 mins.
2. In a frying pan over medium high heat, add 1 tablespoon oil and 1 tablespoon butter. Stir fry the prawns until just cooked. Remove from pan and place over kitchen paper towel to drain surplus oil and butter. Cut into bite size portions or leave whole.
3. In a pot large enough for the fettucine to boil freely, boil sufficient water to cook the pasta over high heat. Add 1 teaspoon of salt. Wait until the water is bubbling freely, then add the fettucine and cook until al dente (just soft but slightly hard or according to instructions on the packet).
4. Whilst the fettucine is cooking, beat the eggs, freshly grated parmesan cheese and the fresh cream in a large bowl.
5. Drain the fettucine pasta when cooked. Put the pasta back in the pot, add a splash of virgin olive oil and mix gently. Beat up the egg, freshly grated parmesan and cream mixture once more and add to the pasta in the pot. Gently mix together. Stir in the prawns and mix gently. Place pot over low to medium heat. Allow to cook over low heat and gently stir mix the pasta with the egg, cream, parmesan cheese and prawn mixture. Gently mix constantly without crushing the pasta. Be careful not to overcook.
6. Allow to cook only until the egg mixture is just done. Serve onto a warm serving dish and sprinkle with some more freshly grated parmesan cheese. Season with black pepper and serve immediately. Enjoy with a seasoned green salad or steamed asparagus.

Crispy Salt and Pepper Squid

Ingredients (Serve 4):
- 500 g cleaned squid tubes,
- ½ cup white flour,
- ½ cup corn flour,
- 1 teaspoon crushed black pepper,
- 1 teaspoon sea salt,
- Peanut oil for deep frying,
- Chilli or garlic sauce to taste.

Method:
1. Cut squid into 3 cm rings. Quarter rings lengthwise. Finish with quarter circle curls about 3 cm long. Alternatively, you can cut squid tube and tentacles to your preference. You can also partly cut diamond shaped patterns on the outer part of the squid pieces.
2. Whisk the flour, cornflour, crushed black pepper, sea salt with just enough cold water to form a batter that would just allow the squid pieces to be dipped in and retain a thin layer of coating when removed from the batter.
3. Heat oil in a saucepan that would allow small batches of the battered squid pieces to be deep fried.
4. When oil starts to sizzle, dip squid pieces into batter one by one, wipe off excess batter against side of bowl. Gently lower battered pieces of the squid into the oil. Cook for about 2 mins or until light golden brown. Do not overcrowd the saucepan.
5. Remove fried pieces of battered squid with a slotted spoon and drain on kitchen paper towel placed on an oven rack.
6. Serve these delicious morsels dipped in freshly made red chilli or garlic sauce.
7. Enjoy.

Crystal Prawns

Ingredients (Serve 2):
- 250 g uncooked prawns, peeled and deveined,
- 2 egg whites,
- 1 tablespoon Chinese wine or dry sherry,
- Pinch of sugar,
- 1 teaspoon of salt,
- Pinch of freshly ground white pepper,
- 60 g cornflour,
- 600 ml vegetable oil,
- 2.5 cm piece root ginger, peeled and finely chopped,
- 2 spring onions, finely chopped,
- 1 cup stir fry vegetables in bite size pieces,
- 25 g frozen peas, lightly boiled and drained,
- 2 tablespoons chicken stock,
- Few drops of sesame oil.

Method:
1. Put the prawns into a bowl with the egg whites, Chinese wine, sugar, 1/2 teaspoon salt, white pepper, and 40 g of the cornflour. Mix together thoroughly.
2. Add the vegetable oil to a wok over low heat. Add the prawns and stir fry gently for about 2 mins, then remove from the oil and drain on kitchen paper towel. Stir fry the vegetable pieces until cooked. Remove and set aside over kitchen paper towel.
3. Pour off most of the oil, leaving enough to coat the bottom of the wok, add the finely chopped ginger and spring onions. Stir fry for a few seconds, then add the peas and the stir fry vegetables, wine, white pepper, remaining cornflour dissolved in the chicken stock. Stir gently to mix well.
4. Put the prawns back into the wok to reheat with the sauce. Stir gently to distribute the prawns evenly within the remaining ingredients.
5. Pour into a heated serving dish and sprinkle the sesame oil over the top.
6. Serve immediately.

Bombay Duck Sauté

Sauté de Bombli

Ingredients (Serve 4):
- 10 dried bombay ducks,
- 3 tomatoes finely chopped,
- 2 medium eggplants diced,
- 1 large onion finely sliced,
- 1 teaspoon finely crushed garlic,
- 1 tablespoon turmeric powder,
- 1 tablespoon ground coriander seeds,
- 1 tablespoon red chilli flakes,
- 2 tablespoons vegetable oil,
- Salt to taste.

Method:
1. Soak the dried bombay ducks in cold water for 20 mins. Remove from water and wash under running cold water. With a sharp knife or scissors, remove the head, tail and any fins. Cut into two or three pieces. Set aside.
2. Wash the eggplants. Remove the stem and cut into 1 cm cubes.
3. Mix the turmeric with the ground coriander seeds and red chilli flakes.
4. In a saucepan or wok, over medium to low heat stir fry the finely sliced onions and crushed garlic in the vegetable oil, until the onion slices become transparent. Add the turmeric, ground coriander seeds and red chilli flakes. Mix well.
5. Add the finely chopped tomatoes and stir into the mixture. Cover and allow the tomatoes to cook for 2 to 3 mins over medium to high heat. Add the eggplant cubes. Stir in, cover and cook for another 3 to 5 mins. Check and stir at intervals to avoid burning the ingredients. If there is not enough water, add a little quantity of hot water. Cook the eggplant pieces to your preference.
6. Uncover, add the bombay duck pieces and stir gently. Cover and simmer for 10-15 mins. Gently stir at intervals. If there is not enough water, add a little quantity of hot water to form a little bit of sauce. You can also thicken the sauce to your preference by uncovering the saucepan and allowing the sauce to simmer and reduce.
7. Season with salt to taste.

Madeleine Philippe with her fans in Melbourne talking Mauritian cuisine

Desserts - Sweets and Cakes

It is an established custom for Mauritians to serve a dessert after evening meals. The word "dessert" originated from the French word "desservir", meaning "to clear the table". Desserts conclude dinners and usually consist of sweet foods, but may include cheeses, nuts and other savoury items. Generally, cakes, tarts, cookies, gelatins, pastries, ice-creams, pies, puddings, custards and sweet soups are served. Sweets are also shared during religious celebrations such as Diwali,

The diversity of Mauritian cuisine has generated an incredible collection of sweets and cakes. The French introduced their rich savoir-faire in pastries, mousses, puddings, cakes and tarts. Sharing a crème brulée, mille feuilles, tarte tatin, éclair au chocolat, charlotte, napolitaine, pot de crème or crêpe suzette after dinner becomes a very special moment. The napolitaine, whilst recognized as a truly Mauritian delicacy must have originated from a clever Mauritian pastry chef, creating the poor man's version of the French macaron.

Your first experience in Mauritius with an Indian dessert would have been with sweets made up of deep fried flour and sugar. During Diwali, the Hindu festival of lights and an annual celebration of good conquering evil, Indian sweets or mithai are served as both a religious offering and celebratory dessert. And they are usually very sweet. Mixed with flour, sugar and often milk products, sweets are flavoured with traditional toppings such as pistachios, almonds and saffron. Other popular desserts served include jalebi, which is a deep-fried swirly dough, drenched in sugar syrup and orange food colouring and gulab jamun, which is deep-fried dough balls also drenched in sugar syrup. Similarly in Tamil cuisine, desserts and sweets are the finale to a sumptuous meal served on special occasions. Payasams, halwas, burfis, appams and adirasam are popular desserts.

Muslims in Mauritius celebrate the Eid festival with sweet vermicelli noodles also known as seviyan, that are either served dry, or in a milk pudding called sheer khurma. Other sweets shared with family, friends and neighbours include barfi, halwa, gulab jamun, rasgoolah, ras malai, safeda, naan katai and sola. During Ramadan, the Islamic holy fasting month, each day the fast is broken at sun down with an array of special desserts. In the Islamic nikah marriage ceremony, the bride and groom share a piece of sweet fruit.

Dessert is not served at Chinese meals in the same way as in other cultures. Generally there is no separate part of a meal that is reserved for eating dessert. However, Chinese cuisine includes many dessert foods, either as part of a meal or as a snack. The sweets include Chinese cotton candy, known in Mauritius as calamindas. It is made of spun sugar and is very sticky. This is sold at street corners or from food stalls in Mauritius, very popular with children. Jellies are also very much part of Chinese desserts. The most famous jelly is the grass black jelly soup sold within the Chinese community compound near the Champ de Mars racing complex in Port Louis, Mauritius. This jelly is made by boiling the stalks and leaves of a mint family plant in potassium carbonate. This jelly can be cut into cubes or other forms, and then mixed with syrup to produce a drink or dessert thought to have cooling (yin) properties, which makes it typically consumed during hot weather. Egg tarts are also very popular. It is also claimed that the "glaçons rapés" sold in Mauritius is of Chinese origin, called "baobing". Shaved ice is compressed around a paddle pop stick and sprinkled with colourful sweet syrups.

Banana Fritters

Beignets de Bananes

Ingredients (Serve 4):
- 2 medium size bananas (ripe but still firm),
- 2 tablespoons lime juice,
- 3 tablespoons white rum or whisky,
- 3 tablespoons caster sugar,
- 250 g self raising white flour,
- 1 egg,
- 200 ml milk,
- 25 g butter,
- Salt to taste,
- Vegetable oil for deep frying,
- White caster sugar.

Method:
1. Carefully peel bananas and cut into two. Place in a bowl with the lime juice and white rum or whisky. Mix well together without damaging the banana halves. Sprinkle with 2 tablespoons of white caster sugar. Turn the banana around from time to time. Soak for 20 mins.
2. Melt the butter and set aside to cool. Beat the egg in a bowl with the milk.
3. In another bowl, add the self raising white flour, ½ teaspoon salt and 1 tablespoon of white caster sugar. Mix well. Slowly pour in the egg and milk mixture, stirring constantly with a spatula. Add the melted butter. Whisk well until the batter is smooth.
4. Add sufficient oil in a saucepan on medium hot for deep frying. Wipe the banana pieces with kitchen paper towel to absorb all moisture and dip in the batter two at a time. When the oil is very hot but not smoking, add the battered banana and fry on all sides. Remove from oil when golden brown and drain on kitchen paper towel.
5. When the fritters are ready, stack them on a dish with some ice cream and serve at once, sprinkled with sugar.

Crème Renversée
Baked Custard

Ingredients (Serve 4):
- 250 g white sugar,
- 2 tablespoons vanilla essence,
- 4 tablespoons water,
- 450 ml milk,
- 250 ml double whipped cream,
- 6 eggs,
- 2 egg yolks.

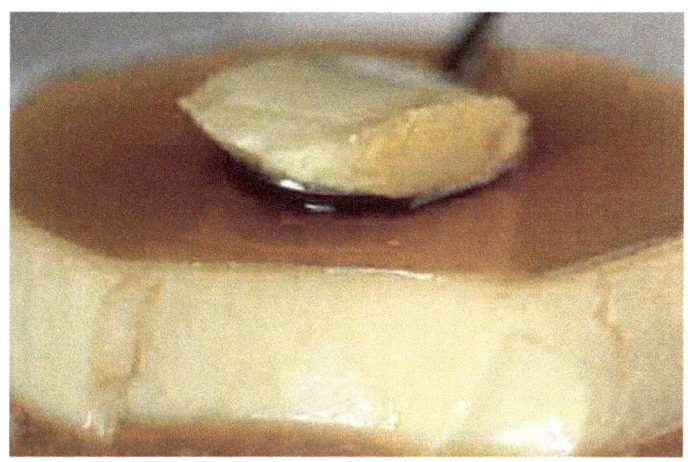

Method:
1. Place 175 g of sugar in a heavy saucepan with the water. Mix and bring to the boil over high heat, stirring all the time to dissolve the sugar. Then boil without stirring until a dark caramel syrup is formed. Immediately pour the caramel into a 1 litre soufflé dish. Be careful with the syrup as it is very hot.
2. Hold the dish with kitchen gloves and swirl to coat the bottom and sides of the soufflé dish. Set aside, to cool and harden.
3. Preheat oven to 170°C.
4. Add the milk, cream and vanilla essence to a saucepan and bring to the boil over medium heat, stirring frequently. Remove pan from heat, cover and set aside for 15-20 mins.
5. Place the 6 whole eggs and 2 egg yolks in a bowl with the remaining sugar and whisk for 2 - 3 mins until smooth and creamy. Whisk in the hot milk and carefully place the mixture into the caramel lined dish. Cover with foil.
6. Place the dish in a deep roasting oven tin. Pour enough boiling water into the roasting tin to come halfway up the outside of the custard dish. Bake the custard mixture for approximately 40 - 45 mins until a knife inserted 2 to 5 cms into the custard comes out clean (the custard should be just set). Remove from the roasting tin and allow to cool for at least 30 mins, then chill in the fridge overnight.
7. Carefully run a knife around the edge of the dish to loosen the custard. Cover the dish with an upside down serving plate and holding both tightly, invert the dish and plate together. Slowly lift one edge of the dish, allowing the caramel to run over the sides, then slowly lift off the dish.

Gâteau Coco

Coconut Sweets

Ingredients (Make 15):
- 1 cup (250 ml) water,
- 1½ cups (375 g) white sugar,
- Pinch of salt,
- 1 teaspoon vanilla extract,
- 1-2 drops food colouring,
- 2 cups (125 g) flaked or shredded coconut.

Method:
1. Place the water in a medium saucepan and add the sugar and salt. Stir and boil on medium heat until the mixture thickens like syrup.
2. Add the vanilla extract and food colouring. If desired, divide the mixture and add different colours to each portion. Mix in the flaked or shredded coconut and stir until all the syrup is absorbed.
3. Drop teaspoonfuls onto a tray lined with a baking sheet. Allow 5 cm space between each piece. Serve when cool.
4. Close your eyes and enjoy. Imagine yourself back in la boutique Chinois Maurice.

Gâteau Patates

Sweet potato cakes

Ingredients (Make 15-20):
- 1 kg sweet potatoes,
- 4 tablespoons white flour,
- 250 g grated coconut,
- 250 g white sugar,
- 1 teaspoon vanilla essence,
- Oil for deep frying.

Method:
1. Wash the sweet potatoes and boil until sufficiently cooked for mashing. Test by pricking with a fork. Peel the sweet potatoes and mash the flesh together until a uniformly smooth paste is obtained. Set aside to cool.
2. Mix grated coconut with vanilla essence and sugar. Cover with cling wrap and set aside.
3. Sprinkle the sweet potatoes with the flour and work to a smooth dough. Add some more flour, if necessary.
4. Make 30 dough balls. Roll individual balls into flat rounds, half cm thick and 6 cms in diameter.
5. Place a little of the coconut filling in the centre of each round. Fold into semicircular shapes and seal edges with the back of a fork.
6. Deep fry over a medium heat until light brown.
7. Remove and place on folded kitchen paper towels to drain any excess oil.
8. Will keep for a few days if placed in an air tight container.

Poutou
Steam ground rice cakes

Ingredients (Serve 5):
- 2 cups coarse rice flour,
- ½ -1 cup grated coconut,
- ¼ cup sugar,
- 2 teaspoons salt,
- 1 cup hot water to sprinkle.

Method:
1. In a large bowl, add salt and sugar to the rice flour and mix thoroughly by hand.
2. Sprinkle water on the flour. Be careful in the mixing. The right combination of water and rice powder gives the best result.
3. Mix thoroughly by hand. The puttu mix should have a bread crumb consistency and not form a dough. To check if the right amount of water is added, take some of the mixture in your hand and clasp it within the palm. If the mixture holds together, it has the right consistency. If it is still powdery and falls off, add some more water. If too watery, add some more flour.
5. In a puttu maker add 2 cups water to the bottom vessel of the puttu maker and simmer till hot. Place the round perforated disc with holes inside the puttu maker such that it fits well at the bottom of the mould.
6. Place 1 layer of grated coconut at the bottom of the puttu maker. Carefully and slowly add about 6 tablespoons of the puttu mix without compacting, followed by another layer of grated coconut. Layer again with 6 tablespoons of puttu mix and another layer of grated coconut. Finish off with 1 layer of grated coconut on the top. Place the lid over the puttu mould and place the mould over the bottom vessel.
7. Steam it for 10 mins. Must be eaten hot.

Poutou (Puttu)
Steamer Method

Ingredients (Serve 6):
- 2 cups coarse rice or puttu flour,
- ¾ cup grated coconut,
- ½ cup sugar,
- ½ teaspoon salt,
- Water as required.

Method:
1. Dry roast the rice flour in a pan for 2-3 mins. Take care not to burn the flour. If puttu flour is used, this roasting step is not necessary.
2. Add the grated coconut, salt and sugar to the rice/puttu flour. Mix well. Add water in little quantities and mix using the fingers, until a crumbly mix is obtained.
3. To check if the right amount of water is added, take some of the mixture in your hand and clasp it within the palm. If the mixture holds together, it has the right consistency. If it is still powdery and falls off, add some more water. If too watery, add some more flour.
4. Fill small cake moulds with the puttu pastry, using your fingers to press the puttu into the moulds so that the particles are held tightly together.
5. Invert the mould and tap slightly. The mixture should come out easily in one piece.
6. With care, transfer the shaped puttus into a steamer.
7. If using a microwave steamer, steam for 3 mins.
8. If using a stove top steamer, steam for 5 mins.

Napolitaines

Very popular pastry cake in Mauritius

Ingredients (Serve 6):
- 250 g sifted white flour,
- 175 g margarine or butter,
- Raspberry jam (about 50 g),
- 2 cups icing sugar,
- 1-2 tablespoons rum,
- 2 drops red food colouring,
- 1 teaspoon vanilla or other flavouring extract,
- 5-6 tablespoons milk or water.

Method:
1. Rub margarine or butter into the flour and work into a soft dough. (Use a little more margarine or butter if necessary but do not use water). Sprinkle with the rum to give it that special Mauritian flavour.
2. Wrap up the dough in plastic wrap and set aside in a cool place for 30 mins.
3. Preheat oven to 180°C.
4. Roll dough out on a lightly floured surface to a thickness of about 4 mm. Cut into small rounds about 5 cms in diameter. Re-roll trimmings and cut more rounds.
5. Place on baking paper in a flat baking tray, in a mid oven position. Bake until cooked but still "beige" in colour, not brown. Remove from oven and set aside to cool.
6. When cool, spread jam over half of the biscuit rounds and cover with the remaining ones.
7. Mix together the powdered sugar, vanilla and milk or water using a fork or a spoon. This icing should still be fairly thick, but it should drizzle easily. A bit of drizzled icing should free flow. Add food coloring sparingly at this stage and blend.
8. Put the icing into a clean squeeze bottle using a funnel. The icing should be thin enough to pour easily. If necessary, add milk or water 1 tablespoon at a time until a thin, pourable consistency is reached.
9. Place the biscuits on a wire baking tray. Individually pour the icing over the biscuits. Any excess icing will drop through thus ensuring that the biscuits are fully coated. Place in a warm open environment and allow the icing to harden.

Bread Pudding

Very popular pudding in Mauritius

Ingredients (Serve 5):
- 680 g stale bread (Pain baguette is ideal),
- 100 g melted butter,
- ½ cup milk,
- ½ cup water (room temperature),
- ½ cup dried sultanas,
- ½ cup rum or whisky,
- 4 tablespoons white sugar,
- 2 tablespoons orange rind grated,
- 2 eggs,
- 3 tablespoons natural vanilla essence.

Method:
1. Soak the sultanas in the rum or whisky.
2. Soak the bread in the milk and water for 30 mins. Break into small pieces. Add the butter, orange rind, eggs and 2½ tablespoons of natural vanilla essence. Hand work the mixture and add more water if necessary to form a firm and smooth dough, but not watery.
3. Add the sultanas and rum (or whisky) and work into the mixture until well distributed.
4. Pre heat oven to 200°C. Have an earthenware or glass pudding bowl ready to receive the caramel coating.
5. Place 4 tablespoons sugar into a medium saucepan, add 2 tablespoons water and ½ tablespoon of the natural vanilla essence. Mix well.
6. Place the saucepan pan over low heat. Stir slowly until the sugar dissolves completely and the mixture starts to bubble. Continue to stir until the hot caramel turns golden brown. Quickly remove saucepan and pour the caramel immediately into an oven safe earthenware or glass bowl. With the help of a heat resistant spatula, spread half way up around the sides.
7. Transfer the bread pudding dough into the bowl and distribute evenly until surface is level all round.
8. Place bowl in oven (middle position) and allow to cook until the bread pudding turns golden brown on top. Reduce oven temperature to 160°C. Test the pudding mixture at intervals with a cake skewer. When the skewer comes out clean, the pudding is cooked. Remove from oven and set aside to cool.
9. When thoroughly cold, use a flat knife to detach the pudding from around the sides of the bowl.
10. Place an upside down serving plate on top of the oven dish. Carefully invert the bowl and the serving plate together in one go.
11. Slowly separate the bowl from the bread pudding. Cut into slices with a sharp knife.

Poudine Maïs

Polenta Pudding

Ingredients (Serve 6):
- 300 g of corn meal (polenta),
- 3-4 tablespoons white sugar (or adjust to taste),
- 500 ml full cream milk,
- 1 teaspoon natural vanilla essence,
- 2-3 tablespoons sultanas (or to taste),
- 3-4 tablespoons finely grated coconut,
- 1 tablespoon butter.

Method:
1. Butter a shallow baking tray (1.5 litre).
2. Place the corn meal in cold water (quantity just to cover the corn meal) and skim off the floating bits.
3. Place the corn meal and cold water mixture in a deep thick bottomed saucepan, over medium low heat.
4. When the cornflour and water start to bubble, add the milk, sugar, sultanas, butter and vanilla essence. Mix well.
5. Simmer and stir constantly to avoid burning the corn flour. Cook until all the liquid has been absorbed by the corn flour mix.
6. Remove from heat and pour into the buttered baking tray. Sprinkle the finely grated coconut over the top.
7. Place in the fridge and allow to set.
8. Cut into serving pieces and use a flat spatula to spoon out.

Vermicelli Pudding

Ingredients (Serve 5):
- 200 g angel hair vermicelli broken into 10 cm lengths,
- 350 g caster sugar,
- 4 tablespoons butter,
- 10 lightly crushed cardamom pods,
- 2 tablespoons flaked almonds,
- 500 ml whole milk,
- 400 ml water,
- 1 tablespoon lemon juice,
- 2 tablespoons slivered pistachios,
- Butter for coating baking tray.

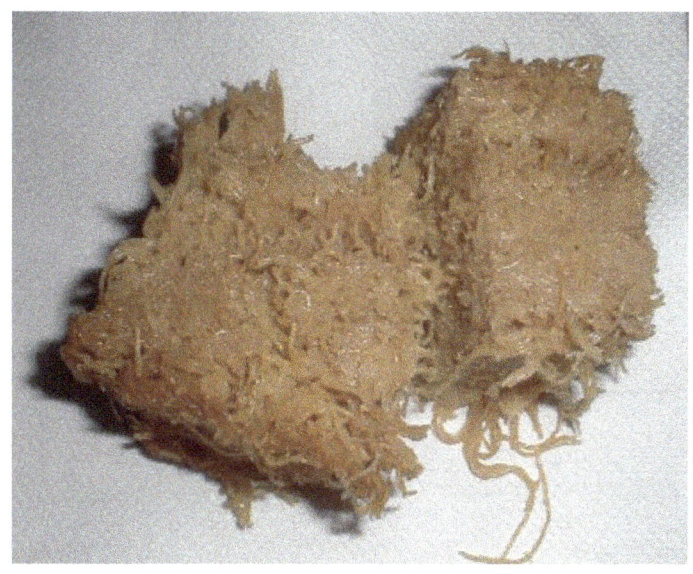

Method:
1. Butter a shallow rectangular baking tray (1.5 litre).
2. Melt the sugar in a pan with the water. Bring to the boil. Remove from heat and set aside.
3. Melt the butter in a heavy bottomed pan over medium heat (a wok is ideal as it allows the water to evaporate quickly). Add the broken vermicelli and the crushed cardamom pods to the melted butter. Carefully mix well using a wok spatula (or similar) without crushing the vermicelli.
4. Fry over medium heat, stir at regular intervals to prevent the vermicelli from burning. Once the vermicelli turns light brown, add the sugar syrup. Carefully mix together.
5. Continue to cook over low heat. Sir at intervals to prevent the vermicelli from sticking to the pan. As the water evaporates, the vermicelli will stiffen and the butter will separate.
6. At this point, add the milk and bring to the boil. Stir in the lemon juice. The milk will be quickly absorbed by the vermicelli. Continue to cook for a minute or two. Add the flaked almond pieces and slivered pistachios. Continue to cook for another minute.
7. Pour into the buttered baking tray.
8. Serve hot or cold. Best served luke warm.
9. You can also cut the cold vermicelli pudding into rectangular pieces.

Oundé

Delicious Ground Rice Savouries

Ingredients (Serve 4):
- 125 g ground rice,
- 3 tablespoons sugar,
- 1 cup of water,
- Vanilla essence or cardamon powder,
- 4-5 tablespoons finely grated coconut.

Method:
1. Add the ground rice to a heavy frying pan and place the pan over a medium heat. Stir the rice and keep roasting until it turns a few shades darker. Remove from heat and set aside.
2. Make a syrup by boiling together the water and sugar. Flavour with either vanilla essence or cardamon powder.
3. When sugar is dissolved, pour in the roasted ground rice and keep stirring until all moisture evaporates and mixture leaves the sides of the pan. Remove from heat.
4. When still warm, form into small balls and roll into the grated coconut.

Banana Tarts
Tartes Bananes

Ingredients (Make 10):
- 200 g white flour,
- 140 g butter or margarine,
- Water (just enough to obtain a smooth mix),
- 8 ripe bananas (medium size),
- 4 tablespoons white sugar,
- 10 tartlets tins.

Method:
1. Preheat oven to 200°C.
2. In a bowl, work together the flour and the butter or margarine until crumbly.
3. Add water sparingly and work dough to obtain a smooth mix without being watery. Place in cling wrap and rest for 30 mins.
4. Crush the bananas and mix with the sugar. Cook over low heat, stir constantly and cook until dark brown. Remove from saucepan and set aside to cool.
5. Roll pastry ½ cm thick and cut into thin rounds to fit the tartlets tins.
6. Butter the tartlet tins and firmly line with pastry rounds. Cut away surplus with sharp knife.
7. Fill pastry with banana mixture.
8. Roll over the remaining pastry, cut into long strips and place to form a criss-cross pattern on all tarts.
9. Brush the tops with milk and bake in oven at 200°C for about 15 mins or until baked golden.

Madeleines

Ingredients (Make 10-12):
- 75 g (½ cup) plain white flour),
- 75 g (½ cup) caster sugar),
- 2 eggs at room temperature,
- 1 teaspoon honey,
- 1 teaspoon vanilla essence,
- 1 teaspoon baking powder,
- 100 g melted butter,
- Madeleine baking tray,
- Butter for baking tray.

Method:
1. Preheat oven to 200°C.
2. Blend together the eggs, honey and vanilla essence, until sugar is fully dissolved. Do not over blend. Set aside.
3. Sift the flour into a mixing bowl with the baking powder. Mix well to distribute the baking powder. Fold in the egg mixture until well combined and smooth without any lumps. Add the melted butter and fold through. Refrigerate for 20-30 mins to firm up the batter.
4. Butter the baking tray to prevent the Madeleines from sticking to the moulds.
5. Spoon and spread the batter into the moulds up to ⅔ depth to allow room for the batter to rise.
6. Bake for 6-10 mins or until the batter has risen (a skewer inserted into the cake comes out clean). Don't overbake and burn the Madeleines.
7. Remove from the oven when a light golden brown. Allow to cool. Carefully tip from the moulds by turning upside down.
8. Enjoy. Perfect with a cup of tea or coffee. Best eaten on the same day.

Massepain

Ingredients (Serve 5-6):
- 175 g caster sugar,
- 175 g plain flour,
- 2 teaspoons baking powder,
- Pinch of salt,
- 175 g softened butter,
- 3 eggs at room temperature,
- Caster sugar for sprinkling,
- 20 x 10 cm or 20 cm dia cake tin.

Method:
1. Butter the base and sides of the cake tin. Line the base with non-stick baking paper. Butter the sides and bottom of the baking tin again. Lightly sprinkle with sugar and remove any excess sugar.
2. Preheat the oven to 180°C.
3. Sift the flour, salt and the baking powder together. Mix together and set aside.
4. In another mixing bowl, beat the butter (preferably with an electric mixer) until creamy. Add the sugar and beat for 5 mins until very light and fluffy. Add the eggs, one at a time. Whisk the mixture until well blended.
5. Fold the flour mixture gently into the butter mixture in three stages. Mix well. Pour the mixture into the buttered cake tin and make sure that no air bubbles are caught by gently tapping the cake tin.
6. Bake the cake mixture for 35-40 mins, in a low oven position to avoid overcooking the crust, until the top is golden and springs back when gently pressed. Alternatively, use a skewer to test the cake. If the skewer comes out clean after being pushed into the cake, the cake is cooked.
7. Transfer to a wire rack and set aside to cool for at least 10 mins. Carefully remove the cake from the tin and cool for a further 30 mins.
8. Remove the baking paper. Cut into slices or wedges.

Colodent
Peanut Brittle

Ingredients (Serve 4-5):
- 300 g roasted peanuts (without shells),
- 500 g white sugar,
- ¼ cup water,
- Greased open tray or marble cutting board.

Method:
1. Remove the skins from the roasted peanuts.
2. Add the sugar and water to a heavy saucepan and slowly bring to the boil over low heat. Stir with a wooden spoon constantly until the syrup starts to thicken.
3. Add the peanuts in two half portions. Keep stirring. As soon as the mixture starts to caramelise to a golden colour, remove from heat and continue to stir.
4. Pour into a greased oven tray or onto a marble cutting board.
5. Allow to cool before cutting into pieces.

Gâteau Coster
Besan Barfi

Ingredients (Serve 4-5):
- 1 cup (250 ml) besan flour,
- 1 cup (250 ml) raw sugar (use palm sugar for caramel flavour),
- ½ cup ghee,
- ½ teaspoon cardamom powder,
- ½ teaspoon cinnamon powder,
- Baking tray 15 cm x 20 cm x 2 cm.

Optional:
Grated coconut to taste.

Method:
1. Melt the ghee and set aside. Use the microwave for 20 secs to melt the ghee.
2. Lightly oil the baking tray.
3. Toast the besan flour in a non stick pan on low heat. Gently stir all the time until you can smell a nutty aroma.
4. Add the ghee to the pan and mix with the besan flour until smooth. Add the sugar and a small quantity of grated coconut (optional). The grated coconut should just add another taste to the burfi without taking over. Mix together and allow the sugar to melt. Reduce the heat if the mixture gets too hot and starts burning.
5. When the mixture is smooth and reaches a semi liquid consistency, remove from heat and stir in the cardamom and cinnamon powders. Mix well.
6. Pour the mixture into the oiled baking tray.
7. Set aside to cool down. Cut into squares or rectangles.

Kulfi Ice Cream

Ingredients (Serve 4-5):
- 4 x 375 ml cans of evaporated milk,
- 300 g of caster sugar,
- 50 g finely chopped blanched almonds,
- 50 g finely chopped pistachios.

Method:
1. Add the milk and caster sugar to a large saucepan over medium low heat.
2. Warm up the milk until all the caster sugar is thoroughly dissolved. Stir constantly to avoid burning.
3. When the sugar is completely dissolved, add the finely chopped pistachios and blanched almonds. Mix together.
4. Place the mixture in 'dariole' or ice cream moulds. Make sure that the finely chopped almonds and pistachios are equally distributed. Place in the freezer overnight to firm up.
5. Un-mould by dipping the base of each mould in warm water.
6. Turn out onto serving plates.

Puits d'Amour

Ingredients (Serve 4-5):
(Pastry):
- 200 g white flour,
- 1 tablespoon water (adjust quantity to obtain a pastry that holds together well),
- 100 g almond flour,
- 90 g softened butter,
- 1 egg yolk,
- 1 tablespoon fine sugar.

Custard Filling (Crème Pâtissière):
- 2 egg yolks,
- 50 g caster sugar,
- 25 g plain flour,
- 1 cup milk,
- ½ vanilla pod (cut in half),
- 6 - 9 cm tartlets tins.

Method:
1. **Making the pastry:**
   Sift the pastry flour and almond flour into a mixing bowl. Mix well. Make a well in the middle. Add the egg yolk, sugar, water and softened butter. Mix with the fingers without heavy kneading until a consistent mix is obtained. Add a little more water to ensure that pastry will stick well together. Collect into a pastry ball. Wrap in plastic wrap and keep in fridge for 1 hour.
2. Preheat oven to 180°C
3. **Custard filling:**
   Heat milk without boiling, add vanilla pod. Mix egg yolk and sugar in a large mixing bowl. Add flour and mix. Pour the hot milk little by little over the egg, sugar and flour mixture. Mix well.
4. Transfer into a small saucepan and cook on medium heat until the mixture thickens stirring continuously (about 1 to 2 mins). Be careful not to overcook. Remove while still slightly flowing to avoid custard getting too thick. Transfer into a mixing bowl. Whisk well and allow to cool.
5. Lightly butter the tartlet tins. Roll the pastry into a sheet about 3 mm thick. Using a tartlet tin as a guide, cut out six rounds, re-rolling trimmings as necessary. Use the pastry rounds to line the tins, then pass the rolling pin over the top of the tins to cut off the excess pastry. Prick the bases with a fork.
6. Line the pastry cases with foil and add a layer of dry beans such as kidney beans (alternatively use crumpled aluminium foil instead of beans). Bake for 15 mins until slightly dry and set, then remove the foil and beans and continue baking for a further 5 mins or until slightly golden. Cool on a wire rack.
7. Spoon the custard into the casings without overfilling. Top with a slight trickle of golden syrup or sprinkle with coarse white sugar.

Carrot Halwa

Ingredients (Serve 6):
- 1 kg carrots grated,
- 600 ml milk,
- 110 g white sugar,
- 85 g brown sugar,
- 1 teaspoon ground green cardamoms,
- 1 teaspoon butter,
- 30 g slivered almonds,
- 40 g raisins,
- 40 g walnuts chopped,
- 1 teaspoon ground cloves,
- 1 teaspoon ground nutmeg,
- 1 teaspoon ground cinnamon.

Method:
1. Wash, peel and coarsely grate the carrots. Combine the carrots and milk in a pan, bring to boil, reduce heat to medium low and cook for 20-25 mins, stirring continuously. Cook until the mixture is nearly dry.
2. Add the white sugar, brown sugar and half the cardamom. Mix together and continue stirring. Cook for 10-12 mins. Remove pan from heat and set aside.
3. Heat butter in a pan over medium low heat, fry the slivered almonds until golden. Stir in the carrot mixture together with the raisins, walnuts, cardamom mix and the rest of the spices, with the exception of half the ground cardamom. Cook until the mixture begins to separate from the sides.
4. Serve hot, garnished with the remaining ground cardamom. This is a traditional Indian sweet served during festivals.

Carrot Halwa
Microwave Alternative

Ingredients (Serve 6):
1. 2 cups freshly grated carrots,
2. ½ cup skim milk powder,
3. 1 cup sugar,
4. ¼ teaspoon ground cardamom,
5. ¼ cup thickened cream,
6. Raisins, fried chopped walnuts and slivered almonds for garnishing.

Method:
1. Place the freshly grated carrot in a microwave safe bowl and cook on high for 7-8 mins.
2. Remove and add milk powder, sugar, thickened cream and cardamom powder. Mix well.
3. Return to the microwave and cook on high for another 7-8 mins.
4. Remove. Serve either hot or cold after garnishing with raisins, walnuts and almonds.
5. Can also be set in the fridge for real "Halwa" consistency.

Crêpes douces by Alain Aliphon (page 32)

Alooda Glacée
Cold Falooda Drink

Ingredients (Serve 5):
- 2 tablespoons basil seeds,
- 1 cup chopped agar agar strips,
- 1 litre very cold milk,
- 500 ml water,
- Crushed ice,
- Vanilla essence,
- Almond essence,
- Sugar to taste,
- Food colouring.

Note:
If you cannot get agar agar strips, use set gelatine jelly, grated or chopped into small pieces.

Method:
1. Place the basil seeds in a flat dish and remove any impurities.
2. Chop the agar agar strips into ½ cm pieces. Separate the strips.
3. Soak the basil seeds and chopped agar agar strips in ½ litre of water each overnight, in separate containers. Alternatively, soak in luke warm water until the seeds are well swollen and the agar agar strips are soft to the touch.
4. Pre-cool your serving glasses in the fridge.
5. Sweeten the cold milk to taste. Pour the sweetened milk into glasses until ¾ filled. Add 2 drops of the almond or vanilla essence and 2 drops of your favourite food colour in each glass.
6. Mix well together. Add 3 - 4 tablespoons of the swollen basil seeds and softened agar agar strips (alternatively the gelatine jelly pieces) in each glass. Mix well together. Top with crushed ice.
7. Close your eyes and imagine yourself in Port Louis market. Give the glass contents a quick stir. Slowly sip and enjoy the alooda.

Gâteau Moutails
Jalebis

Ingredients (Serve 5-6):
For the batter:
- 450 g plain flour,
- ½ teaspoon salt,
- 225 g natural yoghurt at room temperature,
- 1 tablespoon brown sugar,
- 25 g dried yeast,
- Warm water as required,
- Vegetable oil for frying,

For the syrup:
- 10 cardamons,
- 10 cloves,
- 8 cms cinnamon stick,
- 450 g brown sugar.

Method:
For the batter:
1. Sift the flour and salt into a large bowl. Gradually add the yoghurt and a little warm water to form a batter, similar to double cream consistency.
2. Add 1 tablespoon brown sugar, sprinkle with the dried yeast. Stir batter to a uniform consistency. Cover with a clean tea towel and place in a warm place for 6 hours to allow yeast to work.
3. Stir batter again after 6 hours. Set aside.

For the syrup:
4. Bring 1 litre water to boil in a heavy based saucepan together with the cardamons, cloves and cinnamon stick. Lower the heat, add the sugar and stir until dissolved. Increase the heat and boil rapidly, without stirring, until the volume has reduced by half to a heavy syrup. Remove from heat but keep warm.

Making the jalebis:
5. Place the batter into a piping bag (used for cake decorating) with a very small opening, about 3 mm.
6. Add vegetable oil to a deep frying pan over medium high heat. Oil is ready for making the jalebis when a small spoonful of batter immediately starts to sizzle and float to the surface when dropped into the pan.
7. Squeeze whirls of batter about 10 cms in diameter into the hot oil. Cook until the gâteau moutails are golden brown in colour. Remove immediately with a perforated spoon and drain. Immerse the freshly cooked gâteau moutails in the warm syrup for about 5 mins.
8. Remove, drain and serve. Enjoy.

Gâteau Pâte d'Amandes

Almond Flour Cake

Ingredients (Serve 6-8):
- 200 g softened butter,
- 260 g fine white sugar,
- 100 g almond meal,
- 1 egg white,
- 1 teaspoon almond essence,
- 4 egg yolks,
- 2 cups plain yoghurt,
- 260 g white flour,
- 1 teaspoon sodium bicarbonate,
- Icing optional.

Method:
1. Pre heat oven to 180°C.
2. Blend 100 g fine white sugar, 100 g almond meal and1 egg white with a wire whisk. Set aside.
3. Sift the white flour and the sodium bicarbonate together. Set aside.
4. Butter a 20 cm round cake mould. Set aside.
5. Whisk together 160 g fine white sugar with the softened butter until very creamy. Set aside.
6. Using a food mixer, blend the almond meal and butter mixtures from 2 and 5 into a uniform mix. Gradually add the almond essence, egg yolks and blend together. Add the yoghurt and blend.
7. Gradually add the flour from 3. Mix well.
8. Pour into the buttered cake mould. Place on lower shelf in oven and bake for 50 mins. Cover with baking paper and cook for a further 15-20 mins. Test if cake is cooked by inserting a skewer. If it comes out clean, cake is cooked.
9. You can add icing to your liking.

Acknowledgements

The late Madeleine Philippe and I are both grateful to culinary figureheads whom we both had the pleasure to eat with, cook for and enjoy our beautiful Mauritian cuisine with. Their hints and tips that they gave so freely contributed much to the contents of this publication.

When I first met Madeleine, I could not even cook an egg. Her passion for Mauritian cuisine has been passed on to me over the years. Beyond my wildest expectations, she donated to me her immense experience and "savoir faire" in the preparation of delicious dishes that generate so much pleasure and happiness at the table. I am eternally grateful to my beloved Madeleine, who gave me so much. The love we have for each other remains very strong to this day.

I wish to thank those who kept the pressure by continually asking: "When will the book be published?" You kept me going. Many parents want a copy of the book to be passed on to their children, so that our Mauritian culinary heritage is passed on to their grand children.

A special mention has to be made of my editors Liz and Norman Coates, who relentlessly read and re-read the drafts for the book, the recipes and discussed the format and presentation of the contents. Without their contribution and support, the production of this book would not have been possible. Madeleine and I wish to say "Thank you", from deep within our hearts.

I am dedicating this book to the fans of Madeleine worldwide. You kept her spirit present and bubbling like she was. I hope (and I am sure that she does too) that this book will assist you in the preparation of dishes that will delight your family and friends, and secure our Mauritian culinary heritage for future generations.

Like Rick Stein said: *"You lose your culinary heritage, you lose your identity."*

Clancy Philippe

Disclaimer:
The information contained in this book is intended as a general guide. The recipes are based on the authors' own experimentation and research and neither the publisher nor the authors can be held responsible for the consequences of the application or misapplication of any of the information or ideas presented in this book.

Published in Australia in 2016 by the Madeleine Philippe Cancer Foundation (Aus) Inc.

Contact: clancy@cjp.net

All rights reserved. No reproduction, copy or transmission of this publication may be made without permission.

No paragraphs of this publication may be reproduced, copied or transmitted, save with written permission or in accordance with the provisions of the Copyright Act 1968 (as amended). Any person who does any unauthorised act in relation to this publication may be liable to criminal prosecution and civil damages.

Text copyright © 2016 Madeleine and Clancy Philippe

Photography copyright © Clancy Philippe

INDEX

Achar 86

achar bilimbi 88

achar carambole 110

almond flour cake 278

alouda 276

Baked custard 257

banana fritters 256

banana tarts 267

béchamel 103

béchamel poisson 227

beef and potato curry 115

beef bouillon 69

beef bryani 118, 120

beef curry 114

beef roast 137

beef rougaille 136

beef with broccoli 186

beef with mushrooms 116

beef with vegetables 213

bisque oyster and prawn 65

bitter melon stir fry 211

black lentils 178

black pudding rougaille 135

bok choy stir fry 210

bol deviré 131

bombay duck 253

bombli 253

bouillabaisse 225

bouillon malgache 125

bouillon poisson 233

bouillons 63

bouillons brèdes 66, 68

bread pudding 263

brèdes malbar 219

brèdes mouroum 219

brèdes songe 185

bringele frire 35

broccoli with beef 186

bryani beef 118, 120

bryani fish 228

bryani vegetable 198

Cabbage fricassée 196, 197

cabbage with sausages 184

carbonara prawns 250

cari cerf 140

cari dholl 181

cari embrevades 140

cari Jacques 168

cari ourite 248

cari poisson 234

cari tripes et gros pois 139

carrot halwa 274, 275

cassoulet 214, 220

cauliflower sauce blanche 195

chatini bringele 112

chatini ourite sec 111

chatini pipengaille 109

chatini pomme d'amour 108

cheese sticks 29

chick peas boiled 216

chicken and corn soup 74

chicken annabelle 42

chicken cotelettes 50

chicken croquettes 34

chicken curry 122, 124

chicken moulouktani 73

chicken vegetables stir fry 217

chicken wings sticky 54

chicken with green peas 144

chicken with mushrooms 134

chilli cakes 30

chilli crabs 230

chilli paste 99

chilli prawns 231

chillies pickled 105

chinese 23

choko and pork curry 126

choko in white sauce 208

choko salad 205

chokoes boulettes 28

chutney coconut and mint 91

chutney coriander leaves 90

chutney coriander peanut 89

chutneys 85

civet lapin 128

civet lievre 128

coconut and mint chutney 91

colodent 270

condiments 85

contents 1

coriander leaves chutney 90

corn and chicken soup 74

corned beef rougaille 145

cos lettuce stir fry 191

crabs bouillons 67

crème renversée 257

crêpes 31,32

crevettes sauce rouge 243

croque madame 47

croque monsieur 46

crystal prawns 252

cucumber salad 92

curry janot delaitre 127

curry oxtail 164

curry paste 97

curry paste roche cari 100

curry powder hot 95

curry powder mild 96

curry sauce 98

Daube ourite 232

dhall pouris 33

dholl curry 181

du pain frire 35

Eggplant chutney 112

eggplant with pork 194

english 16

Faratas 36

fettucine clancy 174

fish bouillon 71

fish boulettes 43

fish curry 234

fish in sweet and sour sauce 242

fish vindaloo 238

fish with béchamel 227

fish with herbs 240

french 10

fricassée le chou 197

fried noodles 152

fried rice 146

fried rice vegetable 192

Gajacks 25

garlic cream prawns 247

garlic green beans 202

garlic prawns 236

garlic sauce 106

gâteau coco 258

gâteau coster 271

gâteau moutail 277

gâteau patates 259

gâteau pâte d'amandes 278

gram bouilli 216

gratin de morue 237

gratin giraumon 200

gratin manioc 201

green beans 202

Hakien prawns 40

halim soup 75

haricots blancs with pork 180

haricots rouges with minced beef 182

history 3

Indian 18

Jackfruit curry 168

jalebis 277

jardinière de boeuf 213

Kat kat manioc 187

king prawns in red sauce 243

kulfi ice cream 272

Lalos fricassée 209

lamb gajack 61

lamb roast 173

lasagne béchamel 158

lasagne cheese 156

lima beans and tripes curry 139

lindsay noë iii

liz and norman coates vi

Macaroni cheese with minced beef 150

maddy's fried rice 146

madeleine and clancy Philippe v

madeleines 268

main courses 113

mama soup 78

mango kutcha 94

mango pickle 93

manioc gratin 201

manioc kat kat 187

margoze stir fry 211

massepain 269

mayonnaise 102

mazavaroo 104

meat balls beef and chicken 55

mee foon bouillon 70

minced beef macaroni 150

mines bouillis 62

mines frire 152

mint and coconut chutney 91

moon fan 148

moulouktani chicken 73

muslim 21

mustard beef roast 137

Napolitaines 262

Octopus curry 248

octopus dried rougaille 166

octopus dried salad 111

octopus salad 226

octopus stew 232

octopus vindaloo 239

okra stew 209

omelette aux herbes 160

omelette truffles 161

onion fritters 27

origin 4

oundé 266

oxtail curry with eggplant 164

oxtail soup 83

oxtail with carrots 130

Pain perdu 39

palm heart salad 206, 207

pâté chaud 38

peanut brittle 270

peanut coriander chutney 89

peanuts salted 48

pickles 85

pilaf 133

pilau 133

piment frire 35

pipengaille chatini 109

pipengaille with dried prawns 188

pipengaille with pork 189

pipis bouillon 72

poisson aux fines herbes 240

poisson sale 241

polenta pudding 264

pomme d'amour 15

pork and choko curry 126

pork bbq char sui 51

pork chops breaded 172

pork curry janot delaitre 127

pork spare ribs in black bean sauce 169

pork spare ribs in oyster sauce 170

pork with borlotti beans 180

pork with eggplant 194

pork with pipengaille 189

pork with snake beans 183

portugese 9

potato chips 203

potato salad 204

potatoes mashed with corned beef 44

poudine du pain 263

poudine maïs 264

poudine vermicelli 265

poulet aux champignons 134

poulet aux petits pois 144

poutou 260, 261

prawn dumplings 52

prawns carbonara 250

prawns in spicy sauce 246

puits d'amour 273

pumpkin gratin 200

puttu 260, 261

Rasson soup 77

red kidney beans with minced beef 182

red lentils 179

rougaille boudin 135

rougaille corned beef 145

rougaille ourite sec 166

rougaille poisson sale 162

rougaille saucisses 138

Salade chou chou 205

salade palmiste 206, 207

salmon patties 59

salt and pepper squid 251

salt cod with potato gratin 237

salt fish 241

salt fish rougaille 162

samousas 57

sauce blanche chou chou 208

sauce blanche chou fleur 195

saumon maddy 244

sausage rougaille 138

snacks 25

snake beans with pork 183

soup hot and sour 76

soupe mama 78

soups 63

soya eggs 49

spaghetti bolognese 154

spring rolls mini 56

star fruit pickle 110

sweet and sour fish 242

sweet and sour sauce 107

Tamil 20

taro fritters 37

taro leaves 185

tec tec bouillon 72

telegu 20

terrine ham hock 175

terrine pork and veal 142

ti pooris 60

tomato chutney 108

tomato soup 79, 80

tripes and lima beans curry 139

Venison curry 140

vermicelli pudding 265

vindaye ourite 239

vindaye poisson 238

Wan tan bouillon 81

watercress soup 82

Zucchini flowers 58

www.ingramcontent.com/pod-product-compliance
Lightning Source LLC
Chambersburg PA
CBHW042302010526
44113CB00048B/2772